ANGELES
History of a Barrio

UNIVERSITY OF TEXAS PRESS AUSTIN

Dedicado a mis padres, Enrique y Alicia; a mi esposa, Harriett; y a mis hijos, Ana y Carlos

An earlier version of Chapter 6 was published in *Pacific Historical Review* 46, no. 2 (May 1977). Permission to reprint this material is gratefully acknowledged.

First edition, 1983

Requests for permission to reproduce material from this work should be sent to: Permissions, University of Texas Press, Box 7819, Austin, Texas 78712.

Library of Congress Cataloging in Publication Data

Romo, Ricardo.
  East Los Angeles: history of a barrio.

  Includes bibliographical references and index.
    1. Mexican Americans—California—East Los Angeles—Social conditions.   2. Mexican Americans—California—East Los Angeles—History.   3. East Los Angeles (Calif.)—Social conditions.   4. East Los Angeles (Calif.)—History. I. Title.
F869.E18R65 1983   305.8′6872′079494   82-10891
ISBN 0-292-72040-8
ISBN 0-292-72041-6 (pbk.)

Contents

Tables

Maps

Preface

This is the story of the barrio of East Los Angeles during its formative years, 1900–1930. The 1981 celebration of the Los Angeles bicentennial underscores the city's long association with Mexican settlers, for it was a group of northern Mexican pioneers who laid the pueblo's foundation in 1781. While Mexicans have been a part of the city's history for two centuries, they have had their greatest influence in the development of East Los Angeles since 1900. The modern immigrant pioneers who moved to the eastside in the early twentieth century could not have envisioned that their barrio would be the nation's largest Mexican barrio and by 1930 rival in size major cities in the United States.

As the east side is a part of the Los Angeles metropolis, much of its history is interwoven with the development of the city as a whole. The pueblo that the original eleven Mexican families founded was but a frontier outpost in its first half-century of existence. Over the next fifty years the town changed dramatically. Sailors from the Yankee Clippers, trappers off the Santa Fe Trail, Forty-niners, Indian fighters, Civil War soldiers, Chinese railroad laborers, Jewish merchants, and Italian fishermen all came to Los Angeles to begin new careers or, in some cases, to live out their retirement years in "sunny paradise." Coincidental with the infusion of new arrivals was the growing concentration of Mexican residents in a section adjacent to the original site of the pueblo's town plaza. Until the turn of the century, both Mexicans and Anglos recognized "Sonoratown," with its Mexican stores and social activities, as the heart of the Spanish-speaking community. Sonoratown remained the Mexican center of Los Angeles until the First World War, when new industrial forces and urbanization changed the face of the old Plaza community.

The arrival of a massive number of Mexicans in Los Angeles during the early twentieth century corresponded with the key period in the city's drive for industrialization. Although promoted as a worker's paradise, the city fared poorly in attracting European immigrants and American blue-collar workers because of the comparatively low wages and a reluctance among most of these workers to work in a city troubled by labor strife.

This book looks at how Mexicans adapted to industrialization and contributed to the creation of an ethnic community in one of America's fastest-growing cities. In southern California, Mexicans filled a labor shortage created by the absence of domestic and immigrant workers in both the years preceding the First World War and the decade after. By 1920, these newcomers from Mexico numbered over 100,000 and, through their labor in hundreds of occupations, played an important role in the city's drive for domination of international trade in the Western Pacific region.

Mexicans, discouraged from settling in other sections of town, crossed the river and built a new barrio in the vast open spaces, the flat low lands along the Los Angeles River amid old housing tracts belonging to European ethnics of an earlier generation. The east side, with its low rents and inexpensive houses, appealed to the newcomers and grew to be one of the largest ethnic communities in the United States. During the heyday of the interurban railroad and the glorious beginning of the Age of the Automobile, the barrio became a haven for a Mexican population which faced discrimination in housing, employment, and social activities in Anglo parts of the city. On the east side, Mexican residents formed their own organizations, founded several Spanish-language newspapers, and supported businesses and cultural development unique to their needs and experiences. The growth and development of the Mexican barrio, how Mexicans fared in the labor market, problems associated with residential segregation, and educational and social experiences of Mexican immigrants to Los Angeles in the 1920s are discussed in this book.

When the Depression put a temporary halt to economic prosperity, the flood of Mexican migration fell to a trickle. Yet collectively, if not individually, those who had come over the years 1900–1939 had contributed to creating a new barrio. The legacy of those who moved "east of the river" in the early twentieth century lives with us today in East Los Angeles, home to more than a million Mexican Americans and a center of thriving Mexican cultural traditions.

The majority of the emigrants from Mexico who settled in Los Angeles during the late nineteenth and early twentieth centuries referred to themselves as *Mexicanos*. Southern California English-

language newspapers and journals used the term *Mexican* in referring to this population, whether the person was born in Mexico or in
the United States of Mexican parents. Scholars did not begin to use
the term *Mexican American* to describe this group until the post-
Depression years. It is for these reasons that I have chosen to employ
the terms *Mexicanos* and *Mexicans* interchangeably in this study to
refer to those people who settled in this region and who for the most
part eventually became U.S. citizens.

Acknowledgments

In writing this book, I have incurred many debts that I would like to acknowledge. During the course of researching the study, I was helped by the excellent conversations with Stan Coben, Stephan Thernstrom, and Juan Gómez Quiñones. They read early drafts of the manuscript, as did my former colleagues at the University of California, San Diego, Earl Pomeroy, Ramón Ruiz, and Michael Monteón. The blue pencil marks of Greg Allen Grob, Jane Bayes, Cam Miller, José Limón, Rolando Hinojosa, and Norris Hundley, who read all or parts of my early drafts, also aided me in improving the text.

Two Latin Americanists, Jim Scobie and Brian Loveman, gave me extremely useful suggestions concerning urbanization and immigration during the preparation of the final draft. I had learned much from Scobie's brilliant study of Buenos Aires, and his premature death is a great loss of a friend and scholar. At this stage, Chicano historian Rodolfo Acuña also provided some insightful comments on the handling of social history.

I am grateful to Harry Scheiber, Raymund Paredes, William Goetzmann, and Robert Crunden, whose critical suggestions and encouragement substantially contributed to the reworking of my final draft. Scheiber, Paredes, and my wife Harriett all read the manuscript at least twice. Harriett, whose interest in immigration and education contributed to many fruitful discussions, gave generously of her own knowledge and time.

In collecting and preparing the research data, I benefited from the assistance of many individuals, including James Cox and Edith Fuller of the University of California, Los Angeles; William Mason and John Calhoun of the Los Angeles County Museum of Natural History; Elvira Chavaría and Edna Domínguez of the Mexican American Library Program at the University of Texas at Austin; and research assistants Michael Hanson and Mary Isabel Romo of Los

Angeles. The excellent typing of Sandra Inzunza, Sofía Cebrero, Mary Alice Dávila, and Rosemary Neff is greatly appreciated. A special thanks goes to U.T. Press editor Scott Lubeck for recognizing the need to publish a work of this nature and to Carolyn Cates Wylie of the Press for her creative and thoughtful editing.

I am grateful for the research support provided by the Institute of American Cultures at the University of California, Los Angeles, and the Ford Foundation's Graduate Fellowship Program for Mexican Americans. I was able to complete part of the writing through support from the National Chicano Council on Higher Education and a University of California Regents' Summer Fellowship. For all who helped, I am thankful; I alone can be held responsible for errors of fact and mistakes of judgment.

EAST LOS
ANGELES

1 Introduction

The Great Depression that began in 1929 ended an extraordinary generation of industrial and demographic growth in Los Angeles. During the three previous decades, the city had attained national prominence in manufacturing, distribution capabilities, and marketing techniques. Its soaring population growth placed it fifth in metropolitan size, and first among cities in the West and South, by 1929. At the same time the East Los Angeles barrio had gained fame as the largest Mexican community in the United States. In 1930 this barrio with more than ninety thousand residents surpassed in population the capital cities of three of the largest states in the Union: Albany, New York; Sacramento, California; and Austin, Texas.[1] In size and character, the Eastside Barrio was a city within a city. Although this Mexican community and others like it continue to be prominent in the Southwest and parts of the Midwest, little is known of their formative years. The origins and development of the barrio in Los Angeles during the early twentieth century—its social and economic structure, its inner dynamics, and the day-to-day experiences of its residents—are the focus of this study.

Prior to the publication of Stephan Thernstrom's influential study *Poverty and Progress*, most of the urban studies recorded the activities of political and business elites. Thernstrom contributed to the writing of history "from the bottom up" by emphasizing quantitative analysis of working-class people in his historical research. Still, most of the studies that followed Thernstrom's methodology focused on midwestern and eastern cities.[2] An explanation for why immigrant groups such as the Irish experienced limited mobility in Boston while New York Jews rose faster and higher up the occupational ladder than Italians in that city did not really speak to the experience of racial minorities elsewhere in the country. The recent publication of studies dealing with Mexican Americans in Santa Barbara, El Paso, and nineteenth-century Los Angeles, in addition to this study, may enable us to make some suggestions regarding social mobility and residential dispersion in the Spanish-speaking communities of the West.[3]

Certainly one of the most dramatic aspects of the emergence of the twentieth-century West was its urban growth. While San Francisco and Denver, as a result of mineral wealth, registered stunning development during the nineteenth century, only a few cities west of the Rockies claimed populated areas of over fifty thousand. At the turn of the century, one decade after the United States Census Office's proclamation that the continuous western frontier had come to a close, Los Angeles made its bid as the West's premier city.[4]

A direct consequence of this urbanization in the West and Southwest was the evolution of Mexican barrios. These enclaves housed one of the newest, yet oldest immigrant groups. Southwestern barrios gaining large numbers of new residents during the early twentieth century included Los Angeles, San Antonio, and El Paso. Other than these three cities, all other cities in the nation counted fewer than six thousand Mexicans within their boundaries as late as 1920. Ten years later, five cities, all in the Southwest with the exception of Chicago, claimed more than ten thousand Mexican residents.[5] Any study of the urbanization of the West cannot be fully told without considering barrios like Los Angeles' Mexican community.

From the founding of the city by Spanish settlers in 1781 to the American conquest in 1848, slow economic growth and relatively little social change characterized Los Angeles.[6] Wealthy Mexicans owned expansive ranchos in the Los Angeles basin and maintained second homes in town. In the pueblo these rancheros lived close to the main plaza while the poor classes, especially the Mestizos and Indians, lived along both sides of the Los Angeles River. The Mexican merchant class who owned businesses in the plaza frequently lived close to their work, occasionally in the same buildings. Numbering less than fifty families in Los Angeles in 1848, Anglo Americans and Europeans lived alongside the Mexican residents. Since the pueblo was small, the various classes interacted to some extent. Kinship linked many of the residents, while others established close bonds through intermarriage and the *compadre* tradition.

A migration of Anglos, Chinese, Jews, Germans, and Blacks to California followed the Gold Rush of 1849 and statehood in 1850. Even as early as the 1820s, American settlers evidenced strong prejudice toward the Spanish-speaking; after the Mexican-American War (1846–1848) and the gold rush, this intensified. In a short time most Anglo settlers had established residences and businesses beyond the old plaza community. They clustered together and attempted to restrict Mexican voting rights and to prohibit cultural practices native to the Mexican community.[7] The Mexican population did not grow at the same rate as the Anglo population and remained near the center of town. The old plaza offered a Catholic church, bilingual schools, and stores and cafés operated by Spanish-speaking owners. Even though the main Los Angeles business district shifted from the plaza to southwest Los Angeles, the plaza area provided Mexican residents inexpensive housing, boarding opportunities, and close promixity to many jobs.[8]

Unlike the situation in California's northern communities, which Anglo Americans dominated politically and economically, up to the 1870s Mexicans managed to maintain some social and political influence in Los Angeles. The city's urban landscape, social makeup, and political structure, however, changed dramatically following the arrival of the railroads in the early 1880s. Once the town was connected to the eastern markets, its population doubled within a decade. For Mexican residents these changes meant a loss in numerical supremacy and political power in Los Angeles.

Almost daily new businesses and professional offices sprang up in the town. Land prices went up as investors bought up the old ranchos and subdivided them into small lots and new town sites. The resulting economic boom encouraged further promotion by the railroads and other speculators. The Southern Pacific and Santa Fe railroads engaged in a rate war for passenger trade between the Midwest and Los Angeles.[9] For a few days in the mid 1880s, midwesterners could travel to Los Angeles for as little as a dollar. Boosters proudly extolled the many attributes of the city: its excellent climate, warm beaches, and close promixity to scenic mountains.[10] Individuals from all economic classes came in search of new wealth and opportunities.

Anglos and other European settlers who had moved away from the original core area began to refer to the plaza section as "Sonoratown" or "Little Mexico." Sonoratown remained small in comparison to the new Anglo residential communities and business district. Later the interurban railroad and the Santa Fe built depots near the heart of the old Mexican plaza community, attracting new industries and warehouses to the area. Increasing industrial construction finally forced Mexican migrants to spread out from the plaza neighborhood.

Between 1900 and 1930, Los Angeles grew from a town of 100,000 people to a metropolis of over a million.[11] The city attained this spectacular growth by solving energy, water, harbor, and labor problems for a time. The Los Angeles area had an abundant natural supply of oil deposits; the drilling for this oil coincided with the discovery that oil could replace coal as fuel for railroads, ships, and industrial machinery. In the 1920s the construction of dams on the Colorado River 100 miles to the east cheapened the cost of electricity, a factor which appealed to manufacturing interests and provided lights for the whole city. Although the Colorado River supplied the city with fresh water, its resources could not provide sufficient water for an urban area whose hinterland also led the nation in citrus and vegetable output; other water sources were essential. City engineers and municipal leaders turned to the Owens Valley in northern California, trapping water and directing its flow to Los Angeles by means of a 230-mile canal. The dream of a deep water harbor became a reality in the early 1900s when the federal government agreed to provide a share of the construction cost. Once completed, ships from all over the world docked at San Pedro. By the 1920s the Los Angeles harbor handled more tonnage than any other American port except New York.¹² With a first-class harbor, Los Angeles could handle new traffic generated by the completion of the Panama Canal. In essence, with improved industries and communication networks, Los Angeles emerged as an exporter of manufactured goods, processor of agricultural products, importer of machinery and technology, supplier of labor, and distributor of financial capital. In the wake of this spectacular economic transformation, industries in search of skilled and unskilled workers turned to Mexico, a source that railroad builders and fruit growers had already tapped for several decades. Reliable and cheap, Mexican labor became the basis for industrial development.

The growth of industries in peripheral areas stimulated by the new harbor trade and the introduction of an interurban railway system made it easier for Mexicans to take up residence away from the central core of the city. Los Angeles' position as a major financial center and supplier of manufacturing goods to local and foreign markets contributed to a new boom which brought warehouses, banks, and transportation depots to the central core. The central area and the old barrio of Sonoratown, which had been abandoned by the business elites twenty years earlier, became the hub of new manufacturers and financial interests. Thus, by World War I, Los Angeles faced a critical shortage of urban commercial space. Undoubtedly, improved urban transportation hastened the decentralization of the city, as Anglos and European ethnics began moving to the suburbs. This movement freed housing in old ethnic communities on the east side. As White ethnics moved outward, Mexicans bought or rented homes in the old Italian, Jewish, and Russian neighborhoods.

From 1910 to 1920 Los Angeles attracted thousands of new immigrants, principally Mexican, while the influx of immigrant labor slowed in other American cities. More so than in earlier decades, Americans appeared terrified by the spectre of "racial degeneration." The press readily accepted the nativist characterization of Mexicans as lazy, treacherous half-breeds prone to violence.[13] Nationally, restrictionists won an important victory with the passage of the Literacy Act of 1917. The act, introduced as a measure to limit non-Nordic immigration from southeastern Europe, encouraged California nativists to hope that the law would also severely limit the influx of Mexican immigrants. However, it proved impossible to halt Mexican migration because of the open border. Also Congress, pressured by railroad companies, farmers, and ranchers, exempted Mexicans from the Literacy Act less than six months after it was passed as labor shortages threatened to curtail the harvest of crops and maintenance of railroads.[14]

By 1920 Los Angeles' industries had formed a close association, perhaps even a dependent relationship, with the local Mexican labor force. Although some companies in the city openly publicized their reluctance to hire Mexicans, most Spanish-speaking immigrants easily found jobs in unskilled and semiskilled positions.[15] Mexicans, generally desperate for work, accepted low wages, irregular working hours, seasonal employment, and poor working conditions. These factors made them ideal employees for the construction and transportation industries. By accepting these jobs, however, Mexican workers found themselves subjected to violent criticism, and many even risked personal injury from union members as well as nonunion Anglo and Black workers.[16] In the few Los Angeles industries where organized labor had power, unions refused to admit Mexicans and supported the American Federation of Labor campaign to restrict Mexican immigration.

While barrios, like western cities, changed dramatically during the years of rapid urban industrialization, historians concerned with the West have neglected to examine the impact of the urban process on ethnic communities. Robert Fogelson, for example, assumed that Mexicans desired to stay in Los Angeles only long enough to earn some money rapidly and return to the homeland. He concluded that they "had little inclination to improve the town economically or socially."[17] Mexican migrants swept across the southwestern landscape in record proportions between 1910 and 1930, and this northward flow was responsible for the emergence of many of the barrios in this region today. Here we examine their impact on one urban community. Moreover, while it is important to understand the nature of barrio life, it is also crucial to consider how the external forces of industrialization and urbanization affected the economy, physical boundaries, and social outlook of the Mexican communities.

One of the problems associated with explaining the early-twentieth-century origin of Mexican barrios is that most works treat the movements of Mexican Americans to urban areas as a post–World War II phenomenon despite the fact that as early as 1930 more than 50 percent of the Mexican population in the United States lived in urban communities.[18] This historical distortion occurred largely because early studies of Mexicans in this country focused primarily on their rural migration and settlement. Moreover, because Mexicans, at least the vast majority, had arrived in the 1900–1930 migration wave at a time when the West was still economically and politically marginal to the eastern seaboard region, census takers, government officials, and scholars assumed that they were relatively few in number and therefore insignificant. It might be fair to say that Americans knew more about Mexicans in Mexico than Mexicans in the United States.

Considered a relatively "new" city when compared with New York and Chicago, Los Angeles has attracted the attention of few historians. Indeed, the brief mentions that Los Angeles has received have varied widely. In two of the more recent studies of the city, one scholar viewed it as fragmented, while another, commenting on the fact that California during the early twentieth century was the recipient of some two million newcomers, "most of them from rural background," concluded that "it was no accident that Los Angeles resembled a huge village."[19] Ethnic communities, which have been an intrinsic part of Los Angeles history, have received even less attention. Only rare events such as the 1965 Watts riots have compelled social scientists to inquire into life in these communities. As a result, the experience of Mexicans and other ethnic groups has been obscured.

In *The Fragmented Metropolis*, a major contribution to the historiography of Los Angeles, Robert Fogelson referred only briefly to ethnic communities. Although his study concerns the crucial years— 1850 to 1930—when Los Angeles developed from a Mexican pueblo into a sprawling metropolis, Fogelson ignored the Mexican barrio completely and characterized Mexicans as "transient," "maladjusted," and "unadjusted." In another passage he describes them as "unassimilated, unwelcomed, and unprotected" and "so thoroughly isolated that the American majority was able to maintain its untainted vision of an integrated community."[20]

Since historians know little about the urbanization of early-twentieth-century Mexicans, some have assumed that Mexican bar-

rios fit a "ghetto model." This ghetto model, according to one researcher, "supports the generalization that, with the exception of
occasional pockets elsewhere, the rate of deviance increases the
closer one approaches the city center."[21] In the 1910s, Progressive reformers singled out the Mexican barrio of Los Angeles as a blemish
on the city's fine reputation. Contemporary writers maligned the
colonia by focusing on pathological experiences of Mexicans. Journalists linked vices as well as the spread of contagious diseases with
the barrio. Health officials, school administrators, and social scientists joined together to condemn barrio life.

Mexican anthropologist Manuel Gamio, who visited the large
barrios of Los Angeles, San Antonio, and Chicago during the 1920s,
concluded that urbanization weakened the character and spirit of
the immigrants. According to Gamio, as the Mexican moves into
the American city "there arises in him the impulse to get help from
[some] outside mysterious agency, and therefore he pursues con-
fused digressions, so that the result does not represent all the working of his brain nor the total effort put forth."[22] Thus, for Gamio and
other scholars, urbanization had a negative impact on the immigrant. Twenty years later, historian Carey McWilliams followed the
same line of thought when he wrote that because Mexican immigrants came from rural areas, they were "not prepared for a rapid
transition to a society which, at nearly every point, negates the values of their folk culture." McWilliams echoed Gamio's observation
when he wrote that "the Mexican peon faltered and became con-
fused and often demoralized when he came in close contact with a
highly industrialized, urban society."[23]

Indeed, even more recent social scientists have considered the
barrio of Los Angeles static and at best marginal to the larger Los
Angeles community. Distinctions among various ethnic communities have been obscured by the emergence of a general ghetto image that had pejorative racial meaning. This image in turn grew into
a pseudo-scientific "ghetto model." According to this interpretation,
the ghetto represents an urban area where people, because of their
circumstances and characteristics, are forced to live. David R.
Hunter, who considered ghettos "bad from every point of view,"
portrayed residents of these communities as unskilled, poor, non-
White, ill-educated, and ignorant about the means of getting ahead
in American society.[24] Both image and model have been carelessly
applied to the Mexican barrio.

This study proposes that the distorted ghetto image of barrios
ignored the fact that the majority of Mexican immigrants, for reasons of language, kinship, and folk customs, chose to live together in

barrios. These barrios provided a sense of identity with the homeland and a transition into American society. Thus modern ghettos or
barrios are not necessarily homes for losers and sinners. Sam Bass
Warner, Jr., and Colin B. Burke expressed the idea that ghettos have
acted as an "agent of localized acculturation," which has served not
only as a home for the first generation of immigrants, but also as a
place "to which the children of immigrants returned for special
foods, or for the foreign-language theatre, or the national church."[25]
It is also true, however, that while some Mexicans in barrios such as
the one in East Los Angeles had options for spatial mobility to satellite barrio communities, most were prevented from moving to White
neighborhoods by restrictive real estate covenants and prejudices.

Even though some European immigrants had difficulties assimilating to predominantly Anglo-Saxon culture, scholars concerned
with urban residential patterns have sought to explain the evolution
and demise of immigrant enclaves as primarily related to nativism,
economic differences, and period of arrival. In *The Urban Wilderness*, for instance, Sam Bass Warner, Jr., says that over the period
from 1870 to 1920, urban neighborhoods in general "ceased to be [a]
jumble of rich and poor, immigrants and native, black and white" as
they had been in the former area of the big city. Instead, Warner suggests, the neighborhood of the industrial metropolis "came to be arranged in a systematic pattern of socio-economic segration."[26] From
the perspective of Black and White residents or old and new immigrant groups, Warner's analysis may hold together neatly. However,
Mexican immigrants arrived in Los Angeles in the early twentieth
century at a time when racial prejudice strongly limited their housing choices. From 1910 to 1930 the principal Mexican enclaves of
Los Angeles, located in the inner city and formerly inhabited by poor
natives, European newcomers, and Asian immigrants, lost their heterogeneous characteristics and instead of becoming segregated by
socioeconomic criteria became segregated racially.

The evolution of a large ethnic community in a metropolis such
as Los Angeles which by 1900 had gained fame for its homogeneity
in itself merits examination. J. Lilly's 1931 statement in the *North
American Review* that "Los Angeles is to my mind the most American city" in the United States expressed what many other contemporary writers said or believed about this city.[27] Indeed, of the major
cities of the United States, Los Angeles ranked among the top three
for its proportion of native-born White population. Between 1900
and 1930 the city's foreign-born population never surpassed 20 percent. In comparison, New York averaged 35 percent foreign-born

population during the same period, with a high of 40 percent in 1910. Los Angeles' Mexican population ranged from 5 percent in 1900 to nearly 20 percent in 1930.[28] City boosters, however, seldom mentioned the Mexicans' presence. It is no wonder that at a later period Mexicans were referred to as the "nation's best kept secret" or the "invisible minority." Ignored by the rest of society for much of the early part of this century, the barrios of Los Angeles provided immigrants with an environment conducive to family life and the maintenance of many customs and values of the homeland and provided the city with workers that encouraged and supported its rapid growth and prosperity.

One myth, recently popularized by social scientists Leo Grebler, Joan W. Moore, and Ralph C. Guzman in their encyclopedic study *The Mexican American People*, contends that the residents of California had a more tolerant attitude toward Mexicans than did other Americans. Grebler, Moore, and Guzman suggested that Mexicans found greater occupational success in Los Angeles than in Texas, for example, because of the absence of strong historical sentiments against them in Los Angeles. They concluded that a key factor in understanding this tolerance is the fact that the native-born population of Los Angeles has always been largely midwestern in origin. "Unlike the Texas native who was the typical inhabitant of San Antonio, Americans from the midwest probably held few strong preconceptions about Mexicans. This might have been some advantage to the Mexicans in Los Angeles."[29] These authors were obviously unaware of the anti-alien and anti-radical campaign against the Mexican beginning in 1915 and lasting until 1919.

For the study of migration and assimilation, the twenties are crucial. Congressional hearings concerning quota laws and the popularity of the Americanization movement confirm the preoccupation of Americans with ethnicity and migration. The Quota Acts of 1921 and 1924 contributed significantly to the assimilation of European immigrants through increasing the rate of naturalization.[30] Mexicans were not affected by the Quota Acts, and despite some intermarriage, most first-generation and even second- and third-generation Mexican Americans continued to express strong attachment to Mexico. Since the border lay only a few hours away by train or automobile, many Mexicans maintained old country customs and ties considerably longer than Europeans. Some Americans believed that the low level of naturalization rates among Mexican arrivals indicated that the group wished only to exploit America for its economic benefits. Still, the absence of social interaction among Anglos and Mexicans, as well as segregation policies imposed by educators, employers, and real estate developers, badly hindered the assimilation process.

A walk through the Los Angeles barrio in the early twentieth century revealed not only influences of Old Mexico but diversity and adaptation. While outsiders persisted in referring to the barrio as "Sonoratown" or "Little Mexico," it was evident that the community was far from a replica of the homeland. The immigrants accepted the fact that they could not transplant all homeland traditions and values and instead created a new urban culture.[31] By patronizing Mexican restaurants, belonging to community associations, attending Sunday religious services at the old Mexican Plaza church, and maintaining the Spanish language, Mexicans lived a little of the old culture in Los Angeles. In addition, the religious festivals and observation of Mexican holidays in the city brought residents together, providing favorable circumstances to maintain kinship and hometown networks. A variety of community institutions gave new arrivals an occasion to adopt some things and not others from Anglo American society. Still, adaptation occurred at many different levels. Mexican immigrants, for instance, adopted some American sports, such as baseball and basketball, but cared little for football and golf. The barrio of Los Angeles, like many other ethnic communities, essentially acted as an acculturation way station where the recently arrived immigrants could work out their own social and economic adjustment to American life at a pace that suited them rather than that favored by Americanization programs and "cultural custodians."

In exploring differences among ghetto communities, historians have focused on Europeans and Blacks. While Mexican barrios and the European and Black ghettos share many characteristics, several factors distinguish Mexican settlements. With a few exceptions, most of the principal Mexican communities are located within a two-hundred-mile range of the Mexican border. Distance and immigration restriction, especially after 1921, kept most European ghettos from reaching significant population growth. At the same time, the Spanish language and Mexican customs flourished in Mexican barrios. In Los Angeles and other barrios of the border area, Mexicans not only developed and maintained their own Spanish language radio stations, but also continued to listen to radio transmitted from across the border. Newspapers from the homeland survive to this day.[32] Thus proximity to the home country and continuous migration have strongly influenced the character of the Mexican barrios throughout the present century.

Our investigation of selected communities such as Los Angeles' Mexican barrio should contribute to a better understanding of the urban experiences of Mexicans in this country. One unique feature of the Los Angeles barrio was its function as a labor distribution center for Mexican unskilled workers. In Los Angeles, labor agents arranged for Mexican workers to board ships headed to Alaska, railroads bound for the Midwest, and trucks destined for the rich agricultural fields of the San Joaquín Valley. In the years immediately after World War I, this barrio also achieved fame as the nation's principal hub for Mexican cultural and artistic activities, a status which it has maintained to the present day. Mexicans living in the other barrios of the state looked to Los Angeles for its Spanish-language newspapers. In terms of theatre and music, it was considered a pacemaker. In addition, the barrio's location gave residents a unique perspective on how other ethnic groups, including Blacks, Chinese, Russians, and Italians, handled the complexities of acculturation and assimilation.

Yet, like most other barrios of the period 1900–1930, the one in Los Angeles was strongly affected by urban growth and industrialization. Moreover, the heavy migration, residential dispersion, racial disorder, and intensification of segregation policies were probably evident in most barrios of the first three decades of the twentieth century. What is unique and what is common to Mexican barrios, however, may not be determined until there are more Mexican community studies. I hope that this work is a contribution toward that end as well as an examination of a major barrio which lends greater understanding to the urban experiences of Mexicans in the United States during the formative years of the twentieth century.

2 Prelude to the Barrio

The activities of Lt. Edward O. C. Ord and William Rich Hutton in Los Angeles during the hot summer months of 1849 must have struck some of the local residents as unusual. For two months these two surveyors walked about the dusty pueblo counting their steps, peering through lenses, and making sketches for their map of the city. In the late afternoons when Ord sat to summarize his day's work, Hutton took time to make landscape drawings of the pueblo's more picturesque scenes. As if in ignorance of the city's past history as Indian village, Spanish pueblo, and Mexican town, Ord superimposed Anglo names on many of the streets that Los Angeles' residents had long identified with Spanish names. Calle de la Eternidad (Street of Eternity), leading to the cemetery, changed to Broadway, while Calle de las Chapules (Street of the Grasshoppers) became Pearl Street. Once the work had been completed, the city paid Ord a commission of $3,000 and immediately proceeded to sell town property in public auctions. So rapid were the sales that the city civic leaders neglected to set aside land for public offices and in a short time had to buy back property for that purpose. The entire four leagues claimed by the city under the town's Spanish patrimony sold within a few weeks.[1] Like Ord's map, many enterprises of Anglo settlers, contemporary historians, and city officials were attempts to erase Indian, Spanish, and Mexican influences in the City of Angels.

In 1769 the Gaspar de Portolá party, the first group of Europeans to pass through the future site of Los Angeles, came upon a large Indian village which Father Juan Crespi, a member of Portolá's group, described as inhabited by "friendly heathen." "They live in this delightful place among the trees on the river," he wrote. "Their chief brought some strings of beads made of shells, and they threw us three handfuls of them. Some of the old men were smoking pipes made of baked clay and they puffed at us three mouthfuls of smoke. We gave them a little tobacco and glass beads, and they went away well pleased." Unchallenged by those Indians, the Spaniards traveled a few miles north of the village, where they encountered more natives, who offered them food to continue their journey.[2]

The Indian villagers who met Portolá claimed a region settled by their ancestors approximately fifty thousand years earlier. As the Portola party made its way north, Pedro Fages, a member of the expedition, counted seven villages in the coastal route between present day El Toro and the northern end of the San Fernando Valley. Although no more than two thousand Indians lived in this zone, Fages described the villages as "quite populous; some of them so much, that had the Indians borne arms they would have given us great anxiety."[3] The Gabrielinos, as the native population of the Los Angeles Basin became identified following the founding of San Gabriel Mission in the 1770s, relocated their villages quite frequently, generally in response to the availability of food. Their knowledge of the area and their peaceful ways enabled the mission efforts to succeed in the rugged southern California wilderness.

Felipe de Neve, the first governor of Alta California, personally took charge of the founding of Los Angeles, selecting the site in 1777 after exploring the entire coastal region from San Diego to San Francisco. He selected the basin located west of Mission San Gabriel near the Porciúncula River, because, as he noted in his diary, it had "much water easy to take on either bank and beautiful lands." Neve envisioned that the pueblo would shortly meet one of its principal functions: the supplying of food and materials to the coastal outpost, eliminating the need to ship these goods from the interior of Mexico. The padres wanted the pueblo close to Mission San Gabriel in order to have some influence on its growth and development. However, to establish the pueblo's separate identity, the governor planned the new settlement nine miles west of Mission San Gabriel, and a sufficient distance from San Juan Capistrano.[4]

Governor Neve had intended for the new *pobladores* (settlers) of Los Angeles to establish a settlement free of mission influence at a location where Indians exempt from mission obligations might eventually wish to resettle. Indeed, he actually chose a plot of land nearly on top of an Indian village long occupied by the Yang-Na people. Father Junipero Serra, father-president of the missions of California, opposed Neve's plans, arguing that new pueblos were both premature and a potential threat to the conversion of Indians, but the Crown approved the project. The establishment of the Los Angeles settlement came at a time when the Spanish Crown had taken a new defense posture following the inauguration of war with England in June 1779. The mission padres, under Father Serra's direction, reluctantly respected the Crown's wishes to establish a pueblo near the San Gabriel mission. The missionaries treated Governor Neve with kindness and respect during the year he spent in southern California planning the new settlement, but they did not assist him. Soon after settlers and soldiers from northern Mexico arrived at Mission San Gabriel in 1781, Neve left for northern Mexico to proceed with his aspirations of adding several new pueblos in the region.[5]

Alta California in the late eighteenth century held limited appeal for northern Mexican colonists. Captain Fernando Moncada y Rivera, given the difficult responsibility of recruiting new settlers, left for the northern provinces of Mexico with specific instructions to enlist twenty-four settlers and to assist Father Serra in the construction of Channel Island missions. Complicating the search for settlers to Los Angeles was Governor Neve's request that "all were to be married men and to take their families along." The governor also specifically requested a mason, a carpenter, and a blacksmith.[6] In Sonora and Sinaloa, Rivera managed to recruit only sixteen pioneers, eleven of whom eventually made it to Los Angeles. The terms offered to potential settlers seemed generous enough: Each of them could expect five years of payment, beginning at the time of enlistment and consisting of 116 pesos a year for the first two years and 60 pesos a year for the final three years. The *pobladores*, who had to bind themselves for a service of ten years, also each received a yoke of oxen, two cows, a pair of horses, one mule, two lambs, two goats, and all the necessary farm implements, with the understanding that they should pay for the animals and goods with the product of their fields. Finally, Rivera promised the settlers small lots in the pueblo where they could erect homes. In a contract drawn up by the governor of Alta California and dated November 19, 1781, other aspects of the settlers' benefits and obligations are laid out:

> That in addition to the cattle, horses, and mules distributed to the first 11 settlers, as set forth, they were granted building lots on which they have constructed their houses, which for the present are built of palisades, roofed with earth; also 2 irrigated fields for cultivation of 2 fanegas of corn to each settler; in addition, a plow share, a hoe and an axe; and for the community, the proper number of carts, wagons, and breeding animals as set forth above, for which the settlers must account to the Royal Exchequer at the price fixed.[7]

The pueblo prospered over the first two decades, although few reports exist to reveal the daily lives of the early Mexican colonists. After only a year of existence, Felipe de Neve worried that the "fostering of these towns [San José and Los Angeles] demands very special attention; "[it is] most essential that special watchfulness be maintained with respect to the pueblo of Nuestra Señora de Los Angeles." Governor Neve, concerned about a poor first-year harvest, advised his successor that it was "necessary to have an active and exacting man there who will bestir the settlers to cultivate their land, care for their crops, and do everything else connected with farming."[8]

Other than the Indian population that lived near the pueblo of Los Angeles, Mestizos made up the greater share of the first pueblo settlers. Some dispute exists regarding the racial composition of those first settlers from Mexico. C. A. Hutchinson noted that Captain Rivera recruited eight Indians, eight Mulattoes, two Spaniards, two Negroes, one Coyote (Indian and Mestizo), and one Mestizo. Jack Forbes found five Indians, five Mulattoes, one Spaniard, one Black, one Coyote, and one Mestizo.[9]

During the first two decades the migration of Mestizos to the pueblo surpassed that of Mulattoes and Blacks. It should be noted, however, that official population estimates were affected by a tendency among Mestizos, Indians, Mulattoes, and Blacks to "upgrade" their ethnic status when talking to census takers. Mestizos, for instance, preferred to consider themselves Spaniards, while Indians and Mulattoes often registered as Mestizos. In 1790, when the first census of the pueblo was taken, there were a total of 141 residents. Of these, 73 persons classified themselves as Spaniards, 39 claimed to be a Spanish-Indian mixture (Mestizos), 22 stated that they were Mulattoes, only 7 declared pure Indian ancestry, and none admitted to being Black.[10]

According to the 1790 census, 28 of the 141 residents of Los Angeles were adult men. The *pobladores* had constructed adobe houses and amassed a domestic stock numbering nearly three thousand head. However, only 5 of the 28 men owned substantial grazing property. Juan José Domínguez, the first soldier of the pueblo to petition the Crown for a rancho, received a generous allotment of land totaling seventy-five thousand acres. Soon 4 other *pobladores* received land grants, and these individuals began employing both Indians and Mestizos to help run their ranchos. Father Vicente Santa María, a traveler to Los Angeles in 1795, provided a rare glimpse of its pastoral life, remarking that at one of the ranchos "we see nothing but pagans passing, clad in shoes, with sombreros and blankets, and serving as muleteers to the settlers and ranchos, so that if it were not for the gentiles ["civilized" Indians and/or Mestizos] there would be neither pueblo nor rancho."[11]

The pueblo's poor record in attracting new immigrants forced the friars to draw heavily on the native Indian labor force. Historian Hubert Howe Bancroft noted the impact of such action on southern California's labor reserve: "Gentiles still worked for wages at pueblos and presidios, but they were becoming every year more difficult to obtain, and neophytes [Indians] were employed whenever an agreement could be made with the friars who received the wage. The only controversy recorded was that caused by the retirement of a hundred laborers at Los Angeles in 1810 to their mission of San Juan Capistrano."[12]

Unquestionably, the ranchers and farmers of Los Angeles benefited from the large Indian labor pool in the surrounding missions. The mission Indian population at San Gabriel, one of the largest missions of Alta California, grew from 50 residents in 1772 (its second year of existence) to 1,701 in 1814.[13] The padres considered the Indians their wards and preferred to limit the interaction between Indians and *pobladores*. José del Carmen Lugo, a southern California rancher of that era, reported the padres' excessive power over the Gabrielinos: "Indians belonging to the missions could not leave them without special permission, and this was seldom granted. Frequently, they were sent to work in the towns or the presidios under contract. They were not paid for the work they did, but the padres received it for the benefit of the community . . . but we did not know what part of these receipts reached the community."[14]

Like the English settlers on the East Coast who relied on indentured servants and Black slaves to make their town and farms prosperous, these Spanish colonists of Alta California depended upon Indian labor for ranch and mission work.[15] Los Angeles had an Indian population of 150–350 during the first two decades of the nineteenth century, a sizable number, considering that in 1820 the total population of the pueblo stood at only 615. The fact that one-third to more than one-half of the inhabitants of the towns were Indians is an indication of the importance of this group to the pueblo. Although the Los Angeles colonists did not attempt extermination of the Indians as was done in many parts of North America during a similar period, they did cooperate with the padres to exploit Indian labor.[16]

During the Mexican period, hundreds of Indians who had been with the missions of San Gabriel and San Fernando went to work for Mexican *rancherías* (small ranch properties). The rancheros required their vaqueros, the early cowboys, to work six days a week from sunrise to sundown to earn little more than food and shelter. The vaqueros often spent their days grazing cattle, frequently over terrain bordered by dangerous ravines.[17] At the larger ranchos, the rancheros hired *mayordomos*, or supervisors, whose role, explained Pío Pico, one of the pueblo's most prosperous rancheros, was "to take care of the cattle and do whatever [was] demanded," including the sale and delivery of the stock and the supervision of the labor force.[18]

The few available personal reminiscences of the Mexican Californios, although biased in general toward the wealthier classes, also provide valuable insights into the daily lives of others during the Mexican period.[19] The Californios' accounts, recorded decades after the American conquest, place the story in a more balanced perspective than that found in Anglo travel journals. José del Carmen Lugo spoke to his interviewer, Thomas Savage, of "the Californian way of life" when the entire family awoke at three o'clock and men and women worked until dusk. The women worked in the kitchen in the early morning, "sweeping, cleaning, dusting, and so on." They also cooked, milked the cows, and prepared cheese. According to Lugo, "the women's labors lasted til seven or eight in the morning. After that they were busy cooking, sewing, or washing." As for the men, they "passed the day in labor in the fields," some sowing seeds, others reaping or bringing wood.[20] An additional duty of ranch hands, the slaughtering of animals and salting of hides for trade with the Yankee clippers, demanded much expertise. Mariano Guadalupe Vallejo, a California rancher of that era, recalled that each rancho "had its *calaveras*, its slaughter-corral, where cattle and sheep were killed by the Indian butchers. Every Saturday morning the fattest animals were chosen and driven there, and by night the hides were all stretched on the hillside to dry."[21]

Although men tended to dominate the political and economic activities of the Mexican frontier pueblos, women participated more actively in the economy than has previously been recognized. In Mexican California, women ran some of the ranchos, taking charge of the raising of domestic stock and the cultivation of crops. Women also qualified for land grants, as did some of the Indian population of the community. In 1831, the Alcalde of Los Angeles issued a grant of some 4,000 acres to María Rita Valdez de Villa. The city dispensed the grant under the terms of joint occupancy, although within a few years the authorities evicted her partner, Luciano Valdez, and prepared a new deed under Doña María's name. It seems that Doña María had disagreed with Luciano for numerous reasons, including the fact that he wished to plant vineyards. For several decades after his departure, Doña María managed the ranch by herself. In the 1880s she sold her property, Rancho Rodeo de las Aguas, to real estate speculators. The subdivided property at the turn of the century became the site of a new development named Beverly Hills.[22]

During the early years of the development of the Los Angeles pueblo, the population remained predominantly Indian and Mestizo. Two of the first foreign residents came with the trapping party of the legendary Jedediah Smith. Smith is credited with opening a route from the Great Salt Lake to Los Angeles in 1826. While he was in Los Angeles, the padres of Mission San Gabriel attended to his party, providing them with food and shelter. At the pueblo, Smith's men traded furs and other goods for horses and mules. When Smith finally received permission to continue his journey northward, two of his men, Daniel Ferguson and John Wilson, chose to remain.[23] In 1821, another trapper, William Wolfskill, arrived in Los Angeles by way of New Mexico with a party of American fur trappers and decided to stay permanently in Los Angeles. Wolfskill, who had gained Mexican citizenship while in New Mexico, had broad trading privileges. At San Pedro, he built a schooner which he used for nearly a year to hunt otter up and down the California coast.[24]

The beginning of fur trade and schooner traffic along with the Mexican government's desire to encourage population growth in frontier towns such as Los Angeles attracted diverse residents. By 1835, when Mexican authorities officially elevated Los Angeles to the status of a *ciudad*, or town, one-third of the residents held urban occupations. These urban workers included sixteen merchants and numerous artisans and craftsmen employed in work serving both the rural and the urban population of Los Angeles. For example, the seven shoemakers, six tailors, and three hatters drew their trade from visiting sailors of the Yankee clippers as well as from town dwellers. They could also be expected to outfit the cowboys, ranchers, and soldiers of the community. The range of occupations was further influenced by the increasing influx of Americans and other foreigners. Mexicans worked at a variety of jobs during the mid-1830s, many of them specializing in carpentry, masonry, and forging and repairing metal. Others found employment in work related to the shipping and storing of goods, including driving and delivery of goods as well as clerking.[25]

An open port and the beginning of trade with Sante Fe in the late 1820s assured the pueblo residents of lower prices for essential goods and encouraged a few enterprising Californios to utilize the surplus quantities of goods for distribution on a retail basis. Alfred Robinson refers to one such merchant in his book *Life in California*. During Robinson's visit to Los Angeles in the summer of 1828, he "stopped at the house of Don Tiburcio Tapia, the 'Alcalde Constitucional' of the town, once a soldier in very moderate circumstances, but who by honest and industrious labor had amassed so much of this world's goods, as to make him one of the wealthiest inhabitants of the place. His strict integrity gave him credit to any amount, so that he was the principal merchant, and the only native one in El Pueblo de Los Angeles."[26]

Growing affluence as a result of the port and overland trade perhaps encouraged residents of Los Angeles to construct a new plaza in the 1820s. The plaza, as in other Latin American towns of that period, served as an important area of economic and social activity. In the plaza area the Mexican merchants built the first retail stores. In the same general location, residents, using Indian labor from San Gabriel, had constructed the first church in 1820. (Before that, the residents had had to ride or walk the seven miles to the San Gabriel mission to attend services.) Thus, as it underwent transformation from a small agricultural pueblo to an urban area serving surrounding ranches and farms, Los Angeles assumed the urban form characteristic of cities found in Latin America and other areas where Spain had raised its colonial flag. Even the most dramatic change yet to touch the pueblo, the Mexican-American War in 1846–1848, would not immediately disturb the Latin influence of the city.[27]

Compared to the havoc and loss of lives that characterized the fighting between Mexican and American forces in the interior of Mexico and in the Texas campaign, Californios emerged from the Mexican-American War with few physical casualties. The American conquest of Los Angeles cost the pueblo less than two dozen lives, and little property was destroyed. General Robert F. Stockton confiscated the most comfortable and centrally located home in the Main Plaza, but for the most part the wealthy Mexican Californians managed to hold on to their ranchos. Governor Pío Pico, who surrendered the city to the Americans during the first siege of the city, fled to Mexico but returned two years later and quickly renewed his business ties with the once despised "Yankees."[28] The majority of the old California rancheros exhibited peaceful intentions and cooperation, for they had faith in a democratic system that promised them equal protection and privileges. As E. Gould Buffum, a traveler to Los Angeles in 1850, noted, although the Calfornios "fought with a determined resistance against the naval forces of Commodore Stockton they have now, however, become reconciled to the institutions of our country, and will, I doubt not, in a few years make as good a set of democrats as can be found in Missouri or Arkansas."[29]

In the post Mexican-American War years, Los Angeles experienced an unstable political and economic situation. Three major factors contributed to this predicament: (1) the presence of a military occupational force in the city during the period 1846–1850, (2) the exodus of laborers for the northern California gold mines, and (3) the introduction by Americans of new methods of arranging or contracting for labor. As soon as Los Angeles had been captured and even before the ratification of the Treaty of Guadalupe Hidalgo (1848), Americans began to settle in Los Angeles in increasing numbers, a phenomenon that Mexican pueblo residents lamented but could not prevent. Many of the new arrivals came as military support personnel, and for the first few years the military played an important role in the selection of political leadership.[30] The pueblo residents elected two Mexican Californians in 1848 as first and second alcaldes. Colonel J. D. Stevenson, the military commander at Fort Moore in Los Angeles, rejected both choices because, in his opinion, the candidates were "well known to be among the worst of citizens as well as most violent enemies to the American authorities." At Colonel Stevenson's request, Governor Richard B. Mason voided the election and assigned Stephen Clark Foster as alcalde. Foster, a native of Maine, had been a trader in New Mexico and Sonora when the war broke out. He came to Los Angeles in 1846 as an interpreter with the Mormon Battalion.[31] Foster's appointment greatly angered Mexicanos. When the next election for alcalde was held in December 1848, they boycotted the polls.[32]

The military also opposed the influx of new Mexican migrants into the territory. Soon after Colonel Richard B. Mason established a temporary civil government in California following the 1846 defeat of Mexican forces at Monterey, he issued a proclamation denying "Sonorans," the principal Mexican emigrants, the right to migrate to California. His order of December 27, 1847, forbade citizens of Sonora to enter California except on official business. It especially affected Los Angeles, since many of the Sonorans who migrated to California settled there. Mason also directed all Sonorans in upper California to report to American authorities either at Monterey or at Los Angeles for the purpose of making known their business and the date of their arrival in the country.[33]

The nature and the degree of tension in Los Angeles during the years 1846–1848 are further documented in a series of letters written by John S. Griffin. Griffin, a surgeon who had come to California with Kearney's Dragoons in 1846, described the conditions in Los Angeles in 1849 in a letter to his friend, Colonel J. D. Stevenson, the former military commander, who had moved to San Francisco. The city, he wrote, "is thronged with soldiers, quartermaster's men, Sonorans, etc., the most vicious and idle set you have ever beheld." Lest his letter should cause Stevenson to send troops to Los Angeles, Griffin offered reassurances that "our men seem inclined to keep the peace among themselves, and the Sonoranians and Californians seem very much afraid of them." Indeed, Griffin concluded, "A Californian is a rare sight in the streets of Los Angeles." Indeed, following the military occupation of the pueblo, it took some months before Mexican residents felt secure enough to walk the streets without fear.[34]

Another unsettling event occurred in 1848, when the announcement of the gold strike in the north reached the pueblo. Californios flocked to the diggings. Antonio Franco Coronel, a resident of Los Angeles, left for the north as early as August 1848, taking a party of thirty men, Sonorans and Indians. Andrés Pico, brother of the former Mexican governor, also outfitted a party of miners, most of them Sonorans.[35] Walter Colton, a traveler to the Sacramento Valley during the gold strike, wrote that thousands of Sonorans, including many women, could be found in the gold fields by 1849. Immigrants from the northern provinces of Mexico passed through Los Angeles in great numbers between 1849 and 1851. The law prohibiting the influx of Sonorans, instituted during the war years, had lapsed and was no longer a restrictive element in Mexican immigration. Freedom to emigrate and the lure of wealth accounted for many of the eight thousand Sonorans reaching Los Angeles in the fall of 1851.[36]

While many southern California merchants and ranchers profited from the mining activities in the north, the gold rush contributed to a political setback for Los Angeles. Prior to the Mexican-American War, Los Angeles had been California's largest town and had served as the political capital of the province. By contrast, San Francisco had a population of less than 500 people when American forces entered California. The population of California, which numbered 15,000 in 1848, increased to 100,000 two years later, with 90 percent of the people locating in the region between San Francisco and the Sierras. One historian reported that San Francisco became an "instant city" and "gold was the living force that changed a comparative wilderness into the great metropolis of the Pacific." The gold flow gave the city a financial base, while population growth enabled it to command new and influential political power in the state.[37]

As the population in the gold region grew, however, the demand for goods from southern California increased commensurately. Ranchos of southern California enjoyed the greatest prosperity during the decade of the 1850s.[38] Cattle prices more than tripled between the years 1849 and 1851. In the first half of the 1850s, southern California ranchos accounted for sales of more than 50,000 head of cattle. At the same time, Los Angeles also became a major distribution center for horses and mules brought to the pueblo from the northern Mexican states by Mexican vaqueros. This trade drew additional Sonorans to Los Angeles, and the pueblo remained predominantly Mexican well into the 1850s. W. W. Robinson notes that "Los Angeles in 1851 was still a Mexican-California pueblo in looks and feelings. Its homes and shops were one-story adobe buildings, centered about a bare and dusty plaza. Nine-tenths of its three thousand people were Spanish-speaking—either Californios or Sonoran newcomers. The other tenth were mostly recently arrived Americans."[39]

In the meantime, southern California rancheros faced burdening tax problems that eventually caused their loss of power in state politics. Richard Morefield notes that as early as 1851, the twelve northern California counties, with a population of 119,917, commanded forty-four representatives in the state legislature, while the six southern counties, with a population of 6,367, had only twelve. The southern counties, however, paid over $41,000 in taxes during the fiscal year ending in June 1851, while the northern counties in the same period paid only half that amount. Not surprisingly, the disparity in taxation, a result of the high tax assessment placed on cattle, prompted southern rancheros to introduce a bill in the legislature that would have divided the state into two territories. Northern counties blocked this scheme, however, and throughout the 1850s the southern counties paid in taxes as much as thirty-five times more per citizen than their northern counterparts.[40]

The increasing influx of Americans and economic prosperity which resulted from the city's position as a distribution center for goods and supplies to mines and speculators in the north encouraged Angelenos to incorporate. Amid the rapid changes underway in the pueblo, political leaders faced numerous difficulties associated with running a city. The efforts of elected officials to solve the myriad problems of public education vividly illustrate this point. Controversial issues connected with the establishment of public schools included raising taxes to pay for them and finding a method of providing instruction for a community that was overwhelmingly Mexican, yet contained a growing Anglo population.

A man in a position of great influence in the direction of public education was Antonio Franco Coronel. Coronel was elected in 1850 as county assessor. According to state legislation passed that year, the assessor in each county was empowered to serve as pro-tem superintendent of the public schools. His duties in this capacity required that he appoint a school board of three members. It was appropriate that the duty to establish a school board fell on Antonio Coronel, for his father, Ygnacio Coronel, had been the pueblo's first school teacher, beginning his career in 1838. The elder Coronel, in fact, conducted classes in his home until 1854, when the city constructed the first public schoolhouse, a two-story brick building. Antonio Coronel, who had been driven from the gold fields by Anglos in 1849, chose to put the past behind him, selecting two Anglo Americans and one native Californio, Cristóbal Aguilar, for the distinction of serving on the first school board of the city. The two Americans selected, Benjamin Hayes, once the military commandant of the city, and Abel Sterns, rancher and merchant, had strong supporters among the leaders of the community.[41]

In 1853, Coronel, who had by then been elected mayor of Los Angeles, led the movement to establish the city's first public schools. He proposed a system owned and controlled by the city. The council supported his idea, and the mayor and council appointed a superintendent, J. L. Brent, and a new school board consisting of Brent, Lewis Granger, and Stephen C. Foster. The first school opened in 1855.[42]

Los Angeles City Council members (the majority of whom were Mexican) had intended to establish bilingual schools. In 1852, for example, the council had noted that while it supported the opening of a public school, it believed that "such a school ought to provide instruction in [both] English and Spanish." Council members conceded that if a schoolmaster knowledgeable in both languages could not be found, then they would support the construction of two separate schools. As reported in the *Los Angeles Star*, the debate centered on the question of the value of each language. On the one hand, Spanish was important to the Mexicanos, since they could conduct business and maintain social contacts with the older generation whose members did not have the benefit of schooling. On the other hand, the Mexicanos, including the older generation, wanted their children to learn the language by which all government and state affairs were conducted. Supporters of bilingual education lost, as the school board failed to find anyone who could teach in both English and Spanish. When Public School No. 1 opened, only English was permitted for instruction.[43]

While a few members of the Californio elite mixed with Americanos, most remained outside of the mainstream of Anglo society. In addition to the election of Antonio Coronel as assessor, in 1850 Los Angeles citizens elected Francisco Figueroa treasurer and Juan Chávez, Cristóbal Aguilar, and Manuel Requena councilmen. In 1853, Coronel was elected mayor. Over the next generation, however, the number of Mexicanos in elected offices declined drastically. According to historian Richard Griswold del Castillo, the Californios were almost totally excluded from Los Angeles' growth in the three decades after the Mexican-American War. For example, while 60 percent of the Mexicanos in the pueblo owned property in 1850, only 24 percent of the Spanish-speaking residents of the city held property twenty years later. Griswold also reported an overall decline in the wealth of Californios during this period.[44]

Given these transitions in wealth and power, the late 1850s and early 1860s were a turbulent period for Los Angeles in general and its Mexican citizens in particular.[45] Francisco Ramírez, who at age seventeen became the first Spanish-language newspaper editor of southern California with the publication of *El Clamor Público*, followed the daily affairs of Mexicanos with a keen eye for analyzing the process of change that was occurring in the Mexican community. Ramírez published his newspaper in English, Spanish, and French, doing many of the translations himself. He considered himself a Lincoln Republican and an admirer of the American democratic system. Not surprisingly, he championed the rights of the Spanish-speaking. He also favored the emancipation of Black Americans and argued for better treatment of California Indians.[46] Ramírez worked diligently for the systematic publication of all laws, in booklets and in newspapers, in Spanish—a right written into the state constitution but constantly neglected by legislators and governors. Although Ramírez was known to write favorably of American institutions, he proved an able critic of the system. The murder of a Mexicano by the deputy constable of the city prompted him to claim that "it is becoming a very common custom to murder or insult the Mexicanos with impunity."[47] Unfortunately, Los Angeles, which already had the *Los Angeles Star*, seemed unwilling or unable to support a second newspaper. After only three years of circulation, Ramírez published the last issue of *El Clamor Público* in 1859.

Many native Californio ranchers were ruined by the labor problems, tedious and expensive land litigation, and unfair taxation written about by Ramírez. The floods and drought of the early 1860s proved an even more demanding test for the Californios. One of the worst floods in the history of Los Angeles occurred in late 1861, when fifty inches of rain fell on southern California in a period of less than a month. Then came a dry spell of more than two years when southern California received only four inches of rain. The drought caused widespread destruction in the cattle industry. More than fifty thousand head of cattle had to be destroyed, and thousands of mules, sheep, and other domestic animals died as a result of insufficient feed. At the same time the demand for beef, which had peaked during the gold rush period, had subsided. When the drought struck, ranchers attempted to recover some of their losses, offering cattle at low prices. But more cattle than buyers existed, and ranchers who had sold beef for $70.00 per head in the heyday of the mining years could not in 1863 find buyers at the price of $1.50 per head.[48]

The severe drought forced many of the rancheros to borrow at the exorbitant rate of 3–5 percent per month.[49] Julio Verdugo, whose ranch extended from the San Fernando Valley to parts of northeast Los Angeles, lost much of his property in repayment of money extended to him during this crisis. In 1861 Verdugo used his ranch property as collateral for a loan of $3,445.37 at an interest rate of 3 percent per month. Eight years later, still unable to recover from his losses during the drought years, Verdugo owed $58,750. In order to settle the debt, he sold part of the expansive San Rafael Rancho which had been granted to his father, Don José María Verdugo, in the 1790s.[50]

Ranch property became the basis for extensive land speculation in the 1870s. It was in this decade that the seeds of future urban sprawl of southern California were planted. Developers who had acquired much of this property during the period 1850–1870, when taxes, droughts, and floods had made ownership a risky enterprise, were the first to subdivide property for residential purposes. In the 1870s, John G. Downey, Los Angeles' first major subdivider, placed on the market a large amount of property, including sections of the 2,400 acres of land bought from the Domínguez family of San Pedro in 1854. Downey's property eventually became the city of Wilmington.[51] In the spring of 1874, Charles Maclay and several associates purchased the vast San Fernando Rancho, 56,000 acres of land once owned by Pío Pico and embracing the old Mission San Fernando. Less than a month after the purchase, the investors had created a new community and sold hundreds of lots.[52] Ironically, Pío Pico, one of the city's wealthiest native sons, sold much of his rancho land during the 1870s in order to invest in urban property. Pico used more than $35,000, much of it from the sale of his vast rancho holdings, to complete his famous hotel, the Pío Pico House.[53]

Although greatly influenced socially by a growing Anglo population, Los Angeles continued to impress visitors with its strong Mexican character in the 1870s. The city, Miriam Follin Leslie wrote in 1877, "was quite different from any we had seen, having a distinctly Spanish and semi-tropical air that made us feel we were almost in a foreign land." Miriam F. Leslie had arrived in Los Angeles with her husband, the publisher of *Leslie's Illustrated Weekly*, after an extensive and extravagant cross-country excursion. A description of Los Angeles appeared in her 1877 book *California: A Pleasure*

Trip from Gotham to the Golden Gate. In her opinion, Los Angeles had "in ten years become a 'live' American City and might in one sense, date its age at no more than one decade."[54] Another visitor, David Starr Jordan, president of Stanford University, described Los Angeles during the same period as "still a mere village—mostly Mexican . . . " Jordan seemed unimpressed by the subdivision of rancho property that had begun a few years earlier, noting that the "country round was practically a desert of cactus and sagebrush."[55]

When the Southern Pacific Railroad brought Los Angeles its first transcontinental connection in 1886, urban boosters who had worked for such a terminal hailed the event as one of the most important in the city's history. The arrival of the Santa Fe Railroad the following year triggered a fierce battle between the two railroad giants for passengers. At one point, fares from the Midwest to southern California dropped to one dollar, a gimmick that served to further publicize the new migration waves that began with the ensuing rate wars. The railroads, anxious to promote their transcontinental routes to southern California, launched an advertising campaign that succeeded beyond anyone's expectations.[56]

Between 1885 and 1887, newcomers to California participated in a massive buying spree, spending some $200 million on property and climaxing what historians have called the most spectacular real estate boom in American history. Property prices skyrocketed overnight, with some lots changing hands several times daily. Lots within the city limits sold first. Speculators and promoters carved businesses from the valleys and hillsides adjacent to the old pueblo. Twenty-five new townsites sprouted up along the Santa Fe railway between Los Angeles and San Bernardino.[57]

Before the real estate market collapsed in 1888, some enterprising speculators earned enormous profits by offering clients future "harbor property." Near present-day Culver City and Marina del Rey, real estate agents acquired property from the Machados, Talamantes, and Higueras, three families whose ownership predated Mexican independence. In June 1887, promotion of Port Ballona began; advertising called it the "Future Harbor of Southern California."[58] Not to be outdone, a syndicate headed by J. R. Tuffree, having recently bought the large Palos Verdes Rancho, announced the construction of the harbor of Catalina at Portuguese Bend.[59] All this speculation did not deter the city's largest landowner, Henry Huntington, from progressing with his plans to have the city's main harbor constructed at Santa Monica. Meanwhile, San Pedro continued as the city's most utilized port and continued to attract property buyers in large numbers.[60]

The increasing Anglo influences in the city overshadowed much of the cultural life of the Mexican community, although romanticized Spanish-Mexican traditions became quite popular. Helen Hunt Jackson conducted a series of interviews in the 1880s with the Ygnacio del Valle family of Rancho Camulos in preparation for her famous novel *Ramona*.[61] The Southern Pacific Railroad promoted southern California as a romantic region filled with historic Spanish adobe missions graced by beautiful Spanish señoritas. During the recession of 1894, the Los Angeles Merchants' Association sponsored a new event, La Fiesta de Los Angeles, employing Spanish-Mexican themes as a promotional scheme. In the second year of the Fiesta, the Merchants' Association added one Mexican to the planning board. Charles F. Lummis, a transplanted New Englander, also served on the board. According to historian Boyle Workman, Lummis, who founded and edited *Out West* magazine, went so far in romanticizing southern California's past and present that for a time he was the leading cultural chauvinist of the region.[62]

By the late 1890s, Los Angeles had reached maturity as an urban center. The population of the city more than quadrupled in the 1880s, increasing from 11,183 in 1880 to 50,000 a decade later. This urban growth amounted to a 350 percent increase, a rate of growth greater than that of any other city in the country. (By contrast, San Francisco for a similar period netted only a 28 percent population increase.) During this period, most of the new migrants hailed from other regions in the United States, principally the Midwest. In 1890, Los Angeles had one of the smallest percentages of foreign-born White population of any city in the nation: 22 percent, as compared to 39 percent for New York and 41 percent for Chicago. The Mexican population (including all persons of "Mexican origin") doubled over the period 1880–1900, but still comprised less than 15 percent of the total city population in 1900.[63]

The residents of Los Angeles at the close of the century still clustered together in what might be called a "walking city" environment. The close surroundings gave Angelenos ample opportunity to interact and work together, despite racial and class differences. The next generation promised startling transformation. Previews of these changes were reflected in the new subdivisions and extensions of interurban transportation systems. Civic leaders in the 1890s spoke of a port to accommodate world trade. Paved roads and factory smokestacks reminded Angelenos that they had entered a new era. The next twenty-five years promised industrialists a new wave of migrants capable of adding muscle to the manufacturing sector and dollars to commercial enterprises. These newcomers had the benefit of rapid interurban transportation and inexpensive housing. Leaders of Los Angeles faced crucial decisions concerning the lack of water, the absence of coal, and shortages of capital and labor. The labor problem challenged the industrialists over the next thirty years; and in this context, the Mexican immigrants played a crucial role.

3 From Homeland to Barrio

I

Fifty years after the termination of the Mexican-American War and the approval of a treaty which gave the United States half of its southern neighbor's territory, Mexican emigrants began a peaceful "reconquest" of the Southwest. Mexican migration to the United States has been the subject of many scholarly essays, monographs, and novels. Mexico is unique among most countries of the world in that the vast majority of its migrant population, fully 90 percent, has always emigrated to the United States. Few Mexicans leave for other regions of Latin America or Europe. Nonetheless, the migration northward has been selective, with certain Mexican states contributing the majority of the migration stream. Recent scholarship suggests that an investigation into the "local springs of dislocation and emigration" is needed for better comprehension of the causes and consequences of migration.[1] Maldwyn A. Jones succinctly stated this point when he noted that "emigrants should be seen as coming not from vaguely defined countries of origin but from particular provinces and regions, each with its own kind of response or lack of it to the forces shaping emigration."[2]

Los Angeles' emergence as a regional metropolitan center coincided with a wave of Mexican migration that began late in the 1890s and continued unabated until the outset of the Great Depression. Initially many people left Mexico for long sojourns in the United States because of rising population pressures and the introduction of mechanized processes in mining and textiles. Industrialization produced cyclical unemployment in regions chronically plagued by low agricultural production and poor commercial opportunities. These regions also suffered from the increasing expropriation of small farms by hacendados and foreign land speculators, further stimulating the uprooting of rural families.

While the ruling classes in Mexico spoke of progress and a new industrial era, in the period 1880–1910, the Mexican masses received little in terms of better living and working conditions. Indeed, inflation, especially the ever increasing rise in food prices, and the concomitant drop in real wages spurred a massive out-migration among the peasants of the heavily populated interior states. Industrialization contributed to the growth of the national economy but also induced violent labor strikes and prolonged social unrest in the urban areas. Beginning at the turn of the century, political exiles in the United States plotted and financed an attack on the aged, corrupt Mexican dictator Porfirio Díaz. By 1911 the entire country was in revolution. The massive dislocations of the population, which the Revolution caused, also triggered a crisis in food production and industrial output.

In the years following the termination of the Revolution in 1920, Mexico recovered slowly. Chronic unemployment and equally persistent inflation became the principal problems. At the same time, the birth rate, which had dropped off during the Revolution, rose again, and land distribution proceeded at a very slow pace. Moreover, political and religious conflict flared up during the reconstruction decade, events which impelled many residents to seek their fortunes north of the Río Grande. The proximity of Los Angeles and the rich neighboring agricultural regions, together with positive information about wages and living conditions in the United States, produced massive migration northward.

Los Angeles' efforts to attract new immigrants, both native and foreign, had begun with the arrival of the transcontinental railroad in the mid-1880s, at the same time that railroad linkage with Mexico's largest population centers had opened for the American Southwest a relatively accessible source of cheap labor. Under the liberal laws applied to foreign ownership in late nineteenth-century Mexico, in 1885 the Southern Pacific formed the Mexican International Railroad, a line that a decade later extended some 900 miles into Mexico and linked the Texas border town of Eagle Pass with Durango, Mexico. The same year, the Southern Pacific also completed its famous "Sunset" route, offering direct rail connections from New Orleans to Los Angeles. For nearly 1,200 miles the "Sunset" line ran closely parallel to the United States–Mexican border. Passengers boarding at San Antonio for the West Coast could make stops in El Paso, Nogales, Mexicali, and Tecate. The Santa Fe Railroad, a major competitor of the Southern Pacific, during this same period linked the West Coast with Mexico via Guaymas, a port on the mainland side of the Gulf of California. When the Southern Pacific acquired the Sonora Railway to Guaymas in 1898, it presented a plan to the Mexican government to extend the line to Guadalajara. In 1909 the Southern Pacific Railroad Company of Mexico was formed. By 1927 it had completed its line to Guadalajara, constructing 1,370 miles of track in the process. The Nogales-Guadalajara linkage opened new trade routes from the Southwest to Mexico City. This Southern Pacific Mexican line proved immensely valuable to Los Angeles industrialists.[3]

II

Each region of Mexico responded in its own way to the forces shaping emigration. The attractiveness of emigration to the United States as opposed to migration within the national boundaries varied with the geographical position, economic opportunities, and material conditions within the individual rural communities that provided the bulk of the migrants. Manuel Gamio, a Mexican anthropologist, and Paul S. Taylor, a Berkeley economist, both investigated the origin of the Mexican emigrants during the 1920s and found that the majority of them came from the central states of Mexico. Data from 23,846 postal check remittances told Gamio that more than 50 percent of the emigrants in the United States came from Michoacán, Guanajuato, and Jalisco, in that order.[4] Taylor examined 3,132 employment records in Gary, Indiana, and arrived at the same conclusions, only with a different order—Jalisco, Michoacán, and Guanajuato. Mexico City (Distrito Federal), which contributed 5 percent of the emigrants in Gamio's study, accounted for 6 percent in Taylor's.[5] By contrast, Anna C. Lofstedt, who studied 947 cases, concluded that Michoacán and Guanajuato combined accounted for only 9 percent of the total Mexican immigration to Los Angeles. Indeed, in Los Angeles' barrios, Chihuahua, Zacatecas, Durango, and Jalisco represented the home states of 63 percent of the emigrants. Sonora, a state which had held preeminence in emigration to southern California in the nineteenth century, contributed only 7 percent of the Mexican immigrants to Los Angeles in 1922.[6] Thus in general, Los Angeles' Mexican immigrant population came from the central and northern states.

Northern Mexico has several peculiar features that explain its continued importance in the annals of the United States–Mexico migration patterns. Obviously, promixity to the United States border and the existence of an open border, prior to the creation of the U.S. Border Patrol in 1925, influenced the migration patterns of Mexicans. For those wishing to emigrate to Los Angeles, the north was a logical springboard. Moreover, in the north many of the migrants could participate in the seasonal labor pool utilized both by southern California agriculturalists and industrialists and by northern Mexican ranchers and miners. The presence of some of Mexico's most productive mines also acted as a magnet for new labor and capital. During the late nineteenth century, precious metals constituted more than half of the nation's total exports.[7] When mining companies discovered large coal deposits in the early 1880s in the northern part of Coahuila and several other locations near the U.S. border, the future of the North's industrial potential was assured. By the turn of the century Monterrey, in the state of Nuevo León, had become Mexico's chief manufacturing city. It counted among its industries smelters, foundries, cotton and flour mills, breweries, locomotive and machine shops, and steel mills.[8] Moreover, by the turn of the century, the United States was purchasing three-fourths of Mexico's exports, many of them transported by railroad via the northern states.

On the ranches of Chihuahua, Sonora, and Durango, campesinos and vaqueros earned wages 10–50 percent above those paid to unskilled laborers in the central states. The research of Friedrich Katz has shown that in prerevolutionary Mexico, the northern rural workers were probably better off than those in other parts of the country. Hacendados paid higher wages in the North than in the South, and northern farmers offered sharecropping contracts which surpassed terms provided in other parts of Mexico by as much as 25 percent.[9] Northern sharecroppers had employment options not readily available to their counterparts in other regions of the country. In the event of bad harvests, they either went to work in the mines or crossed the border to find seasonal work in expanding economic areas such as southern California. Of central importance was the fact that many of the sharecroppers could take on casual or seasonal work without ending their relationship with the hacendado and without necessarily having to move their families.[10]

Over the period 1890–1930, Durango, one of Mexico's northern states, contributed significantly to Los Angeles' Mexican community. Much of Durango's wealth was tied to agriculture and silver, although by the late nineteenth and early twentieth centuries the state also attracted investments in numerous cotton mills, tanneries, flour mills, and several factories which produced soap, cottonseed, and glycerine. Beginning with the world silver crisis of 1893, Durango began to suffer from economic boom-and-bust cycles. In 1903, for example, the mining industry of Durango em-

ployed 10,481 people. But with the drop in silver purchases during
the world economic crisis of 1906–1907, the labor force dropped to
5,256 in 1907.[11]

Despite the uneven growth of one of its principal industries,
Durango continued to show population increases. Between the years
1895 and 1910, Durango recorded a male population increase of
45,000 for the 16–50 age group. The state's agricultural labor force
rose sharply over the years 1900–1910—from 71,821 to 125,227.[12]
Yet as the agricultural export trade expanded, causing a need for
more laborers, the number of small farmers decreased. For the peasants, the maldistribution of the land and the entry of foreign companies into large-scale agricultural production became the burning
issues prior to the outbreak of the Revolution. In the Laguna region,
Durango's richest agricultural area, hacienda owners controlled
more than 4.5 million hectares of land, or most of the best acreage in
the state.[13]

Most of the laborers employed in the haciendas in Durango
worked for foreign-controlled joint-stock companies. In contrast to
the early-nineteenth-century hacienda system, these companies encouraged the formation of a floating proletarian work force. Agricultural workers employed by the joint-stock companies earned
average daily wages of 51–57 centavos in the years 1909–1911; but,
unlike the campesinos of the traditional haciendas, they managed to
move about quite freely.[14] In the Laguna region, cotton dominated
the agricultural economy. Its cultivation required only a seasonal labor force, thus eliminating the need to attach the laborer to the soil
by debt peonage.

While Durango recorded significant population growth during
the late Porfiriato, by comparison, Guanajuato, one of the principal
central states, registered population losses of nearly 22,000 in the
16–50 male age group for the period 1895–1910. A typical emigrant,
Juan Berzunzolo, a native of Ojos de Agua, Guanajuato, left the state
in 1908 and settled in Los Angeles, where he found work with the
Simons brickyard. As a young man he had labored with his father
sharecropping a small farm. After his father's premature death, he
had hired himself out as a peon earning 25 centavos (12 cents U.S.) a
day working from sunrise to sunset. His friends encouraged him to
emigrate north in 1908. After crossing the border at El Paso, Texas,
he accepted a job with the Southern Pacific line doing track maintenance. Eventually, he moved to Los Angeles, where he found work in
the brick and tile industry.[15]

Mexican government statistics provide clues that explain the
tremendous volume of internal migration common to every rural

area between 1895 and 1910. The rates of migration resulted in large measure from the growth of towns and centers of concentrated industry. Contemporary observers and scholars failed to document properly the internal migration of Mexicans, giving attention instead to the flow of workers traveling toward the U.S. border. Albert Alexander Graham, a Topeka, Kansas, attorney and businessman, spent two months in Mexico in 1906. When he traveled northward from Mexico City to El Paso, Graham was impressed with the crowded passenger trains headed for the United States: "Cars containing as many as two hundred Mexican laborers . . . men leaving the country against the will of the government and the desire of the landowners, with every discouragement placed in their way."[16] The internal migration patterns of rural workers in Mexico for the period 1900–1910 clearly indicated that Mexicans who left for the north did so as a last resort. In that decade four northern Mexican border states combined absorbed a migrant population of 159,000. Over the same period the four most populated states of the Central Plateau recorded an influx of over 360,000 new residents (Jalisco, 97,386; Guanajuato, 102,696; Zacatecas, 112,949; Michoacán, 48,802).[17] Nonetheless the owners and managers of the railroads, the mines, and the factories argued that they found it difficult to secure sufficient laborers. As long as wages in agriculture remained at one-third to one-half of those paid in industrial work, one could not expect an end to the mass movement of the rural population of the central and southern states to more industrialized regions.

The migration of laborers to other states signified an important first step toward eventual emigration. N. O. Winter commented in 1900 that "a constantly increasing number of the peon class are moving to the industrial centers."[18] The principal cause of this migration in the prerevolutionary years was linked to the differential rates of industrial and urban growth.

In 1883 the Mexican Congress enacted a new land law which empowered land companies to survey public lands for the purpose of settlement and subdivision. The Díaz government, convinced that these laws would promote foreign colonization of rural Mexico, gave the land companies the right to claim one-third of the land surveyed and to purchase the remaining two-thirds at substantially less than the market price. The law proved disastrous for those living on village lands, or *ejidos*. While many of these small farmers had lived on the land all of their lives, as had their ancestors, few held formal titles to the property, and thus they became victims of the massive expropriations that occurred between 1883 and 1910. Although it resulted in higher wages than had formerly prevailed in the Central

Plateau, this expropriation of communal village lands had grave social and economic consequences. George McCutchen McBride estimated that by 1910 the rural inhabitants of Mexico who held no individual property were probably more numerous than they had been at any previous time in the modern history of the country.[19] In Jalisco, Michoacán, and Guanajuato—three states that contributed a significant number of Los Angeles' Mexican immigrants—the rural population topped 2.5 million (2,537,625) in 1910.[20] The percentage of rural heads of families holding individual property averaged only 3.2 in 1910.[21] The loss of land, much of it occurring during the years 1876–1910, forced the majority of rural workers into tenant farming, migrant labor, or employment in the mines. Nationwide, up to 5 million campesinos lost their right to the use of communal lands during the Porfiriato.[22]

For those workers employed under the wage scale, underemployment and inflation were the major problems. Although the government reported an increase in money wages from 1890 to 1910, real wages actually fell sharply because of inflation; and prices for the entire period of the Porfiriato increased by at least 30 percent.[23] Already burdened by the seasonal nature of the work, the region's 1.5 million laborers, half of the total national work force in this occupation, suffered additional problems with the steady elimination of small farming units. The larger plantations required a surplus labor force, a factor which contributed to underemployment. Thus most workers considered themselves fortunate to find work six months of the year.

Although the land grabbers received favorable tariff exemptions and tax concessions, nonetheless, they exploited their sharecroppers. Elías Garza, a cement worker in Los Angeles, recalled the perils of tenant farming during the days of his youth in Michoacán: "The owners gave us the seeds, the animals, and the land, but it turned out that when the crop was harvested there wasn't anything left for us even if we had worked very hard. That was terrible. Those land owners were robbers.[24] The sharecroppers most feared the unannounced visits and confiscation of the tenant farmer's harvest. Against such actions, the sharecroppers could hold no realistic expectation of judicial redress.

Probably no other state in Mexico contributed more immigrants to Los Angeles than Jalisco. This seems ironic, since Jalisco was one of the wealthiest and most productive states in the Republic. Mexicans liked to refer to it as the granary of their nation. The state led the nation in the production of corn, beans, and milk. In fact it produced sufficient corn during the late Porfirian years to export well over 200,000 tons to other regions, including a sizable portion to the United States. Jalisco also led the nation during Díaz' last years in the value of livestock, although it had only one-fourth as much grazing land as its second nearest competitor, Chihuahua.[25]

Jalisco's inability to keep its residents from leaving their homeland stemmed from three principal causes: (1) population pressures on land that had been increasingly subdivided; (2) massive expropriation of communal lands by private entrepreneurs; (3) a drop in real wages and increases in food prices. The first factor, population pressures, also affected many other central states of Mexico; but for Jalisco, the second most populated state in the Republic, overpopulation, or the threat of it, reached serious proportions after 1890. By 1910 Jalisco, with a population of 1.2 million, had ten times as many residents as its neighbor Aguascalientes.[26] Friedrich Katz has recently contended that "the number of laborers available to central Mexican haciendas greatly increased from 1876 to 1910, as the massive expropriations of that period created a new landless proletariat, which limited industry in most parts of central Mexico could not absorb."[27] Moreover, the custom of equal division of inheritance and the tendency among the Jaliscans to have large families caused an increasing subdivision of the land. By the turn of the century thousands remained landless in a society that placed great significance on farming and land ownership. Finally, food prices reached record levels as private land companies turned traditional food production regions toward cultivation of sugar, sisal, and cotton, Mexico's major agricultural exports.[28] At the same time, average daily wages in Jalisco in the years 1907–1910 came to the equivalent of twenty cents (U.S.).[29]

For the middle-class sector, Jalisco had been economically stable throughout the late nineteenth century, and opportunities in commerce, farming, and professional services had not been wanting. Jalisco was second only to the Federal District (Mexico City) in the number employed in commerce and professional occupations. In 1910 the state not only was first in agricultural production, but also led in construction. Unlike the neighboring states of Colima and Nayarit, where economic opportunities in 1910 were limited to agriculture and some livestock raising, Jalisco had a diversified economy, which provided a degree of upward mobility for most members of the middle-level, educated classes.[30] It is quite probable, however, that by 1910 a new generation of youth from the nonagricultural sector had become victims of limited openings and underemployment in industry and professional service.

Overall, the consequence of capital investments, foreign trade, and industrial expansion in the central and northern states over the years 1880–1910 created new problems for the semi-agricultural and industrial laborers who constituted a large part of the working force.[31] As often is the case during the initial years of industrialization and the creation of capital-intensive units, cyclical fluctuations plagued the developing industries. The results were that workers faced long periods of unemployment or underemployment.

The consequences of cyclical fluctuations in industry are best exemplified by the mining industry. In 1899, a record number of miners were employed in Mexico—some 106,536 (nearly half in the northern states). In a short span of three years the number dropped to 85,333, nearly 90 percent of the job losses occurring in the north and central states. The unpredictable status of this industry played havoc with the workers' goal of full and steady employment.[32] Whereas 92,176 persons found employment in mining in 1900, only 26,890 held mining jobs in 1921.[33] Industries in the southwestern United States experienced similar cyclical fluctuations during approximately the same period, but the expanding economy north of the border provided workers with numerous employment options not found in Mexico.

Migration to the north also increased following the shutdown of manufacturing plants during Díaz' last decade in power. Factories producing *aguardiente* (brandy) declined from a high of 2,211 in 1899 to only 1,674 ten years later. Likewise, tobacco companies registered a drop in the number of plants from 766 in 1899 to 437 in 1908. In four of the five major regions of Mexico, the number of persons employed in the manufacturing industries declined. Moreover, even when factories did not close, declining production had a major impact on the work force. Between the years 1899 and 1909, for example, the number of textile mills declined very slightly, from 144 to 142. During this same period, however, the number of workers employed varied from a high of 50,132 in 1901 to a low of 26,149 a year later. On the average, the number of textile workers remained at a level between 27,000 and 33,000. Such figures certainly demonstrate the instability of the Mexican industrial economy for this decade.[34]

Such was not necessarily the case for agriculture. In the same decade, 1899–1909, sugar production more than doubled, from 68,218 tons to 145,790 tons. Cotton producton was also at a record level, increasing from 20,702 tons in 1899 to 41,277 in 1909.[35]

In some of the central Mexican states, agricultural production advanced with the development of large plantations. The creation of the plantation system, however, generally eliminated the necessity for tenant farming. Owned principally by foreign interests, these agricultural units operated much like factories. Carlos Ibáñez in Zacatecas at the turn of the century experienced the life of a peon before emigrating to Los Angeles. He received a small food allowance and a few cents a day for his labor; an amount so little "that I don't even remember how much it was," he was to state twenty-five years later in Los Angeles, where he worked as a laborer. He cited the low wages as a principal reason for his decision "to leave [Mexico] in search of fortune" in California.[36]

When Díaz permitted foreign monopolies to expropriate communal Indian lands on a massive scale and allowed the enslavement of thousands of workers, he failed to consider the long-term consequences: the displacement of small farmers and subsequent creation of a new pool of unskilled labor. Many of the displaced rural workers flocked to the cities, where they could find only casual day work. Unskilled and poorly educated, the landless proletariat found themselves in a weak bargaining position. Many from this class found employment in the textile factories of Mexico City and the East Coast region, while others stood at street corners and offered their services as casual laborers. These workers suffered in particular during periods of production fluctuation. The industrial sector employed three thousand fewer people in 1910 than in 1900. The total percentage of agricultural laborers rose several points in the years between 1895 and 1910, when it reached 68.1 percent.[37]

Many urban workers who could not earn a living in agriculture emigrated to the United States. Percy F. Martin, an English author who visited Mexico in 1906, observed that for some years there had been a great shortage of stone and brick masons, carpenters, painters, and other skilled laborers of the building industry. He concluded that many of the urban workers had migrated to Texas, where the cotton fields and railroads absorbed "many thousands of Mexican labourers by reason of the high wages offered."[38] Martin arrived in Mexico during an especially critical era. In Mexico City and other urban areas, the years between 1905 and 1907 were marked by high inflation, notably in food and rents, as well as by an absence of wage increases.

Emigration was not restricted to the peon class. In the relatively small middle class, reasons other than economic destitution accounted for individual decisions to migrate north. For example, Ramón Lizárraga, whose father owned a small ranch in Sonora, fled neither famine nor civil strife when he followed his music teacher to Los Angeles in 1901. There he labored in the fruit packing sheds during the day, playing bass violin for a Mexican orchestra in the evenings. He stayed less than two years on his first trip across the border and after returning to Mexico in 1903, he waited another twenty years before returning to Los Angeles. Another migrant to Los Angeles, Abundio Chacón, the son of a successful tobacco merchant, left Mexico in 1910 just months prior to the outbreak of revolution in spite of his father's pleas that he had no reason to leave Guanajuato. Chacón, who was sixteen at the time, was encouraged to emigrate when he heard from his best friend about the high wages and good life in the United States. He later recalled his father's main argument for not going to the United States: "The men go there— you will starve to death [in the U.S.]." Still Chacón persisted, and finally with his meager savings of forty pesos (twenty dollars U.S.), he left with a friend who had been to the United States previously as a railroad laborer.[39]

The exodus of so many citizens troubled Mexican officials, although they knew they could do little about it. A. A. Graham noted that Mexican authorities were making every effort to discourage emigration to the north, continuously giving out false information that no work could be obtained in the United States and "telling stories of great suffering among the Mexicans" across the border. These reports, however, did not deter them, Graham reported, because "they had no remunerative work at home, and they certainly could not be influenced, in view of their condition at home, when told of suffering abroad."[40]

The consequence of intense foreign capital investment and industrial expansion over the years 1880–1910 created serious problems both for President Díaz and for the semi-agricultural and industrial work force. Díaz came increasingly under attack by Mexican citizens for giving foreigners such generous concessions. In a biography of Díaz published in 1908, Rafael de Zayas Enriques prophesied: "Mexico is headed straight toward revolution. Discontent, hatred of office-holders, and of foreigners to whom so many special privileges have been granted, long deep-seated but quiescent, are now openly manifest. A spark may kindle a conflagration that in devouring the governing classes will at the same time destroy the fruits of industry and reverse the progress of the country."[41]

In 1910 Díaz invited journalists from Europe and the United States to participate in Mexico's Centennial celebration. The government did everything possible to impress the thousands of foreign visitors who attended the ceremonies. It was Díaz' finest hour. The Mexican capital itself stood as a monument to the accomplishments of Díaz' regime. Electric trolleys, fancy restaurants offering French cuisine, a bustling population—all demonstrated evidence of Mexico's entry into the Western club of industrialized nations.[42] None present could have guessed that Díaz' political tenure was to end within several months. As Díaz and his cabinet entertained their guests in opulence, political exiles in Los Angeles, San Antonio, and other U.S. cities stood ready to challenge Díaz.[43] Revolution was in the wind.

III

The Mexican Revolution was the most spectacular circumstance promoting emigration during the period 1900–1930. It was not, however, the principal cause of Mexican migration to the United States for this era. During the years 1910–1930 approximately 925,000 Mexicans crossed into the United States. Twice as many emigrated during the 1920s as had left in the decade of revolution. Over the period 1910–1920, the median yearly average number of Mexicans crossing the U.S. border was 25,000. Ironically, in the years 1913–1915, considered by Mexican historians to have been the worst years of fighting, Mexican emigration actually declined, as battles became more frequent and travel throughout Mexico became more dangerous, if not impossible, because of the near destruction of the rail transportation network.[44]

In the period 1910–1920, emigration to cities like Los Angeles was in part a response to the crisis of war: single men were threatened by conscription; families were worn down by food shortages; inflationary prices caused economic hardships; workers were impatient with the revolutionary government's slow delivery on the promise of better days for the working classes. In addition, the factors most essential in determining Mexican emigration in an earlier decade—loss of land, cyclical unemployment, and runaway inflation—persisted throughout the 1910s. The conditions responsible for attracting workers to the U.S. Southwest—expansion of agriculture, mining, ranching and urban industries—also persisted.[45]

Mexicans who arrived in Los Angeles during the decade of revolution were often different from earlier arrivals. Many had never before left their native villages. Some, pressed into military service against their will, stole across the border, previously having given only slight consideration to leaving Mexico. Like earlier generations of German and Irish immigrants and a later group of Cuban refugees, most came with the intention of staying only for a short time. They were optimistic about the prospect of finding temporary work and homes in southern California. Some were deserters from the warring Mexican armies in conflict, which altogether numbered some 300,000 men and women. Others were members of that vast majority of the nation's 15 million inhabitants who became dislocated by pressures set in motion by political forces they had little control over.

The threat of conscription into the warring Mexican forces and frequent army desertions had an impact on the labor resources of employers on both sides of the border. When the Liberal Army of Baja California seized Tijuana from Federal troops in May 1911, it interrupted construction of a railway connecting the Imperial Valley with San Diego. Building the railroad line involved laying forty-four miles of track within Mexican territory. When Mexican rebel forces attacked Tijuana, the Los Angeles construction firm of Sherer and Company lost 80 percent of its work force as their laborers fled upon hearing rumors "that the Mexican government intended to impress all citizens into the army." On one occasion a rebel sergeant made an impassioned speech to workers coming in as replacements, convincing twenty-two to join him and his comrades.[46] The search for new recruits often brought representatives from the warring rebel forces to points across the border. The *Los Angeles Times* reported several instances where Mexicans living in the city were urged to return to Mexico to join the Revolution.[47]

For Americans in the border communities of the Southwest, violence associated with the Revolution became a frequent occurrence that often touched their own lives. In the spring of 1910 Margaret L. Holbrook Smith recorded in *Overland Monthly* her experiences in witnessing the capture of "Tia Juana" near San Diego by rebel forces. Following the battle, she wrote, "On the American side close to the custom house many Federal wounded were cared for. . . . On our side, also, was the refugee camp. Often whole families herded under one bit of canvas stretched out to shelter them. . . . Many poor women walked all the eighteen miles into San Diego, carrying babies in their arms."[48] Other victims of the insurrection fled toward Ensenada, a coastal city eighty miles to the south.

The border cities did not always turn out to be the haven that refugees sought. The border exploded with activity during the years of civil war.[49] In 1911, four months after Madero's entry into Mexico, the U.S. government ordered twenty thousand troops dispatched "without delay, at points on the border."[50] Los Angeles, San Antonio, and Galveston were coordinating centers for the massive movement. Fort Rosecrans in San Diego, 125 miles south of Los Angeles, served as a headquarters for U.S. army personnel stationed to protect the twelve-mile border territory between Tijuana and San Diego. The troops at Fort Rosecrans, many of whom were recruited and trained in Los Angeles, flushed out rebel forces in Tijuana between 1911 and 1913. Marion Ethel Hamilton, writing for the *Overland Monthly*, vividly described the capture of rebel forces during a battle where soldiers of the U.S. 115th Company and 8th Infantry captured 105 "insurrecto" members in Tijuana. As the war dragged on, residents of the Mexican border towns affected became impatient, with many choosing to leave for points further removed from the conflict.[51]

Border communities such as San Diego and Los Angeles served as a first stopover for political refugees and new emigrants. The *Los Angeles Times* commented on March 27, 1914, that "thirty-three Mexicans, including the wealthiest inhabitants of Hermosillo, Sonora, who were forcibly deported to the United States several days ago, told their troubles yesterday to Consul Juan R. Orci through a delegation of their number. More refugees are to reach Los Angeles today." Arrival of political refugees and migrant laborers concerned some American officials, but because they contributed in an important way to the labor needs of major industries and commercial agriculture, few restrictions were placed on their immigration.[52]

Some of the emigrants who came to Los Angeles during the revolutionary period expressed no desire to return to Mexico once the fighting had terminated. Pedro Nazas, a stockyard worker in Los Angeles during the 1920s, had left his home in Zapotlán, Jalisco, in 1918 following the collapse of his small business. His father had been a farmer there; however, when his parents died, the family suffered extensive losses in settling the small estate. He tried making a living from a store that he owned, but, plagued by high taxes and inflation, he closed down. The time had arrived, he noted, "to come to seek my fortune in the United States." In Los Angeles he earned thirty-five dollars a week, enough for him to support himself and to conclude: "I don't want to go back to Mexico because I couldn't earn there what I am used to earning in Los Angeles and besides, one can buy more things with a dollar than with a Mexican peso."[53]

Destruction of Mexican railway lines connecting the interior of Mexico to southwestern cities such as Los Angeles during the revolutionary years dashed the hopes of many potential emigrants and made it that much harder for others to leave their homeland. As early as 1913, reports surfaced that numerous towns in the central states had been cut off from the border towns. Reports on the rail conditions were often inaccurate, and travelers learned to expect delays and dangers. One correspondent wrote in 1915, "Thousands of miles of railway have been destroyed, bridges and station-houses have been burned at every step."[54] A *New York Evening Post* writer,

David Lawrence, traveled to the site of the Constitutional Convention in the summer of 1917 and found conditions far more favorable, although "Along the railroad line a few burnt stations bore testimony to the ravages of revolution. . . . Trains, to be sure, did not run on time; they were often eighteen and twenty-four hours late [and] freight was not moving."[55] The reduced state of transportation that these journalists reported no doubt forced many of the emigrants to travel by foot or carriage. One American reporter wrote:

> If anyone has any doubt about the volume of this class of immigrant a visit to South Texas would reveal the situation. In a day's journey by automobile through that region one passes hundreds of Mexicans, all journeying northward on foot, on burroback and in primitive two-wheel carts. They are so numerous as to almost fill the highways and byways. When questioned many of them will tell you that they fled from Mexico to escape starvation. In a great number of instances the refugees have friends or relatives in this country who have told them of the wealth and prosperity of the wonderful *ESTADOS UNIDOS*.[56]

The trip by boat took time, and inadequate transportation facilities forced many of the seasonal migrant workers stationed in the United States to remain longer than they had originally anticipated.

Curtailing railway communication between Mexico and the border created new problems for both rural and urban dwellers. The uncertainty of food deliveries and the unstable Mexican peso drove prices far above what the working class could afford. The *New York Times* reported 2,000 percent price increases for corn and beans between July 1914 and July 1915. Responding to the inability of many Mexicans to feed their families, the Red Cross opened soup kitchens in Mexico City in 1915. In one month alone volunteers fed twenty-six thousand families. Still, many in the rural areas looked to the cities as havens. As a result of the great influx of people, rents in Mexico City rose more than 50 percent in 1915 and thousands of workers lived under the dread of famine.[57] Author Thomas Edward Gibbon reported that government officials sought to discourage new migrants from moving into urban areas but that they had little success, since so many of the campesinos believed "that it [was] not safe for them to live out in the country and work their farms."[58]

In the early years of the Revolution, numerous attempts were made by the warring factions to gain control of the Republic's major cities and production centers. Jalisco, a contributor to the nation's food production and an important source of new recruits, became a battleground in the spring of 1914. In a major battle, Carranza's Constitutional army surrounded the capital city of Guadalajara in an effort to flush out the Federales. Twelve thousand Federal soldiers protected the city, but in the ensuing battle, Constitutionalists handed them a terrible defeat.[59] Two thousand Federal soldiers died, and another six thousand were taken prisoner. For the Constitutional forces, the victory at Guadalajara cleared the Federales from Jalisco and made the road to Mexico City, for them at least, easier. The victors, however, had destroyed the railway lines over a large area in the central region, leaving the residents of Jalisco without connections to Mexico City. Once cut off from Mexico City, which at this point had fallen under the control of Francisco Villa, refugees fled northward.

In 1914 the Revolution reached Monterrey, northern Mexico's largest city, for the first time. Following a three-day battle, one witness told how "a cloud of gloom and apprehension brooded over the city." The attack had caught the residents by surprise, for few had expected that the recently organized Constitutional forces would take their fight into the northern urban areas. For months after the attack residents lived in fear. Reports during the battle confirmed the impact and dislocation caused by the fighting. "The city is full of troops now," wrote a reporter.[60] The soldiers occupied public buildings, theatres, empty private houses, anywhere officials could find space. Eventually the rebel forces failed in their attempts to capture the city. They succeeded, however, in blowing up the railroad tracks outside the city, thereby cutting off communication between Monterrey and Mexico City. The danger of traveling and moving about the countryside during these years forced many from Monterrey to remain in the city until after 1915 when the battlefronts shifted to other localities.[61]

In the Central Plateau region, where the majority of the earlier emigrants to Los Angeles had originated, the Revolution had a momentous impact. Haciendas closed as peasants scattered either to join the rebellious armies or to search for a living in other, more stable areas of the nation. In 1913, a year before the rebels initiated the crucial military stages of the conflict, an observer for the *Outlook* commented on the devastating effects of the fighting on the economy of the central region.[62] North of Zacatecas, one of the richest mining states in the Republic, there was "not a mine or manufacturing industry of any kind that [was] running, and south of Zacatecas there [was] nothing doing ten miles away from the railway."[63]

Enrique F. Vásquez, interviewed in Los Angeles fifty years after he had migrated to the United States, recalled losing his job in his home state of Zacatecas when the Revolution caused the collapse of the mining industry.[64] Nonetheless, he remained another three years working in a number of jobs in an effort to support his family. For twenty-five centavos a day (twelve cents U.S.) he labored as a mule driver transporting oranges to local markets. He later worked on an hacienda as a watchman. On duty twenty-four hours a day, seven days a week, he earned less than two pesos a week, the standard wage in Zacatecas for unskilled labor. In 1913, already a young man of twenty-three, he left for the United States. After working several years in the midwest, first in the railroad yards and later as a merchant, he settled in Chicago. His stay in the United States came to an abrupt end in 1931, when he became one of thousands repatriated to Mexico by the American government.[65]

Coinciding with the new military situation in the interior of Mexico was the stepped-up recruitment of Mexican laborers by railroad agents. Warfare had reduced the number of emigrants leaving on their own to the United States over the years 1913–1915. Acting on behalf of American railroad companies, these agents visited Jaliscan villages and dozens of other communities in central Mexico in search of track hands. Paul S. Taylor noted that several workers were recruited from Arandas, Jalisco, months prior to the battle of Guadalajara and that the agents took them by auto to the railroad depot and placed them on a northbound train. The agents paid for the villagers' expenses to the American border, although such practices were prohibited under U.S. immigration laws.[66]

Ernesto Galarza, author and labor organizer, recalled that his family had been recruited to work on the railroad under similar circumstances. Galarza lived with his mother and two uncles in Tepic, Nayarit, during the early months of the Revolution. Galarza remembered the night that his Uncle Gustavo announced "that he had talked with a labor recruiter for the Southern Pacific Railroad." The agent signed both of Galarza's uncles. "The arrangement was that Gustavo and José would give us the advance from the Southern Pacific on which we would live temporarily." Recruiting by such measures continued until the late 1920s.[67]

Under the strain of the rebellion, the Mexican national economy staggered. At a time when industries and agriculture in Los Angeles were absorbing thousands of new laborers yearly and offering wages for unskilled workers of ten to twenty dollars weekly, salaries in Mexico dropped year by year over the period 1910–1920.[68] Statistics for this period are meager, and scholars must rely on estimates provided by contemporary observers. Wages varied significantly in

different regions of Mexico. Speaking of the public utilities industries in Mexico City, in March 1916, E. D. Trowbridge noted that the
average daily wage for about three thousand employees was less
than eight cents U.S. Numerous scholars who visited Mexico several years later projected similar profiles. Paul S. Taylor estimated
that agricultural workers earned between twelve and sixteen cents
U.S. daily in the period 1914–1915. Former Díaz appointee Francisco Bulnes estimated that the wages of the peon had dropped to
eighteen centavos, or approximately nine cents U.S., while the
skilled worker could expect to earn slightly more than a peso.[69]

A sizable number of immigrants arriving in Los Angeles during
the 1910s left Mexico with the thought of working for a short period,
accumulating some savings, and returning to Mexico after peace had
been restored. As one observer put it, "They saw their brothers and
friends return from the United States wearing shoes and good suits
of clothes."[70] One war refugee, Jesús Moreno, arrived in Los Angeles
in 1915 at the age of nine with his parents and three brothers and
sisters. His experiences are typical of many who came during this
period. Moreno's recollection of El Paso, where the family stayed for
several months before settling in Los Angeles, was that of a city in
constant flux. "We were running away from the rebellion," Moreno
noted, and, "there were so many [other] Mexican refugees at that
time in El Paso." The Moreno family rented a small house in East
Los Angeles, expecting that the Revolution "would be over in a few
months." They did not enroll their children in Los Angeles public
schools for almost a year because they believed that they would be
returning to Mexico at almost any moment. Jesús attended school
for only two years and eventually landed a job as a delivery boy in a
drug store. Like hundreds of other immigrants in Los Angeles, the
family decided not to return to Mexico when the fighting terminated in 1920.[71]

Labor contractors contributed to the movement of workers to
Los Angeles, but the Mexican government's failure to impose a restrictive emigration policy was also influential. During the Revolution the governments of Victoriano Huerta and Venustiano Carranza
focused their attention on other priorities; both leaders lacked the
resources to prevent the exodus of Mexican laborers from the Republic. Manuel Gamio, an influential member of Carranza's Department of Development, suggested in his study *Forjando patria* (1916)
that the government could improve the national economy by sending "our workers to foreign industrial centers that they may incorporate foreign experience with their traditional industrial aptitudes."[72]
By 1918, the Mexican government believed that if any workers had

heeded Gamio's suggestions, they should now return. *La Prensa de Los Angeles* published numerous articles that year extolling the excellent opportunities for Mexican workers in Mexico. Such propaganda referred to the Mexican government's successful efforts in finding jobs for "thousands of Mexicans who have returned to our country during the past few months." The governors of Baja California and Coahuila declared that jobs existed for more than eight thousand men. "For those workers not wishing to remain in the states of Durango and Chihuahua—all arrangements have been made including transportation and food for work in Yucatán, where the highest salaries in Mexico are paid."[73]

Carranza recognized that Mexican migrants encountered great hardships in the United States, and as president he made several attempts to work out a mutual agreement between the labor movement in Mexico and that in the United States. At the urging of AFL President Samuel Gompers, Carranza's representatives journeyed to Washington in 1916 for a meeting to discuss the formation of an international union of workers. The purpose behind the creation of this organization was to facilitate the unionization of Mexicans in the Southwest and Americans in Mexico. When the war in Europe came to a conclusion, however, Gompers, concerned that aliens had pre-empted thousands of jobs that belonged to Americans, lost interest in a cooperative labor venture with Mexico.[74]

World War I (1914–1918) gave impetus to unprecedented economic activity in southern California and subsequently increased tremendously the need for unskilled labor in that region. This contributed to the decision by many Mexican laborers to forsake the urban areas in Mexico for more promising prospects in Los Angeles and other U.S. cities. Such emigration became evident especially in 1917 and 1918 when, despite the growing hope among Mexicans that the Revolution was coming to a conclusion, living conditions in Mexico still had not improved. Thomas Edward Gibbon, a resident of Los Angeles, visited Mexico City in 1918 and reported that its population had reached one million, a factor which had caused rents and food prices to increase.[75] Other reports noted that, as of 1917, commercial businesses had been especially handicapped "by the lack of a credit system and the restricted currency" which, according to informed sources, amounted to only one-half the prerevolutionary total.[76]

World War I did stimulate exportation of oil, cotton, and henequen to the United States, but the number of additional persons needed in these sectors had only a slight impact on the unemployment rolls. Indeed, most of the workers in the oil fields in 1917 were

Americans. The increased exportation of goods, most of it by rail, kept the rail traffic between Mexico and the United States open, giving many emigrants an opportunity to use the trains for the trip north. Sales of war goods to the United States also prompted the maintenance and repair of the railroads connected to the oil fields and highly productive areas of cotton and henequen. One commentator noted that regular train service from Laredo to Mexico "had continued for some months [in 1917] with only rare mishaps."[77]

Mexico's economic recovery, stimulated during the war years, was most evident in the production of raw materials. Cotton reached a record production during the war years, accounting for 79,000 metric tons in 1918, three times as much as had been produced at the turn of the century under Díaz.[78] The most dramatic demonstration of Mexico's taking the successful path to economic recovery was in the production of crude oil. Oil production, which totaled 12 million barrels in 1911, reached 156 million barrels in 1920.[79] The war industries opened new jobs for Mexican workers, although workers in these industries continued to explore the possibility of selling their labor north of the Río Grande.

The war also proved a boon to the Mexican henequen industry. Although grown principally in two states, Yucatán and Campeche, henequen from the 1880s to 1920 was second only to cotton as Mexico's most important agricultural product. Prior to World War I, sisal hemp was used almost exclusively for binder twine in harvesting American and European wheat. When the war broke out, it came into great demand for use also in ships and bagging industries. While production remained high, many of the workers who had fled the plantations during the Revolution chose not to return.[80]

IV

Following the deaths of Zapata in 1919 and Carranza in 1920, the violence that accompanied the Revolution began to ebb. National elections in 1920 signaled a new era. Nonetheless the forces that led a record number of Mexicans to abandon their homeland in the decade after the Revolution demonstrate that for millions of landless peasants the end of the revolutionary era promised only a slightly better future. Economic factors continued to constitute the single most important reason why the migrants left Mexico, although other "push" factors carried some importance.[81]

In the 1920s, Mexican leaders, citing the 1917 Constitution, promised the masses greater labor privileges, religious freedom through separation of church and state, and the redistribution of land. Yet, according to one Mexican historian, "while key goals of labor survived nominally on the statute books, native businessmen and foreign corporations enjoyed special privileges."[82] Certainly, on the labor issue, Mexican leaders promised better days to come. "The truth is," President Plutarco Elías Calles told a reporter from *El Demócrata* on April 18, 1924, "that until the present, industry, agriculture and mining in Mexico have been founded and carried on at the expense of the stomach of the workers, that is to say, on the basis of the lowest compensation which would enable the workers to live." Yet Calles recognized that the guarantees offered to labor under the 1917 Constitution were not broad enough to improve their lot. Speaking to a partisan audience in Morelia, Michoacán, in 1924, Calles said: "I want to see the industries flourish and develop. I only ask that the relations between the industrialists and the workers be placed upon a more humane basis. I ask that the industrialists reckon the worker as something a little less than a machine and a little more than a beast . . . "[83]

How the Mexican workers actually fared during the 1920s is perhaps best demonstrated by wage levels. In the depressed Mexican economy of the early 1920s, agricultural workers earned less than a peso (approximately $.50 U.S.) per day. In 1925, Nathan L. Whetten found that the poorest paid rural workers in Mexico—those of the central states of Guanajuato and Michoacán, who were paid from $.35 to $.41 (U.S.), the lowest daily wages in the Republic—earned hardly enough to maintain an average family. Mexican government statistics indicate that miners, among the highest paid industrial laborers in Mexico, earned only $1.25 (U.S.) per day during the 1920s. In Arandas, Jalisco, Paul S. Taylor calculated that the wages for urban workers, which had reached a record high of $.75 (U.S.) in 1915 because of the rise of war industries, had actually increased very little, averaging $1.00 a day by 1928.[84] Ernest H. Gruening, a U.S. senator who visited Mexico in 1928, found that urban workers earned three to four pesos daily if they were unskilled and six to ten pesos per day if they qualified as skilled workers.[85]

José Novoa, who earned his living in Los Angeles during the late 1920s working for the Santa Fe Railroad, was one of many emigrants who left Mexico in the postrevolutionary decade. In 1924, the year of his migration, he was working as a trash collector for the municipio of Maravilla, Zacatecas. Working seven days a week for a daily wage of 1.25 pesos ($.62 U.S.), Novoa yearned for a better life. Aided by an uncle already working in the United States and accompanied by his grandfather, a seasonal railroad worker, young José crossed the northern border at Juárez, Chihuahua.[86]

It was not uncommon for immigrants to Los Angeles to have been a part of the migrant stream in their own homeland, as was the case of Carlos Almazán. Almazán, who grew up on a small farm in Zamora, Michoacán, migrated as a young man to Mexico City, where he managed a butcher shop. He later became fruit peddler. When he lost all of his investments in that venture, he migrated north. Crossing at El Paso in 1923, he found his way to Los Angeles, where, after only two days of job hunting, he landed a laborer's position with the Simons Brick Company in East Los Angeles.[87]

Critics of the Mexican government viewed emigration as a sign of Mexico's inability to resolve economic problems. One such critic, Marcelo Villegas, wrote in 1928, "The Mexican people, with industries dying and the land not being cultivated, are crushed, starved, and driven out of their country."[88] A severe decline in population from 1910 through the early 1920s in many Mexican states reflected the heavy emigration of workers to the United States. All but two of the major emigrant-sending states sustained large population losses. The highest out-migration occurred in Guanajuato, Michoacán, Jalisco, and San Luis Potosí, states which contributed heavily to Los Angeles' Mexican *colonia*. The two exceptions, the Federal District (Mexico City) and Coahuila, lost Mexican emigrants to the United States but still had small population gains from 1921 to 1930. Durango, which had registered a 2.64 percent population growth between 1900 and 1910, suffered a 3.22 percent drop in population between 1910 and 1921, and experienced an almost normal population increase of 2.16 percent between 1921 and 1930. At the same time, the border state of Baja California recorded population increases nearly double those of any of the principal emigrant-sending states of the Mexican interior.[89]

Few single women emigrated to Los Angeles during the twenties. In nearly every city which registered significant Mexican immigration, men came over in greater proportions than women, and women seldom left Mexico alone. In most cases, either a family migrated together or the husband crossed to the United States on his own and sent for his wife and children when he had found work and a place to live. There were exceptions, however, as in the case of Elisa Silva, who in 1924 at the age of twenty left her home in Mazatlán, Sinaloa, with her widowed mother and two sisters. Their decision to sell everything they owned for the purpose of emigrating to the United States resulted from information they received "that there were good opportunities for earning money in Los Angeles, working as extras in the movies and in other ways."[90]

Labor unrest continued to plague political leaders of the Republic during the 1920s. In 1925, Moisés Sáenz, the Undersecretary of the Mexican Department of Education, offered statistical data showing a decrease in the number of strikes in the years 1922–1925 as proof of "the growing tranquillity of the working class." Yet even Sáenz, who noted that the workers' salaries had increased, concluded that "while there has been a decided betterment in salaries, what the average working man is now receiving is not sufficient to meet the most elementary needs of civilized man."[91] The central issue, as many saw it, concerned the number of concessions that the government was willing to make to workers. As the historian Ramón Eduardo Ruiz noted, during the early 1920s, President Alvaro Obregón "kept the capitalist system intact, usually favored the employer, hampered the development of labor unions, perverted the ideas of federalism, and mocked the ideals of the Revolution."[92] All these policies militated against increases in real wages for the industrial workers.

In addition to the weakness of the labor movement, the past inequities of the educational system also greatly contributed to the workers' low wages and consequently to their tendency to emigrate to the United States. In the prerevolutionary years, only the upper classes had been afforded the luxury of postelementary schooling. In the 1920s, Mexican leaders placed an unprecedented number of resources in the hands of educators in order to eliminate illiteracy. The obstacles of bringing education to the masses and eliminating illiteracy were indeed formidable. Government statistics showed that, during the twenties, 60 percent of the population could neither read nor write. Further, only a small minority of the Mexican population had an opportunity to attend university classes in Mexico in the decade after the Revolution.[93]

Reform in the postrevolutionary years concerned not only education but nearly every major national institution. Soon after the Republic had celebrated its first five years of peace, unrest came in the form of a feud between the Roman Catholic Church and the political reformists in the government. The religious conflict engulfed Mexico for nearly three years, pitting two powerful groups over the issue of "who controlled the Mexican people." In education, land distribution, and the organization of labor, the Catholic hierarchy and politicians were at odds.

President Plutarco Elías Calles' decree of June 14, 1926, calling for the rigid enforcement of constitutional provisions pertaining to religion triggered the confrontation between church and state. These statutes made it unlawful for foreign priests to perform religious functions, forbade church involvement in education, and outlawed the operation of monastic orders and nunneries. Mexican Catholics "responded with vehemence to the publication of the decree."[94] The controversy touched on numerous issues, and neither side seemed willing to compromise. One contemporary scholar reported that Catholic clergy had accused President Calles of Bolshevist policies in trying to bring about a complete change in the life and legal regimen of the Mexican people. At the annual convention of the Knights of Columbus, Catholic leaders called upon the membership of the organization for a million dollars to launch a campaign of education "to the end that the policies of Soviet Russia shall be eliminated from the philosophy of Mexican life."[95] The church supported and organized an economic boycott that produced few tangible results; business continued as usual. The U.S. government, at this time conducting high-level meetings with Mexico concerning the legal ramifications of the Constitution of 1917 for American privileges in the drilling and ownership of oil fields, chose to step lightly on the church controversy. On August 15, 1926, however, U.S. government agents took sides with Calles, arresting the leader of the Catholic faction, General Enrique Estrada, former secretary of war under President Obregón, together with 174 supporters, at San Diego, California. Most of the men had been recruited near Los Angeles.[96]

In Jalisco, homeland of thousands of emigrants to Los Angeles during the 1920s, the church recruited many supporters, and the state became a major battleground in the religious confrontation, known in the U.S. press as the Cristero revolt. Stories of rebellious activity in Jalisco circulated throughout Mexico, while Mexican officials had to contend with rumors that the Coolidge administration "was making plans either to foment a revolution in Mexico or to bring about a war with that Nation." In July 1927, Mexican army officials declared an eight-thousand-square-mile area of Los Altos, Jalisco, as a "neutral zone" and ordered everybody to concentrate "in twelve named towns or be considered rebels." Carleton Beals, an American anthropologist doing field work in Jalisco during the conflict, reported that the consequences of this action by the military placed a heavy burden on small farmers and the laboring classes in general. The poor people, Beals noted, "have had to leave home and security. All they have left behind them is at the utter mercy of roving bands and looting soldiers."[97] In Arandas, Jalisco, Paul S. Taylor found that a large number of persons emigrated to the United States during the Cristero revolt. He estimated that 400 emigrants left Arandas in 1926, 600 in 1927, and 200 in 1928.[98]

The Cristero revolt peaked in April 1927. The turning point came after the Catholic rebels attacked a Guadalajara–Mexico City passenger train. The rebels, numbering some 500, derailed the train and fired upon it, killing guards and passengers, then poured oil on the train coach, burning those too severely wounded to be moved. The rebels fled after taking 150,000 pesos from the mail car and all baggage. Confirmation from the rebel camp that the attack had been led by two priests produced a predictable uproar in the press. The total number of passengers and guards killed has never been determined, and estimates vary from 100 to 150 dead.[99] From that day on, the Catholic forces found themselves unpopular with the masses and the target of violent government reprisals.

These internal conflicts compounded the Mexican government's problems in administrative reorganization. President Calles had complained during the church controversy that the clerical questions came at a time when he was "deeply preoccupied with the resolution of the great national problems," including "public education, the industrial and agricultural development of the country and the contemporaneous social movement."[100]

The government met its greatest challenge and enjoyed its least success on the issue of agrarian reform. The Constitution of 1917 had promised land to the peasants. Under President Obregón, the Mexican Congress had passed the Ejido Law, which promised distribution of forty million government-controlled acres to the campesinos. However, by the mid-1920s, the government had distributed only 3.2 percent of this land.[101] Frank Tannenbaum, an American historian visiting Mexico in 1928, wrote that "even at this day approximately 75 percent of all communities in Mexico are located upon private estates, and . . . in some of the states the proportion will be as high as 90 percent of the total inhabited places."[102] Such a high concentration of land in a few hands and the fact that more people toiled in the fields in the 1920s than in 1910 gave proof of the absence of fundamental changes under the first two chief executives of the Republic. Indeed, much of the land distributed during the 1920s as a means to quell the mood of agrarian discontent was land which had never been farmed previously. Lacking modern equipment and sufficient irrigation, the small farmers found that the small plots given to them seldom provided more than a subsistence-level existence.[103]

Speaking in 1924 before a partisan audience in Morelia, Michoacán, a region saddled with high unemployment and a near absence of agrarian reform, Plutarco Elías Calles proposed that the great landowners would profit by distributing lands to all the villages in the Republic "because then they themselves [landowners] will be compelled to cultivate all of the land which remains to them, thereby converting themselves into true farmers under the spur of necessity."[104] Such logic carried little weight with those accustomed to owning large haciendas. Land distribution would not become a reality in Mexico unless the federal government put its resources fully behind it.

One individual case, that of Ramón García, illustrates how the small farmer fared in the Central Plateau during the 1920s. García, born in 1906, spent his early youth helping his father care for a small herd of cattle and raise a food crop. Although the family survived the revolutionary period without any major setbacks, the postwar years brought them the prospects of only a slightly better future. By the time that Ramón García reached the age of eighteen, his family had grown to eleven members. At this stage, Ramón's burden of responsibility grew heavier. He felt tormented that he could not contribute more to the family income. For the first time he listened with interest to the stories told by several of his friends about the abundance of work across the border. That year, 1924, he decided to leave Jalisco. First he traveled to Aguascalientes by mule. There he paid thirty-six pesos (eighteen dollars) and boarded a train for the international border. He eventually arrived in Los Angeles, where he landed a job with the Southern Pacific Railroad. He was more fortunate than others like him, because in Los Angeles his work was year-round. Ramón García had left Mexico with the dream of eventually returning to his homeland. He chose instead to build his dream in the United States and did not even return to Mexico for a visit until the mid-1950s. Thus García's decision to emigrate was related to the lack of economic opportunities and poor material conditions within his rural environment as well as to the promise of favorable circumstances in other areas.[105]

In contrast to the difficulties experienced by laborers such as Ramón García in the central states, workers in northern Mexican states found more steady employment and wages one-fourth to one-third higher. The northern states of Baja California, Sonora, Tamaulipas, and Nuevo León recorded high population increases mainly through in-migration, a sign that they were undergoing prosperous periods. Baja California demonstrated a 25 percent increase in the number of persons in the labor force between 1900 and 1930. During the same period, Zacatecas in the central region registered a sharp drop in the number of persons with full-time employment. As one writer noted in 1924: "Wages have always been higher in the north of Mexico than they have in the south and there has been a steady drift of labor from south to north. Today in southern Mexico unskilled labor gets from 0.50 to 1.00 dollar United States currency per day. In northern Mexico it gets from 1.50 to 2.00 dollars per day, and just across the border in the United States wages are about double what they are in Northern Mexico."[106]

Throughout the early twentieth century, the northern region offered Mexican workers ample jobs in mining, ranching, and transportation. From 1900 to 1930, the population of Sonora grew by 30.0 percent and that of Tamaulipas, by 36.4 percent; by contrast, Jalisco's population grew by only 8.1 percent, and Guanajuato's decreased by 6.9 percent. These statistics clearly demonstrate the vast demographic changes occurring because of economic trends.[107] New workers migrating north in turn produced new demands for food production and other goods. Along the Río Grande, small commercial distributors found border towns ripe for commercial exploitation. The north, which had also suffered from the Revolution, quickly rebuilt its towns and opened railway connections with the interior and the U.S. border. It made rapid adjustments to the breakup of large cattle ranches. By the early 1920s, ranchers in the north once again sold to Mexican and American customers. Moreover, Mexican and American goods shipped to the interior of Mexico from the border region required a legion of distributors and packers, while craft workers commanded good salaries.

Nevertheless, even though conditions in the northern states were much better than those in other parts of the country, workers continued to emigrate to the United States. For example, Manuel Terrazas, a resident of the border state of Chihuahua, first considered leaving home at age eighteen when a friend tried to persuade him to emigrate with him to the United States. It was 1919, and the city of Chihuahua had been devastated by revolution. Unable to convince his mother to allow him to go north, he remained in Chihuahua until an opportunity arose in 1926 for his family to go to Juárez for a temporary stay. Once settled in the border city, Manuel Terrazas fulfilled his dream of working in the United States when he crossed from Juárez to El Paso later in 1926. Having heard much of the physical demands placed on railroad crew workers, he rejected an offer to work in that capacity and instead took a job as a laborer in El Paso. He learned about job opportunities in southern California from a friend, and within a year he had signed on with an *enganchista* (labor contractor) for work in the Golden State. Eventually he

Table 1. *Population Growth of Major Border Cities, 1910–1930*

City	Population 1910	Population 1930	Percentage of Growth
Juárez	10,621	39,666	273.5
Mexicali	462	14,842	3,112.6
Tijuana	7,330	8,384	14.4
Piedras Negras	8,518	15,878	86.4
Matamoros	4,444	6,001	35.0
Villa Acuña	933	5,350	473.4
Villa Frontera	2,109	5,601	165.6
Nogales	3,117	14,061	351.1
Nuevo Laredo	8,143	21,636	165.7
Monterrey	75,528	132,577	75.5

landed a job with a petroleum company in Los Angeles as an un-skilled worker, a job he held for nearly twenty-five years.[108]

The tremendous influx of Mexican migrants into the northern Mexican states during and after the Revolution had its greatest consequences in the growth of urban communities on the border. As Table 1 shows, some cities recorded remarkable increases between 1910 and 1930. Mexicali, on the California border, grew by over 3,000 percent, benefiting by the expansion of railroad connections into the region. In the years before the Mexican railroads reached Tijuana, Mexicali functioned as one of the major ports of entry for emigrants destined for California. Juárez and Nuevo Laredo, the largest border towns in Mexico, did not grow in such spectacular fashion at that time. The population in these two border communities spilled over to their twin cities, El Paso and Laredo, Texas.

During the 1920s, the majority of the Mexican emigrants arriving in Los Angeles passed through the Texas border towns. During the same period, the flow of migrants to the Mexican northern states also helped the rapid rise of new towns in that region. Between 1921 and 1940 the number of towns in the north grew from 14,637 to 27,655, a rate of growth significantly greater than that of towns in the central region.[109]

Emigrants arriving in Los Angeles before the Mexican Revolution often returned to Mexico during the winter months when work in the agricultural fields was difficult to find or employment in railroads slacked off. During the revolutionary years, this seasonal migration became dangerous, if not impossible, because of military operations. Mexican census data listed the entry of immigrants in two different categories: (1) *repatriados nacionales e inmigrantes extranjeros* (Mexican citizens returning as repatriated persons and foreign-born immigrants); and (2) *visitantes, inmigrados, turista nacionales y extranjeros y transmigrantes* (visitors, immigrants, foreign- and native-born tourists, and transmigrants). In 1910, for instance, Mexico recorded an entry of 86,909 immigrants from the United States in the first category. This figure dropped to 20,381 in 1914, the year of heaviest fighting, and peaked in 1924, when 150,507 persons (mostly of Mexican citizenship) entered Mexico. Over the years, the percentage of migrants employed in seasonal labor varied from 30 to 50 percent. Despite the high number who moved back and forth across the border, a sizable number of Mexicanos remained in the United States. A quantitative measure is provided by the 1930 U.S. census, which noted that the Mexican population increased by almost 100 percent, from 729,992 in 1920 to 1,422,533 in 1930.[110]

V

In summary then, it might be said that from 1900 to 1930, dissatisfaction with economic and social conditions in Mexico and relatively easy access to the United States caused thousands of Mexicans to emigrate to Los Angeles. During this period, Mexico underwent an enormous transformation. Those who left Mexico during this generation began to do so during an age of tyranny and despotism. The migration increased with the fall of the dictatorship, peaking in the years of civil strife, when industries in the U.S. Southwest began to handle massive orders for World War I. The decade of reconstruction saw a record number of Mexicans, impatient with the institutions of reform and delays in stabilization of the economy, arrive in Los Angeles. More than at any earlier period, unemployment, inflation, religious conflict, low wages, and civil disorder encouraged Mexicans to investigate reports from friends, relatives, and labor agents that better opportunities awaited them across the border. Those Mexicans who settled in Los Angeles, planning to return with new-found wealth to a more stable political situation in their homeland, began to realize that such a return was neither so easily accomplished nor so desirable as it had once seemed.

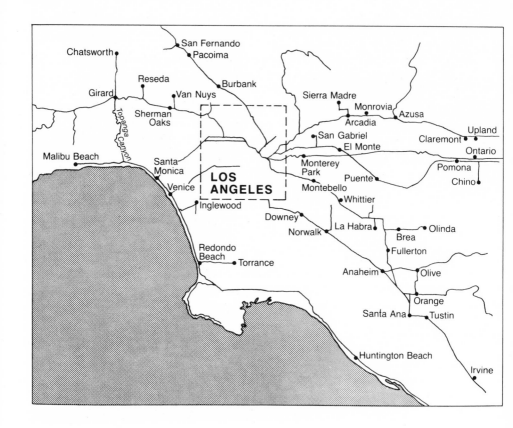

Map 1. *Los Angeles and the Surrounding Area*

4 Creating the Eastside Barrio

During the first quarter of the twentieth century, the already existing ethnic diversity of Los Angeles escaped the attention of most White Angelenos. In 1926, at Congressional hearings concerning the restriction of Mexican immigration, Charles P. Bayer of the Los Angeles Chamber of Commerce testified: "We do not have a varied group of different kinds of nationalities in southern California such as they do in some of the larger eastern cities."[1] Nonetheless, Bayer estimated the Mexican population of the city at ninety thousand and admitted that most of the unskilled labor in southern California was performed by this group. To *Saturday Evening Post* readers, Garet Garrett asserted in 1930 that Los Angeles residents were "native Americans almost in total,"[2] mostly from the Midwest. The permanency of the Spanish-speaking population also figured into the restriction debates. Many Americans assumed that Mexicans were casual laborers who, like "homing pigeons," returned to the old country after short work stints in the United States. This was a misconception, however, for in Los Angeles by 1930 Mexicanos had created the largest "Mexican city" in the United States, a stable and growing community that rivaled in size principal cities of most other states.

During the period 1910–1930, rapid suburbanization and industrial growth pushed Mexican residents of the old Plaza community to the east, where the barrio recorded spectacular growth. Four factors help explain the development of this Mexican residential concentration. First, rapid increases in migration from Mexico generated a need for new housing areas. In the years between 1910 and 1920, the city's Mexican population grew from 5,000 to more than 30,000; by 1930 that figure had more than trebled.[3] Second, the introduction of industry and commerce in the old Mexican plaza crowded out the residential areas there. Following the construction of a deep-water harbor and completion of the Panama Canal, the demand for industrial and commercial sites in the central business zone increased significantly. North and south of the Plaza, railroad depots attracted warehouses, wholesale distributors, and light industry. A third factor, the development of interurban transportation, contributed to the decentralization of industries and middle- and upper-class homes. Long Beach almost tripled its population, from 55,593 in 1920 to 142,032 in 1930, and Hollywood gained 150,000 residents during the same period.[4] Finally, a rise in racial tension and subsequent efforts to segregate Mexican residents prevented the movement of these immigrants into the north and west sections of the city. In the postwar years, these forces drastically affected physical change in Los Angeles.

The new wave of Mexican migration during the first quarter of the twentieth century was part of a general migration that transformed small towns in the Southwest into urban industrial centers. Mexicans came to Los Angeles by train directly from Mexico through Nogales, Tijuana, or Mexicali, or indirectly from other southwestern points such as El Paso, Douglas, Laredo, and Del Rio. A few came by ship, landing at either San Diego or San Pedro, and a smaller number traveled by automobile. Industrial growth, which caused the expansion of rail services eastward and across international borders, figured heavily in attracting Mexican laborers.

The makeup of Los Angeles' population in the period 1900–1920 indicates that Mexicans constituted one of the few major foreign-born groups in the city. In 1900 only one of five residents (18 percent) of the city had been born in a foreign country, a figure considerably lower than that for most other large American cities. As migrants, however, Mexicans need not have felt out of place. Two-thirds of the population in 1900 were from other areas of the United States. While New England had been the birthplace of more California immigrants than any other section of the nation in 1880, by 1900 most newcomers to Los Angeles came from the nation's midwestern heartland. Especially prevalent among migrants arriving in 1900 were farmers from west of the Missouri.[5] Mexicans had little in common with these eastern and midwestern American migrants of the 1910s and 1920s, although they did share some experiences with the many migrants who came to California from the American Southwest.

While thousands of Anglo newcomers favored Los Angeles as a retirement haven, the new arrivals from Mexico were different. Carey McWilliams observed that "after 1900 the tide of [Anglo] immigrants to southern California increasingly represented people of moderate means who came west to retire, to take it easy rather than to have a good time."[6] In contrast, 90 percent of those crossing into the United States from Mexico in the years 1910–1925 were under the age of forty-five and pursued jobs and better economic situations than they could find in Mexico.[7]

The reputation of Los Angeles as a city of transplanted Anglo midwesterners and easterners was well cultivated by the Los Angeles Chamber of Commerce during the postwar years. Indeed, Los Angeles did attract a great many such migrants and there was a great deal of truth in this image. Edgar Lloyd Hampton wrote in 1926 that of all the people who moved west of the Rocky Mountains during the years 1916–1926, one-third settled within fifty miles of Los Angeles. Nonetheless, despite its image as an Anglo American town, Los Angeles had other ethnic communities. Northern and western European immigrants made up the largest foreign-born group in the city from 1900 to 1930, but the southern and eastern European population doubled between the years 1920 and 1930. Russians and Italians represented nearly 60 percent of the Europeans who settled in the city.[8] Other ethnic communities, mainly Black, Jewish, and Mexican, could be found in the southern and eastern sections of town.

The evolution of a distinct Black district, like that of the Mexican barrio, may be traced to the first two decades of the twentieth century. Historians mark the real estate boom of 1887–1888 as the beginning of Black migration to the city. But Blacks were only 2.5 percent of the total population in 1890, numbering only 1,258. Over the next two decades the Black population grew to 7,599, still only 2.3 percent of the total population. There was then little indication that Blacks would concentrate in significant numbers in any one area. When Mexican construction workers went on strike in 1903, the Southern Pacific Railroad imported 2,000 Blacks to the area. But action by the railroad did not signify a trend, and by 1920 the Black population had increased to only 15,579 residents.[9]

In the early years of Los Angeles' development, Blacks, much like Mexicans, lived in a few isolated communities. On the east side, Blacks occupied a section adjacent to the Mexican community in Boyle Heights. The area, although small, had two thousand residents by the 1920s and consisted of a neighborhood bounded on the north by Brooklyn Avenue, on the east by the Evergreen Cemetery, on the south by Michigan Avenue, and on the west by Mott Street. A contemporary scholar described the area as "originally undesirable territory, a cheap land area, located near the downtown business district and surrounded at the time of its origin by brick yards, railroad yards, and manufacturing plants."[10]

In the 1920s Central Avenue became the heart of the Black community. About 40 percent of the Blacks in the city lived in the Central Avenue district in 1920. According to *The California Eagle*, a Black Los Angeles newspaper, newcomers had been attracted to Central Avenue by the low rents and inexpensive hotels where they could live until they found housing. There were, in addition, Black-owned stores, theatres, clubs, and pool halls, as well as some Black churches. During World War I, White residents, many of them Jewish emigrants of an earlier generation, began an exodus from that area that continued until 1930, when the Black population reached 38,894. By the mid-1920s the Central Avenue Black community had become one large ghetto. Extending southward thirty blocks from downtown Los Angeles and nearly fifteen blocks wide, it became the largest Black community in the West.[11]

Blacks living in Los Angeles during the 1920s found economic opportunities there superior to those they had known in the South. In some industries the new migrants found little resistance to their participation and advancement, and even skilled positions were not out of their reach. Perhaps because Mexican workers were more numerous and employers held stronger negative attitudes toward them, Blacks were preferred over Mexicans in certain industries. As one representative of a meat-packing company observed, "There is no opposition to Negro labor on the part of the company. They make better butchers than the Mexicans and there is no trouble between the various race groups."[12] As their numbers grew, however, the opportunities for Blacks in the semiskilled and skilled industries lessened. In many instances, even in the unskilled jobs, they found the door closed to them. As a spokesman for the Los Angeles Railway Company put it, the reasons for not hiring Black workers were quite simple: "We use a few Negro helpers. We use mostly Mexican workers because they work better and for less."[13] Scholars assumed that bigotry and deeply rooted prejudice of White employers were responsible for the fact that a smaller percentage of the industrial jobs went to Black workers in Los Angeles than in most northern cities during the 1920s. Such setbacks in the western labor market also placed the Black worker at a disadvantage in the Los Angeles real estate market. A Black family faced housing discrimination and inflated prices for a home outside the ghetto. As a result only a few were able to move to areas outside the Central Avenue District.

At the same time that Blacks were in the midst of creating an urban homeland on the West Coast, across town on the east side, Jewish immigrants had initiated similar efforts. Although the first Jews had settled in Los Angeles during the Gold Rush era, two historians of the Jewish community postulated that in 1900 "there were too few Jews to form a definitely Jewish district."[14] Between 1900 and 1910, a period of considerable Jewish immigration, the Los Angeles Jewish population more than doubled, from 2,500 to 5,795. The Jewish community actually had its beginnings in East Los Angeles over the years 1910–1920. It grew in response to industrial expansion in the downtown core region where many Jews had settled. In six short years, between 1917 and 1923, the Jewish community increased substantially, from 10,000 to 43,000. Although quota laws of 1921 and 1924 cut by more than half the influx of Jews to the United States, the Jewish community of Los Angeles still prospered in the twenties. Jews moving out of the downtown area in the 1910s and early 1920s relocated in three principal communities: the Brooklyn Avenue–Boyle Heights section; the Temple Street section; and the Central Avenue section. Boyle Heights, which had counted 3 Jewish families in 1908, grew to an estimated 1,842 Jewish households in 1920 and nearly 10,000 by 1930. In 1920, Jews considered Boyle Heights the heart of their community. At least a third of the 65,000 Jews living in Los Angeles in the mid-1920s lived in Boyle Heights. Attracted to this area by inexpensive housing and the prospect of easy access to downtown by interurban railway, most of the Jews living in Boyle Heights worked in the central business and industrial district. Easy access to job opportunities in these areas made the Boyle Heights community attractive to other foreign-born groups as well. In addition to becoming the site of the Jewish settlement, Boyle Heights became an immigrant community where Italians, White Russians, Poles, and Mexicans lived side by side.[15]

A second Jewish enclave evolved during the same period, north of Brooklyn Avenue at a section known as City Terrace. The Boyle Heights Jews viewed these neighbors as a more prosperous group. The new residents of City Terrace were more "orthodox" in their religious beliefs and more likely to be homeowners. Other affluent Jewish families settled in westside areas, especially in the Wilshire, West Adams, and Hollywood communities. West Adams reported 1,534 Jewish households by 1926, an increase of over 100 percent in a period of a decade. Wilshire grew even faster, demonstrating a rise from 310 Jewish households in 1914 to 2,410 by 1926.[16]

The Russian community of Los Angeles consisted of two groups, the Molokans, or Pilgrims, of Russian-Town near Boyle Heights, and the Russian Colony of Hollywood. The two groups were quite distinct. Numbering about 1,500 during the 1920s, most of the Hollywood emigrés represented the cultural elite of the old aristocracy. In the mid-1920s, according to George M. Day, they were organized tightly around the Russian Orthodox Church, and accustomed to exhibiting group solidarity. Day, who studied the Hollywood colony during the 1920s while a doctoral student at the University of Southern California, observed that they embodied "a remnant culture that will die out with the present 'Kulturtraeger,'" who had passionately devoted themselves to the "cause of grafting the culture of the old regime upon American stock."[17]

The best-known and largest Russian colony in Los Angeles lived in the "Flats" in Boyle Heights—an area located between the Los Angeles River on the west and Boyle Avenue on the east. This community originated in 1905, when members of the Molokan Sect began leaving Russia, following the outbreak of war between their country and Japan, to avoid conscription and religious persecution. Guided by a vision of religious freedom and the formation of a communal colony, they emigrated in large groups. Nearly seven thousand Molokans, almost one thousand families, arrived in Los Angeles in less than two years' time. When they first arrived, they settled near the Bethlehem Institute on Vigres Street.[18] Later, as the settlement grew, they moved to the "Flats." This area, which was within walking distance of the central Plaza district, was a congested but pleasant community near downtown that had earlier been settled largely by Asian immigrants and then by Mexicans. Pauline Young, a visitor to the "Flats" during the 1920s, wrote:

> Life in the "Flats" is a strange conglomeration of immigrant
> peoples living side by side though speaking a veritable babel of
> tongues. The outsider particularly notices the Mexicans, who
> are numerous and everywhere in evidence. Mexican boys spill
> out on the streets for lack of room at home. Old Mexican
> women—dark-skinned, with shawls over their heads and a
> subdued, faraway look in their eyes—wander down the untidy
> streets or browse about the market.[19]

Centuries of persecution in Russia had bound the Molokan group closely together, and in Los Angeles they struggled to remain closely knit. Among the first generation of emigrants, few married outside the group. Nearly everyone in the community was related by blood or marriage. In the initial years of the founding of the Russian community, the group also participated in a limited occupational sphere. Lillian Sokoloff found that "of all the Russians in this city, about 75 percent of the working men were employed in lumber yards up to the outbreak of the war. Then the majority entered the shipbuilding industry." The residential clustering of this group was evidenced by the concentration of their churches, businesses, and social clubs and by the fact that about 40 percent of the student body of Utah School (1,000 total enrollment) were Russian Molokans.[20]

Molokans and Mexicans did not interact socially, but the two groups had much to do with each other in business affairs. The Molokans considered homeownership one of their most important goals, and it very often happened that Mexicans rented or became boarders in Molokan homes. Sokoloff observed, "Almost all the Russians who own their homes, do not occupy any more rooms than are absolutely necessary . . . The remaining rooms they rent to others. In almost all cases, there are two or three families occupying one house." The Molokans had been in Los Angeles less than fifteen years when Sokoloff found that out of a group of fifty families, twenty-six owned property. The value of these homes ranged from $800 to $4,000.[21]

The Molokans settled originally in the "Flats" because they found low-cost homes and lots, an environment that readily accepted the foreign born, and easy access to the various industries and commercial shops immediately east of downtown. By the mid-1920s, however, life in Russian-Town had begun to change. Most noticeable was the expansion of the railroad yards to the edge of their community and the construction of dozens of warehouses and factories in the region surrounding the Boyle Heights neighborhood. This threatened to convert the residential section into a semi-industrial district. With this increasing industrialism, the Molokans complained of the encroachment of cheap amusement houses and saloons into the "Flats" and adjacent communities.[22]

Following the introduction of a modern interurban railway system, dispersion of the ethnic communities increased. As most European immigrants left their inner city dwellings for new single-family homes in the suburbs, new groups of immigrants, in many cases Mexicans, took the old immigrants' places in communities such as Boyle Heights, Lincoln Heights, and the adjacent community of Hollenbeck Park.[23] The development of the interurban rail system thus contributed greatly to the process of change that occurred in communities absorbing Mexican residents between the years 1900 and 1930.

Introduced in 1887, the electric trolleys had a modest beginning. Investors interested in land speculation opened the Hollywood line from the downtown area to a nearby rural section west of Vermont and Pico streets. Led by Charles J. Howland, the investors intended to promote land sales in this section of town. Property sales increased, but not sufficiently to make the line a successful venture. Although the Hollywood line failed, the idea persisted, and over the next ten years other individuals invested in several interurban transportation ventures.[24] The most profitable line, operated by Eli Clark and Moses Sherman, connected downtown Los Angeles with Pasadena. Following the success of the Pasadena line, Sherman and Clark established a rail line to Santa Monica. The new trolley greatly boosted Santa Monica real estate values and population. The interurban railway system had arrived in Los Angeles, but it lacked the financial backing required to shape a new future. The much needed thrust came with the involvement of San Francisco financiers Collis P. Huntington, president of the Southern Pacific, his nephew, Henry E. Huntington, Collis' heir apparent, and banker Isaias W. Hellman. After Collis Huntington's death, Henry Huntington sold the Southern Pacific stock he had inherited and invested the money to build a land and railway empire in southern California.[25]

Although Huntington sold his share of the trolley system in 1910, already having become a wealthy man as a result of buying and selling property that was serviced by his interurban rail lines, he left his mark on the city's urban transportation system. The impact of the interurban network on residential dispersal was already evident in 1910. Pasadena, for instance, tripled in size, from a population of 9,117 in 1900 to 30,291 ten years later. Other cities more than doubled: Santa Monica, Maywood, and Redondo Beach all grew by more than 100 percent between 1900 and 1910. In the same decade, Long Beach's population exploded from less than 2,500 to 17,809. By the 1920s the interurban trolley offered passengers twenty-seven routes, and more than a thousand miles of track crisscrossed the city. At the peak of trolley operations, in 1924, the "Red Cars" carried over 100 million passengers. The lines extended to San Pedro and Santa Monica in the west, to Balboa and Santa Ana on the southern coast, to La Habra, Covina, and Glendora in the east, and to Glendale and Mount Lowe in the north.[26] Huntington designed the route to the east side, a route that extended to Boyle Heights and Maravilla. The lines to these outlying areas started the massive exodus of Mexicans from the Plaza to the east side. Many of them were workers who depended on inexpensive public transportation to get from their new residences on the east side to jobs in the urban industries.

Construction of these interurban lines provided jobs for thousands of unskilled Mexican workers. As one of the major industries of the city, Huntington's Pacific Electric Railway introduced the practice of recruiting laborers from Mexico. The majority of these workers came through El Paso, where thousands of unskilled workers stood ready to accept jobs in railroad work. Although the railroad companies, including the Pacific Electric Company, paid wages slightly lower than other industries, they offered free transportation and provided the workers and their families with company housing. In southern California, the railroad companies paid their Mexican workers from $1.00 to $1.25 for a ten-hour day, while offering other nationalities up to $1.75 for similar work. In parts of southern California, Mexicans working for the Southern Pacific earned an average of $1.25 per day, while Greeks earned $1.60 and Japanese $1.45 daily for the same work. In Los Angeles, where Huntington had to compete with the Southern Pacific and the Santa Fe Railroad companies for track hands, the Pacific Electric initially paid Mexican workers $1.85 per day.[27]

Mexican laborers recruited to Los Angeles by the Pacific Electric became the first group of immigrant residents whose residential locations were directly related to interurban transportation. At every major junction or end of the line, the company constructed labor camps for track hands. In Santa Monica, a community promoted as a resort paradise, a labor camp at the outskirts of town kept the rail line operating from that location to downtown. In Pasadena, Long Beach, and Santa Monica, labor camps slowly grew in the postwar years. Many workers left their railroad jobs and joined other industries but maintained residency in the labor camp communities. As the communities around the labor camps grew, small oases of Mexican residents became surrounded by suburban residents of a different class and nationality. In the middle of suburbia these small Mexican communities evolved into isolated urban satellite barrios outside of the political and cultural mainstream.[28]

The development of Watts as a Mexican enclave in Los Angeles had such a beginning in 1902. The railroads recruited four hundred Mexican laborers to work on track construction extending from central Los Angeles to Long Beach and Los Angeles Harbor at San Pedro as well as the expansion of two other lines to Santa Ana and Redondo Beach. According to a longtime Anglo American resident of Watts, the Mexican laborers "first lived in box cars with their families, later in tents, and finally in rows of four-room houses, each house occupied by two families with a common shelter for wash days for the women." This was the "Latin Camp."[29] The railroad companies that owned the small houses later relocated the camp in another part of Watts. At the new *colonia*, investigators found that of seventy-six households, only one family lived "in good conditions." Thirty-one percent were found to be living in small three-room houses. The Board of Health inspector stated: "Because of the low status and low wage of the Mexican family, it is impossible to enforce the state law" concerning the living space of the homes owned by the Pacific Electric Company.[30]

Substantial disagreement surfaced among those investigating the housing needs of Mexicans. Certainly the "experts" could seldom agree on the often-used categories of "good," "fair," and "poor" conditions. Other problems concerned questions of space and the location of the Mexican community. John Kienle, the executive secretary of the Los Angeles Housing Commission, conducted the first study of Mexican housing status in 1912. After visiting seven hundred habitations, he reported that 18 percent of the families lived in one-room houses and 60 percent in two rooms. Only 16 percent resided in three-room dwellings and 6 percent in more than three rooms.[31]

Encouraged by the arrival of the interurban trolleys, developers subdivided rural land adjacent to the rail line and sold the lots at modest prices. The real estate people of Watts made great efforts to sell to the Mexican population of Los Angeles, including offering an installment plan in 1916 of $1 down and $1 per week.[32] Tract homes were placed on the market for a small down payment and as little as $25 per month. Promoting Watts with the exuberance of a public relations agent, journalist Bertha H. Smith wrote in 1916 that the community was "the type of tenement Los Angeles has adopted to ward off the dangers of those other tenements that are the curse of all great cities."[33] Another old-timer described Watts as "undesirable, but cheap, an area low, sandy, and damp." Still the lots sold at a brisk pace, with developers encouraging buyers to build temporary quarters on their property while they arranged to have their "dream homes" constructed.[34]

With the earnings saved from daily wages of $2.65, one Mexican laborer purchased two lots for his "dream house" in Watts in 1922. He bought the lots for $500, paying $100 down and $15 per week. He constructed a four-room frame house, where he lived with his wife and six children. They cooked their meals on a wood stove, used a kerosene lamp for lighting, and maintained a small garden next to their house.[35]

The majority of the Mexican population of Los Angeles, however, did not move to Watts and other suburbs until the twenties. Prior to the twenties, newcomers from Mexico continued to settle in the old Mexican Plaza area. This area also attracted a large share of the non-Mexican foreign-born population, representing more than twenty different ethnic groups. Mexicans and Italians emerged as the principal groups, accounting for approximately 76 percent of the population of the Plaza community.[36] When World War I began, immigration from Europe came to a halt, and Mexicans began replacing Russians, Italians, Jews, and even Anglos in "Sonoratown." Thus they once again became the major ethnic group in this section, in effect reconquering the Plaza.

An examination of marriage records for the years 1917–1918 confirms contemporary surveys that placed the heart of the Mexican community during the war years in the Plaza community (Macy School Section).[37] A sample of 275 Mexican families living in Los Angeles in 1917–1918 shows that a larger number lived in this section than in any other single section, and moreover that the largest percentage (60 percent) lived west of the Los Angeles River. The marriage record survey reveals that the Mexican community prior to the 1920s resided largely in heterogeneous ethnic groupings and had yet to make a significant impact on the area east of the Los Angeles River. The heart of the Mexican business district was in the North Main (Plaza) district.[38] The area also contained numerous religious and self-help agencies aimed toward the immigrant. In the center of the district was Our Lady of Angels Roman Catholic Church, the principal church for the Mexican community. In a study of the Mexican population of the city, one University of Southern California researcher observed that an average of 400 Mexicanos visited the Plaza Park across from Our Lady of Angels on a typical Sunday.[39] The Plaza Community Center, the Bloom Street Project, and the Bauchet Street International Mission served the Mexican community. Other immigrant community centers and mutual-help agencies in the area included the Hibernian Center, the Garibaldi Society, the Maccabees, the Druid Society, the Syrian Society, St. Peter's Benefit, and the Sons of Italy Hall.

Growth of the Plaza area had leveled off with industrial development and the encroachment of commercial establishments. The old Mexican section deteriorated to some extent and, according to some contemporary accounts, lost its appeal as a family neighborhood. An examination of insurance surveys for the years 1905–1921 shows an increase in commercial shops, warehouses, and small hotels.[40]

As mentioned earlier, one of the principal forces drawing increasing numbers of Mexican laborers to Los Angeles in the World War I years and the 1920s was the railroad companies. The largest employers of Mexicans were the Southern Pacific, Santa Fe, San Pedro and Los Angeles–Salt Lake, and Pacific Electric companies. A survey by the Los Angeles Housing Commission in 1916 revealed that some 267 of the 928 men employed in the Mexican Plaza district earned a living from the railroad industries.[41] Frequently the railroad companies provided small shacks, boxcars, and lots at no cost to the laborers. In 1912, John Kienle found workers in the Plaza area living in deplorable conditions and observed that "one of the motives of the railroad companies for offering free or low cost housing is that they desire to keep the men near the yards in case of an emergency at night. Besides, it is cheaper to build poorly constructed houses for these people than to add a few cents to their wages. The difference has been a saving to the railroad companies."[42] Almost twenty years later, Emory S. Bogardus, a sociologist at the University of Southern California, concluded that the tendency for many Mexican workers to live in boxcars resulted from the fact that they were "continually on the move." In any case, whether they lived in boxcars or in railroad company housing "along the track," the housing conditions were poor.[43]

Although Mexicans also lived in railroad camps, private homes, boarding houses, apartments, and low-cost hotels, investigators took special interest in the conditions of the Mexican residents in the house courts. In these quarters, three to thirty small houses occupied a common lot, and the residents shared a common yard as well as toilet and washing facilities. The courts of the Plaza community, for example, gave evidence of the cramped and poor conditions of such facilities in the city. A court there consisted generally of ten to twenty houses, half on each side of the lot, with toilet facilities in the center. Lots were usually 40 by 170 feet and offered only limited space for children to play or for social activities. In 1920 tenants paid six dollars per month for a 300-square-foot two-room house. Residents of a typical court had the use of ten hydrants with sinks and six toilets. Overcrowding was prevalent: in one court, for example, fifty-seven residents made their home—twenty men, nineteen women, ten boys, and eight girls—although only nineteen of the twenty-seven houses were occupied.[44]

One research project found the existence of some 630 courts in 1913 accounting for 10,000 residents, with the number of individual houses numbering about 3,700. "Mexicans, Russians, Italians, Slavonians, Austrians, Chinese, Japanese and a scattering of some 20 other nationalities" lived in these house courts.[45] While not actually promoting the construction of house courts, city officials considered them the answer to the growing city housing shortage. In 1912, in the 700 block of New High Street, considered at the time to be the heart of the Mexican barrio, developers constructed twenty-two one-story habitations on a lot occupying a space of 44 by 171 feet. As required by law, the owners left 30 square feet of the lot vacant, but the court was jammed tightly against adjoining lots. On each side of the lot stood eleven houses, all of them two-room dwellings, 15 feet wide and 12 feet deep. The total cost of the house court was placed at $1,000 and rent for each house brought the owner $6 a month, or $132 in all.[46] Families of four or more typically lived in these small habitations, which often sheltered eight or nine individuals each. City regulations required only that the house courts have at least one men's toilet for every ten men and one women's toilet for every ten women. Older house courts also existed where a hard rain or a cold night made the residents miserable.[47]

Although adequate housing continued to be an issue, raising a family in Los Angeles was seen by many immigrants as desirable. Nonetheless, employer groups testified in Congress that Mexicans came as single workers. A January 1915 study of 1,202 house court units in the city, many of them occupied by Mexicans, revealed that they housed a total population of 6,490 men, 4,920 women, and 5,100 children.[48] Elizabeth Fuller surveyed fifty Mexican homes in the Central Plaza district in 1920 and found an average of 5.78 persons per household (including 3.10 children under age ten). The Mexican, Fuller concluded, "comes here as a young husband and a young father," not as a single individual. The family, she believed, would find "steady improvement" under the "influence of church, school, mission or settlement." In the fifty homes in Fuller's survey, the Mexican tenants paid an average monthly rental of $9.80—a considerable amount when one takes into account their low wages and irregular employment.[49]

The heavy new Mexican immigration during the war years resulted in an overabundance of unskilled labor in Los Angeles. State investigators examined the work pattern of residents of the Plaza community in 1915 and concluded that unemployment was high and those who worked held poor-paying jobs in occupations that called for hard manual labor. The investigators found, for example, that of 246 Mexican men eligible for employment, 106 held jobs, 131 were unemployed, and the remaining 9 were either unaccounted for or away from their homes. Exactly 100 of these workers earned their living in blue-collar jobs, 93 of them as unskilled laborers. Only a small percentage of the Mexican women in the community worked outside the home. Of the 25 Mexican women employed, 8 worked in laundries and 7 kept boarders as a means of earning a living.[50]

Although the thirty-three major industries in the Plaza community employed a total of 1,499 workers in 1915, workers could expect to experience long terms of unemployment or underemploy-

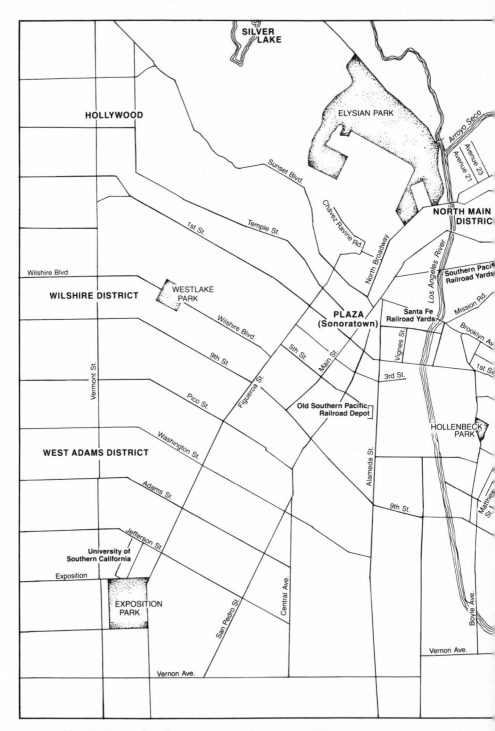

Map 2. *Central and East Los Angeles, 1915–1930*

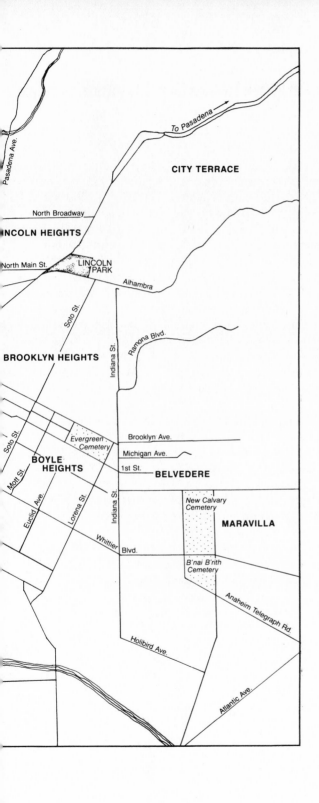

ment. A survey of 359 families in 1914–1915 revealed that 228 men were without jobs. Only 146 men in the survey confirmed that they were working.[51] Sixty-two percent of the laborers in the community earned less than $15.00 per week, or less than $2.50 per day for a six-day week. Only a small minority, 21 workers, earned weekly wages of $22.50, or between $3.00 and $4.00 daily.[52] The study, conducted during the four months of December 1914 through March 1915, no doubt counted many seasonal workers who labored during the harvest season in the outlying areas and who had resettled in the city in hopes of finding casual work. The railroad industries also had slack months during the winter period; and since the community bordered the Southern Pacific and Santa Fe railroad yards, it is probable that jobless railroad hands were counted among the unemployed.

That the immigrant residents of the Plaza community were able to make ends meet, considering their meager income and irregular employment, was a credit to their fortitude and willingness to make great sacrifices. Even those who worked regularly earned low wages. The largest industries in the community in 1916 included two beef packing houses which employed 876 men, the Los Angeles Pressed Brick Company which employed 143 men, and the Los Angeles Gas Works with 182 men. Daily wages averaged $1.75–$4.00 at the beef packing houses, $2.00–$4.00 at the Los Angeles Pressed Brick Company, and $2.00–$2.40 at the gas company. By way of comparison, a machine and foundry company in the community which employed only a few Mexicans paid $.35 per hour, or $3.50 for a ten-hour day. The machine company, however, listed 40 of its 58 workers in the skilled categories.[53] Civic leaders blamed unemployment and low wages for the increasing social problems in the Plaza barrio.

To the chagrin of local residents, the area north of the Plaza had emerged at the turn of the century as the city's principal redlight district. Through zoning laws and corrupt practices, city officials had allowed nearly all of the gambling houses and brothels and one-third of the city's saloons to be located in the space between the Plaza and the heart of Chinatown (immediately northwest of the Plaza). Responding to complaints of church and civic leaders, progressive reformers, including the local housing commission under the sponsorship of the health department, managed to close down most of the "sin shops" in the mid-teens and ordered the razing of scores of old buildings and houses.[54] This encouraged light industry to move into the space created by the urban clean-up. During the first two decades of the twentieth century, Plaza homes and commercial property sold at reasonable prices, and much of this property was bought by railroad repair shops and depots, a factor which increasingly attracted warehouses, slaughterhouses, and kindred industries.

The shift of the central business district away from the Plaza coincided not only with the rise of interurban transportation and the intrusion of light industries, but also with wholesale construction of suburban homes. During the month of September 1910, nine hundred building permits were issued citywide, fully 60 percent for single-family homes. In reference to the significant growth in housing, one booster commented that "cities five times the population of Los Angeles cannot point to an achievement of equal proportion."[55]

In the war years the Plaza community, already crowded by the influx of new immigrants, expanded even more, spilling into the area immediately east of the river. This expansion had been encouraged since the turn of the century, when Pacific Electric had built a freight depot one block north of the Plaza and two blocks from the water. In the immediate vicinity, the early industries included two macaroni factories, the Pacific Biscuit Company, the Maier and Zobelein Brewery, and the two largest lumber yards in the city. Two of the largest employers of Mexican labor in the pre-1910 era, the Cudahy Packing Company and the Southern Pacific Yards, also maintained their shops in the old Plaza community. At the opposite end of the Plaza, several new industries—including the Lewellyn Iron Works, the Southern Refining Company, and the Standard Oil facilities—provided additional employment opportunities for unskilled laborers. Finally the Western Lumber Company and the Los Angeles Framing and Milling Company located their offices two blocks south of Chinatown next to the property of Don Manuel Requeña. Requeña, whose family predated the American conquest, was one of the few Mexicans to retain property in the downtown section.[56]

Following the outbreak of World War I, Los Angeles' economy greatly expanded as a result of the growth of war-related industries. The wartime rise in production and sales of goods ranging from ships to fruits generated a new demand for workers. No longer able to find housing in the Plaza colonia, the Mexican newcomers went northeast in search of living quarters. Within a few years, the Elysian Park neighborhood (also called the Ann Street District) north of the Plaza (bordered by Elysian Park on the north, North Broadway on the west, Avenue 20 on the east, and Alhambra on the south) grew in reputation as a heterogeneous working-class community. Researchers found that by 1916 Mexicans and Italians constituted 80 percent of the ethnic groups in this neighborhood. In a survey conducted by the Los Angeles Society for the Study and Prevention of Tuberculosis, some 1,650 individuals in 331 homes were questioned about their health situation. Fifty-one percent of the respondents were Mexican and 30 percent Italian. As in other Mexican communities, youth was a common denominator. Only 2 percent of the

Mexican residents were over thirty years of age, compared to 13 percent for the other groups. Although the average Mexican family consisted of five members, more than half of them lived in small apartments in house courts. The cramped living and recreational space especially affected the Mexicans, since 56 percent of the 855 members of this group were between the ages of five and nine. The move to this neighborhood illustrates the fact that the Mexican community moved in a northeast direction at the same time that it was beginning its major thrust to the east side.[57]

As early as 1920, numerous other signs pointed toward the movement of Mexicans to the east side of town. G. Bromley Oxnam suggested in 1920 that "It is quite likely that the Mexicans now situated around the Plaza and in the Macy School District, will be forced to go to other parts of the city within the next five years."[58] It was already certain that the state railway commission had looked into placing the Union Pacific passenger depot in an area adjacent to the Plaza community. This area, with boarding houses, small hotels, and one- and two-room shacks had been extremely popular among the new immigrants. Although a civic group had proposed the construction of the railroad passenger terminal in the area east of the Los Angeles River, this alternate plan never appealed to the railroad giants. To Oxnam, it seemed likely that the Plaza site would be chosen. As he explained the consequences, "This means that between five and ten thousand Mexicans will have to move to other sections of the city. It is thought that a large number will go to the Palo Verde region . . . that a larger group will cross the river and locate around Stephenson Avenue, in what may be called the South Boyle Heights section. Still another group will seek the new Industrial District just south of city limits."[59]

Jobs, inexpensive housing, and community life accounted for the move of Mexicans to the east side. This resettlement, however, would have been of small consequence without the regular service and inexpensive fares provided by the interurban railway system. The electric interurban trolley made it possible for Mexicans to spread to residential areas several miles from the central business district and industrial areas. The movement of Mexicans toward the "new" east side occurred at the time when the Los Angeles Pacific Electric Railway opened new lines to Brooklyn Heights, Boyle Heights, and Ramona. Indeed, the existence of rail service to outlying communities such as Maravilla and Belvedere made it possible for many working-class families to leapfrog the older Mexican communities immediately east of the Los Angeles River. These scattered communities of the east side soon became one. In contrast to the

overall population of Los Angeles, which lived in a "fragmented metropolis par excellence," the Mexican community emerged by 1930
as a group tightly clustered residentially and socially.

Mexicans built the interurban railroad system, and they were its
most consistent users. But while the Mexicans continued to rely on
the Red Cars, the Anglo population turned toward the automobile in
increasing numbers. The rise and popularity of this new mode of
transportation had a remarkable impact on the urban structure of
Los Angeles. Auto registration soared, especially in the years after
World War I. By the middle 1920s, 1 of every 7 Americans owned an
automobile; 1 of every 4 Californians were car owners; and in Los
Angeles, hailed as the auto capital of the world, the rate was 1 car for
every 2.25 people. Car owners had greater mobility; and as auto registration increased, the population naturally gravitated toward outlying areas.[60] Like other cities around the country, Los Angeles an-
nexed many of the new communities. A city of 100 square miles in
1910, Los Angeles claimed 441 square miles by 1930.[61] As the population of the city spread, vast tracts of single-family homes emerged.
By the 1920s, the auto had contributed not only to a mass movement
of families to outlying areas, but also to the increasing dispersal of
manufacturing industries.

Although the new Mexican *colonia* on the east side began to
grow, still other Mexican enclaves survived the enclosure created by
suburban development. One such community, itself split into three
sections, was located in Pasadena, one of Los Angeles' largest suburbs and a predominantly Anglo area. According to a 1922 survey,
the three barrios of Pasadena accounted for 1,736 Mexicans, or 395
families. Christine Lofstedt, a university researcher, described one
of the southern section Pasadena barrios as being "located in that
narrow strip of land south of Colorado Avenue, traversed by two railroad tracks, having gas tanks, electric power plants, several factories, laundries, and a heterogeneous huddle of abodes."[62] In Pasadena, Mexicans who lived in the southern section and other barrios
found seasonal agricultural work in nearby citrus farms and ranches.
"Most of their work," Lofstedt wrote, "is in orchards, picking fruit,
gardening, stone work, cement work, digging, hod carrying, and
laundering."[63]

In another southwestern barrio of Los Angeles, another investigator, Elizabeth F. Hymer, found housing conditions little better
than those in the Mexican *colonia* of Watts, although the residents
seemed better off economically. The community, she wrote, is "a
heterogeneous racial group, with Jewish, Negro, and upper class
Mexican predominating." To the casual visitor, the residents of this

neighborhood appeared to have a "definite attitude of thrift, aspiration, and self-respect." Hymer's survey revealed that nearly two-thirds of them wanted "American" neighbors, an indication that they have "a definite desire to become a part of the fabric of the American social order."[64]

As Los Angeles diversified its industries, new areas came under development and others under the bulldozer. Tire industries and meat packing companies, for example, viewed the inexpensive land, low taxes, and ample labor force of the outlying areas as ideal for relocating their plants. For companies relying on ocean shipping, the harbor area surrounding San Pedro and Wilmington (south of Los Angeles) seemed a logical choice. For companies doing major business by rail, the area just east of the city's center offered many advantages.

Rapidly developing tire manufacturing was found predominantly on the east side. The industry had begun in the post–World War I years when the automobile gained popularity in the United States, in particular in southern California. By the mid-1920s, the industry employed eight thousand workers and produced an annual payroll of $14 million. One major factory, the Samson Tire Company, acquired forty acres from the Union Pacific Industrial Park on Atlantic Boulevard. This area had a high concentration of Mexicans by the early 1920s and continued to expand.[65]

Growth of all these Mexican communities was influenced by increasing immigration of Mexican workers. In the mid-1920s, the phenomenal in-migration of Mexican families to Los Angeles contributed to its rise as the new "Mexican capital" of the United States. From 1920 to 1930 the Mexican population in the city tripled, from 33,644 to 97,116. Such growth gave Los Angeles the lead for the first time over San Antonio, traditionally the nation's largest Mexican city. In the entire county, moreover, Los Angeles counted 167,000 Mexicans, a number significantly greater than the population of all but a few cities in Mexico.[66] The greatest growth occurred in areas east and south of downtown Los Angeles, especially in the Central Plaza District and the Boyle Heights community (referred to as Assembly Districts 60 and 61 in 1930). In District 60, which in 1930 included the Central Plaza, Lincoln Heights, and sections of Boyle Heights, the Mexican population numbered nearly 35,000, or approximately twice the size of the second largest barrio located in District 61. District 61 bordered the Anglo community of South Pasadena, the predominantly Mexican community of Belvedere, and a small Black district extending from the Central Avenue neighborhood.[67]

As the Mexican population shifted eastward, so did many of the social and religious centers involved with this group. The Brownson House Settlement, the oldest center for Mexican immigrants in Los Angeles, relocated its facilities in 1928 to Pleasant Avenue on the east side in order to continue to serve the Mexican population. Built in 1901, the original Brownson House was located near the Plaza just west of the Los Angeles River. Mary J. Desmond, head resident of the settlement house, recalled that when it was first established "it was in a valley surrounded by pleasant homes and attractive gardens, but in recent years the encroachment of commercial enterprises was so rapid that the settlement house found itself entirely surrounded by factories and carried on its work directly beneath three huge towering gas tanks."[68]

By the late 1920s the community of Belvedere, with thirty thousand residents of Mexican descent, had the largest concentration of Mexicans in the Los Angeles metropolis, surpassing other communities closer to the central core such as Boyle Heights and Lincoln Heights.[69] Mexicans had begun to move to Belvedere in the late 1910s, a period when lots and houses there were significantly cheaper than in Boyle Heights, a Jewish and Italian district at that time. Like Santa Ana, this eastside community was served by an interurban railway system that made movement into the city inexpensive and relatively fast.[70] By the early 1920s, a Pacific Electric line running from the Slauson Junction (near downtown Los Angeles) to Orange County via Belvedere, Los Nietos, and La Habra gave Mexicans greater options in their quest to obtain property. Belvedere, even closer to the Central core than Watts or Santa Monica, flourished in the post–World War I decade. Unlike the southwest communities of Los Angeles, where Mexicans and Blacks together constituted a majority, in Belvedere there were only 13 Black residents listed in the 1930 census. In Belvedere in 1920, native White residents and Whites of mixed foreign parentage were equally represented. The fact that there were few Blacks on the east side presumably increased the job opportunities for Mexican workers, especially workers seeking jobs in the brick, lumber, clay, and heavy manufacturing plants in the adjacent districts.[71]

As industries set up new locations in the communities east and south of Belvedere, Mexican residents filled an important labor void. Companies restricted to areas outside of the residential sections, such as meat packing, steel, and auto assembly, as well as those companies seeking to remain near the more extensive railroad lines of the east side, established manufacturing headquarters in Vernon, Maywood, Commerce, Bell, and Cudahy. These plants gave Mexicans employment opportunities in industry-related jobs. Yet, despite what seemed to be an abundance of employment options, social worker Mary Lanigan noted that second-generation Mexicans in Belvedere by the late 1920s remained disillusioned, having "become accustomed to segregation and (referring to) Americans as white people." They had come to understand, Lanigan wrote, "that there are certain types of jobs for Mexicans and certain kinds for Americans." As to integration, she concluded that "America has repulsed the Mexican immigrant in every step he has taken toward that goal."[72]

Most new Los Angeles subdivisions, some 1,400 in the county during the 1920s alone, catered to native Anglo Americans and immigrants of northern European ancestry. In an article entitled "The Land of Sunny Homes," one booster of Los Angeles warned: "For the man whose capital consists principally of his bare hands the opportunities in southern California are limited. Though the district has made a remarkable industrial growth, thanks to cheap oil fuel and cheap electric power, though the number of factories is doubling every five years, still the influx of labor usually exceeds the demands."[73] Thus most of the "golden opportunities" hailed in Los Angeles benefited skilled and semiskilled workers. Capital profits made possible by cheap unskilled laborers allowed many of the Anglo blue- and white-collar workers to move into more and more affluent subdivisions.

The Interchurch World Movement of Los Angeles found considerable improvement in the housing situation in 1920, although Mexican communities remained crowded and isolated. The Interchurch study found that only 1 percent of the Mexican families lived in one-room quarters and 50 percent lived in four- and five-room residences, an improvement over conditions reported by the city's 1912 study, which had shown only 5 percent in the larger residences. These advancements seem remarkable indeed and have subsequently been refuted by other studies. Nonetheless, although the church survey found that progress had been made in housing, it recommended "that a reasonable rental commission be appointed to investigate the exorbitant rent now charged Mexicans."[74]

The rapid growth of Mexican businesses in the barrio, numbering about 239 in 1922, reflected a sense of permanency and dispelled the myth that Mexicans in Los Angeles contributed to the economy only through seasonal work. Most Mexican business establishments, at least up until World War I, operated in the Plaza community. As the Mexican community spilled over to the east side in the postwar years, many of the businesses followed, for they too faced the prob-

lem of higher rents and lack of space. Moreover, greater business opportunities awaited Mexicans in the new communities. This was especially true of neighborhood stores such as those selling groceries
and tortillas. By 1920, ten of the sixty-six grocery stores owned by
Mexicans were located on Brooklyn Avenue on the east side, and
dozens more opened over the same period on streets near Brooklyn.
The grocery business was the most popular one for Mexicans; grocery stores constituted one-fourth of all the commercial activity in
the community. The next two most popular businesses for Mexicans
in the twenties were restaurants and cleaning establishments. The
popularity of these two businesses may have resulted from the presence of many single men in the barrios.[75]

The Plaza area, however, continued to dominate in recreational
and cultural activities. Mexican workers frequented pool halls, movie
houses, and penny arcades of the downtown area. Mexican men especially favored the pool halls of North Main as gathering places. On
a typical afternoon, some 150 men played pool or simply visited the
pool halls of this area. The pool halls catered to particular ethnic
groups; and although segregation policies did not prevail, as a rule,
Mexicans preferred to gather in areas with others of their class and
background. In the post–World War I period Mexicans frequently pa-
tronized four pool halls operated by Japanese. Additionally, five of
the most popular Mexican theatres in the city were located on North
Main. During the 1910s, the Hidalgo Theater drew the largest audi-
ences. For one Saturday show, for example, an investigator reported
that 525 customers packed the theatre and that 75 percent of them
were Mexican.[76]

Demographic data show that the movement of Mexicans to urban areas of California had a marked impact on the general population. According to the *Monthly Labor Review*, Mexicans in California in 1929 accounted for 17.7 percent of all newborns in the state.
The excess of births over deaths among the White population of the
unincorporated area of Los Angeles County in the years 1921–1927
was only 241, while the Mexican excess of births over deaths for the
same period was 4,070. Over a similar period, 1918–1927, the total
excess of births over deaths in Los Angeles was 43,066, of which
10,189, or 20 percent, were Mexican. A study of 769 Mexican households in this same period confirmed the high birthrate of Mexican
families. The study revealed that the average number of children per
family canvassed was 4.3. In fact, 45.3 percent of the families had
five or more children while 40.4 percent had fewer than three.[77]

The study also affirmed the low wages earned by the Los Angeles Mexican working class. Of the 701 Mexican families for which

reports on average monthly income were available, 69.2 percent averaged less than $100 per month; 10.5 percent between $100 and $150; 5.9 percent between $150 and $200; and only 4.4 percent $200 or over. As a result, every capable person in these families was encouraged to contribute to the household income. A study of 435 families revealed that 35.2 percent reported children working at least part time.[78]

While some of the outlying communities continued to attract Whites as well as Mexicans, distinct patterns of Mexican and White neighborhoods became clearly visible with increasing Mexican population. For example, in Watts, according to Clara G. Smith, "Main Street divided the community into two sections; north of Main Street became settled by white people, mostly those who segregated themselves, while the greater part south of Main Street was occupied mostly by the Mexicans and later by both Mexicans and Negroes."[79] Although Mexicans resided in every district of Los Angeles, housing discrimination by Anglos against Mexicans prevailed in many southern California communities. Prior to World War I, Anglo residents of the Central Avenue District of the Plaza successfully resisted the "invasion" of Mexicans, as well as Blacks and Asians, through their own personal efforts or by the use of restrictive clauses in mortgage contracts. Further south in Watts, Smith concluded, "When the Mexican buys property in the white district, he becomes an outcast of his former group and is rejected by his American neighbors."[80]

Like Blacks and Asians, Mexicans experienced segregation in housing in nearly every section of the city and its outlying areas. In Santa Ana, one woman explained how the Mexican population came to live near the railroad tracks in an area known as the Santa Fe District:

> The Mexicans went down there to live because the rents were cheap. Then, too, there was a terrible feeling among the white people in Santa Ana at that time. They did not like to live near the Mexican people. A white man would let his house stand vacant all of the time before he would rent it to a Mexican, even if the Mexican and his family were clean and could pay the rent. So whether or not the Mexican people wanted to live in a district by themselves, they had to. There was no other place they could get a house to live in.[81]

In the Santa Ana community, the desire of Mexicans "to put their children in schools with Americans" caused additional shifts in the residential patterns of the new immigrant population. According to Helen Walker, a social worker in the community, "many of the Mexicans feel that the Mexican schools, with their old and ugly buildings are not as good as the schools to which the Americans go."[82]

In 1927 the Los Angeles Chamber of Commerce asked surrounding incorporated cities to report on such issues as population growth and industries. The responses recorded shed much light on the problem of segregation and the attitudes of community leaders toward the movement of Mexican residents to their districts. The coastal city of El Segundo stated in a boastful manner that its city "had no negroes or Mexicans." Lynwood, one of the new industrial areas southeast of the central area, reported in 1930: "Lynwood, being restricted to the white race, can furnish ample labor of the better class." Every city that wished to attract new settlers apparently felt compelled to congratulate itself on having few foreign-born or racially mixed groups. Long Beach, a community that in the late 1920s actually had a large Mexican population of nearly 13,000, advertised haughtily, "Long Beach has a population of 140,000—98 percent of whom are of the Anglo-Saxon race."[83]

Most of this hostility was directed at the poor working-class Mexican immigrants. Real estate agents and homeowners were willing to bend the unwritten rules of segregation when it appeared that the interested minority had attained the "proper" class. Once having established their movie careers, Ramon Novarro and Dolores del Rio, two of Hollywood's most successful stars in the 1920s, bought homes on the nearly all-White west side. A few other affluent Mexican immigrants also settled on the west side, amid fashionable homes on Adams and Wilshire boulevards. These westside residents, who had been members of the ruling elite of Mexico during the presidency of Porfirio Díaz, lived comfortably in private dwellings with spacious gardens reminiscent of days in prerevolutionary Mexico. The *Los Angeles Times* reported that on West Adams Boulevard near the popular Centro Hispano Americano, Mexican *señoritas* mixed with the city's upper crust.[84] Some of Mexico's wealthiest exiles made their homes in Los Angeles during the period 1910–1930, including the ex–land baron of Chihuahua, Luis Terrazas, who had once ruled over a cattle and mining empire valued at $200 million, and the ex-governors of Baja California and Oaxaca.[85]

The impact that segregation had on the Mexican residents is difficult to measure. Certainly some of the newcomers chose to live in ethnically segregated communities, and such selection may have made their adjustment to new life styles easier. At a conference dealing with the immigration question, Orfa Jean Shontz, a former referee of the Juvenile Court of Los Angeles, spoke about "Mexican Family Relations in a Changing Social Environment." In her opinion, raising children was certainly no easier in the United States than in Mexico and as a whole, she found Mexicans "as a class, the best mannered, the most obedient, and the least quarrelsome of the nationalities" in California. Mexican family life, under strain in a new urban industrial environment, seemed to hold together, because, as Shontz noted, "Mexicans have a universal respect for childhood and old age" and family relationships among them "are closer, warmer, and more sacred than with us."[86] No doubt living in the barrio made it easier for Mexicans to maintain these relationships.

How the media and the public viewed Mexicans affected the responses of agencies and institutions toward this group. The California Development Association, among other organizations, would have liked for the public to believe that Mexicans employed in the state were mainly engaged in agriculture and returned to Mexico at the end of the harvest season. Their misconceptions or efforts to deceive the public resulted from attention given by the United States Congress to the question of restricting immigration from Mexico. The association's argument that "The Mexican coming to California has evidenced little mass tendency to remain in permanent colonies" was aimed at assuring the Congress that there was little need to place Mexico on the quota list as it had done for Eastern European countries.[87]

Some of these false perceptions held by Los Angeles residents concerning the Mexican population also resulted in large part from attempts of local industrialists to portray Mexicans as a casual labor force. The Los Angeles Chamber of Commerce contributed to this myth of the transient Mexican laborer. An extensive report written in 1929 by Dr. George P. Clements, a prominent spokesman for the Chamber, to Vanderbilt University Professor Roy Garis reveals misconceptions held by Angelenos as well as attempts to mislead proponents of the immigration quota. Of the three categories of workers—permanent, casual, and climatic—Clements placed the Mexican in the latter two divisions, noting that Mexican laborers in the casual sector met both agricultural and public utility demands, while "climatic labor calls for a class of workers who are by habit and ability capable of standing up under desert conditions." Clements asserted that the casual labor needs of the region, which "are totally un-American since they are nomadic, are supplied by Mexican people both immigrant and American citizens of Mexican stem." The latter part of his statement reveals a common misconception: that even the American-born Mexican held no claim to American society. To the question posed by Garis, "In industries, to what extent have cheap unskilled immigrant laborers (especially Mexican) replaced American laborers?" Clements replied: "In general industry, alien labor—especially Mexicans—are drawn upon to supply a short labor market in industry. An American laborer willing to work has the first preference." The Mexican, Clements concluded, "comes to America primarily to sell his labor for American money that he may return to Mexico and be a landed citizen."[88] Like most of his contemporaries, Clements ignored the realities that Mexicans raised families, bought homes, sent their children to school, and were becoming an increasingly stable contingent of the Los Angeles work force.

In a study published in 1929, Robert N. McLean, a religious leader and author, challenged the characterization of the Mexican as a nomadic individual who returned to Mexico during the winter months. In a dozen settlement houses from San Antonio to Los Angeles, McLean found that of 1,021 individuals studied, 833 had been in this country for five years or more. Of the same group, 982 remarked that they intended to live permanently in the United States; 15 were not sure; and 24 said they desired to return eventually to Mexico. Of the group, "not a single one stated that it was his habit to spend the winter in Mexico."[89] An earlier (1918) study by Gladys Patric had revealed that 31 percent of 495 Mexicans surveyed in one northeast community of Los Angeles had lived in the city between five and nine years, while 34 percent had been in the city for a period of ten to nineteen years. Of this group, only 8 percent had been born in the United States.[90]

Some insight into the settlement and migration patterns of Mexicanos surfaced in one survey of the mid-1920s in which 50.7 percent responded that they expected to return to Mexico to live. Another 35 percent chose not to answer the question. In response to a related question, 29 percent expressed a desire to "remain permanently in the United States while 49.2 percent chose not to answer this particular question."[91]

Los Angeles had tackled the issue of restricting Mexican immigration in a conference sponsored by the "Friends of the Mexicans" held on November 11 and 12, 1927. Mexican Vice-Consul Joel Quiñones and Professors Malbone W. Graham of the Political Science Department at UCLA and Emory S. Bogardus, director of the School of Social Welfare at the University of Southern California, gave key addresses. Conference participants voiced concern over "the tendency of Mexican labor to congest in Los Angeles, San Bernardino and other centers," and the failure to maintain proper living facilities. Still, they recognized the uncertainty of regular employment in rural sections which forced many migrant laborers to urban areas and agreed that the Mexican population of the Southwest essentially needed to be more "properly distributed." A special committee concluded that the public needed accurate facts concerning the Mexican population. At the end of the conference, delegates warned that public opinon might force immediate drastic legislation detrimental to agriculture, industry, and transportation. They made numerous recommendations regarding the establishment of minimum wage standards and "minimum standards of wholesome housing and sanitation for Mexican workers."[92]

With changing economic conditions, Mexicans also came to view their migration and settlement in new ways. In the pre–World War I years when jobs in industry were few and low-paying, many Mexicans discovered that only crowded and inadequate house courts accommodated their families. In the twenties, suburban developers found it profitable to cater to a lower-income market and pursued Mexican buyers. Although a smaller proportion of Mexicans owned their own homes than native Anglo Americans and European immigrants, many nonetheless found in the new barrios of the east side at least a partial opportunity to make a better life for their families.

5 The "Brown Scare"

Accelerating urbanization and industrialization in Los Angeles after 1910 brought a change in the city's social and demographic base. The vast numbers of Mexican migrants settling in the city during the period 1910–1920 contrasted with the region's traditional patterns of immigration. Prior to 1900 most immigrants to California had originated in Northern Europe, especially England, Ireland, Scandinavia, and Germany. After 1910 the majority of the newcomers to the Golden State came from Mexico and the southern regions of Europe. The influx of people from other parts of the United States as well as this increasing foreign immigration accounted for Los Angeles' rapid population growth.[1]

These factors, along with other social conditions during the 1910s—an economic depression, the transition from a commerce and trade economy to one of industry and manufacturing, a large influx of alien population, mainly Mexican, which crowded old communities and established prominent ethnic enclaves, Mexican-U.S. border conflict, labor turmoil, and war-related hysteria—produced a situation which promoted strong nativist sentiments. Nationally, the years 1910–1921 witnessed the rise of radical labor movements and of extremist organizations espousing racial hatred; the passage of immigration quota laws based on race and nationality; and political repression.[2]

Some scholars consider nativism a social movement whose occurrence and timing are closely related to the level of disillusionment among the majority of the population. Under these circumstances, its principal aim has been "to purge the society of unwanted aliens, or cultural elements of foreign origins, or of both."[3] Other scholars see nativism as simply an ideology which propagandists have manipulated in order to serve their own purposes. In either case, nativists place the blame for the major ills of society on an alien or external group. When nativist sentiment surfaces, it becomes a crusade against foreigners, and usually results in increased political repression of a minority. In periods of social crisis or increased individual stress, nativism translates into "a zeal to destroy the enemies of a distinctively American way of life."[4]

California's unique blend of nativism, which surfaced periodically during the latter half of the nineteenth century, touched the lives of Mexican residents of southern California during the early twentieth century. Californians, mostly recent arrivals themselves, expressed a deep xenophobia, which surfaced in the racial nativism of the Gold Rush era and later in the demands for anti-Chinese laws during the 1870s and 1880s.[5] An anti-Mexican nativist crusade, unrelated to the anti-Asian campaign and directed against Mexican aliens and radicals, began early and developed peculiar dimensions on the West Coast. Among other things, during World War I Mexicans were alleged to stand on the verge of a revolution which would reclaim the entire American Southwest for Mexico. An understanding of the causes and meaning of this phenomenon in Los Angeles must take into consideration three principal factors: the fear of radicalism—political and labor-related—associated with Mexican immigration; anxiety over the spread of the Mexican Revolution and apprehension of revolution by Mexican-Americans in the Southwest; and the suspected collaboration between Mexicans—in and out of the United States—with Germany, especially during the war years.

At the national level, attempts to restrict Japanese immigration in 1905–1907, passage of the Alien Land Law in 1913, and a call for more stringent deportation and exclusionary laws figured prominently in California nativism.[6] Additionally, during the 1910s Californians, influenced by sentiments held more generally in the United States, began to associate aliens with radicalism. Political repression of labor leaders and radicals demonstrated in police action against the Industrial Workers of the World (IWW) and socialists in California during the years 1910–1921 involved elements of hysteria and violence unknown in the Golden State since the anti-Chinese movement of the mid-1870s.[7] In California, and in Los Angeles in particular, what has for many historians of the Southwest been seen as a transitional period—a lull before the stormy era of the Red Scare—actually constituted a crucial era for repression of aliens and radicals. During the period 1913–1918, a Brown Scare hysteria fully as great as that aimed at Communists and other radicals elsewhere, was directed at Mexicans living in Los Angeles.

As the industrial sectors in Los Angeles underwent rapid expansion and far-reaching adjustments, frequent unemployment and violent labor disputes erupted. A notable example of unrest occurred in 1911, when a mysterious explosion rocked the *Los Angeles Times* building. The *Times* had been a stinging critic of organized labor in the city, and *Times* editorials encouraged a widely accepted assumption that labor supporters had been behind this reprehensible deed. Under strange and still unexplained circumstances, two radical labor leaders took responsibility for the bombing.[8] This violence precipitated an enormous labor setback, for over the next three years manufacturers won a prolonged battle for an open shop city. In efforts to reduce the influence of organized labor, southern California industrialists stepped up recruitment of Mexican labor. Nativists, however, attempted to stem the flow of immigration from Mexico, claiming that Mexicans were unassimilable and likely to ignite new labor conflict. Although at times the two groups undermined one another's objectives, over the years 1914–1918, Mexicans in Los Angeles became the principal scapegoats, along with alleged labor "agitators," for economic and social dislocation.[9]

During this industrial transition, nativists paid close attention to U.S. international affairs. When the United States entered World War I, the fear of German intrigue in Mexico and in the Mexican communities of the United States surfaced as an additional "threat" to the safety of U.S. citizens. It was an era, as one historian has noted, when individuals groped "for national unity, alarmed at unheeded or widening rifts of class, or race, or ideology."[10] Nativist leaders, especially politicians, called for immigration restrictions and U.S. military intervention in Mexican affairs.

Increased Mexican immigration did not escape the attention of nativists. This immigration came on the heels of political confrontation over Japanese immigration. The movement of Mexicans into Los Angeles, moreover, occurred during a period of intense rural-to-urban migration. In southern California, Mexican laborers filled a labor vacuum created in numerous agricultural communities by the restriction of Asian workers.

During the depression of 1913–1914, California nativists found immigrants a prime economic scapegoat. Jobs which had been considered menial or unworthy a year earlier attracted hundreds of Anglo applicants at this time. Immigration restriction had broader implications than merely jobs, as nativists raised the spectres of disease, illiteracy, and high welfare costs as the main weapons to influence public opinion.[11] They often referred to the "learned opinions" of academic researchers to bolster their case. Samuel Bryan of Stanford University, for example, wrote in 1912, "Socially and politically the presence of large numbers of Mexicans in this country gives rise to serious problems."[12] Bryan visited the Mexican community of Los Angeles and concluded that the Mexican quarters had become "the breeding ground" for "disease and crime." He summarized his findings in this manner: "Their low standards of living and of morals, their illiteracy, their utter lack of proper political interest, the retarding effect of their employment upon the wage scale of the more progressive races, and finally their tendency to colonize in urban centers, with evil results, combine to stamp them as a rather undesirable class of residents."[13]

To nativists, the influx of Mexican refugees represented a serious problem. In a story of the ordeal of several hundred refugees from the Mexican Revolution who had crossed over to the U.S. side of the border under great duress, the *Los Angeles Times* warned that providing care for the "uninvited guests" would prove very costly, as officials of the State and War departments "cast about for means to defray the expense of maintaining these thousands of strangers." Chiding those who failed to seek federal assistance, the *Times* speculated that Los Angeles officials were reluctant to go to Congress for funds for fear that such an action might "precipitate an undesirable Congressional discussion on the whole Mexican problem."[14]

Politically active refugees caused even more alarm. White Angelenos initially gained awareness of Mexican radical activity in their city through the presence of the PLM (Partido Liberal Mexicano or Mexican Liberal Party), whose exiled members established a headquarters in Los Angeles in 1907.[15] Originally dedicated to the overthrow of the Díaz dictatorship, PLM members during the revolutionary decade worked toward social and political reform in Mexico. Indeed, during the period 1907–1911, the PLM, headed by Ricardo Flores Magón, was the most active anti-Díaz organization operating within Mexico and the United States. Flores Magón and others proposed the creation of secret PLM cells inside Mexico in order to gain the financial backing of oppositionist newspapers and impoverished or persecuted liberals inside Mexico.[16]

Soon after arriving in Los Angeles, the Magonistas began publication of *Revolución*, a bilingual newspaper which called for political and social reform in Mexico.[17] In political rallies hosted by the Socialist Party of Los Angeles, Flores Magón asked his Mexican compatriots to return to Mexico to overthrow Díaz. From Los Angeles, PLM leaders laid plans for the first offensive against the Díaz dictatorship. The PLM sensed that the Díaz regime was in political trouble and in 1907 called for a revolution on September 16. As PLM members in Mexico and Los Angeles worked to finalize their plans, private detectives arrested several PLM leaders. Not bothering to secure an arrest warrant, the detectives broke into their East Los Angeles headquarters and took three members of the Junta to the city jail.[18] The police charged the PLM members with being fugitives from justice. Flores Magón spent nearly two years in the Los Angeles County jail while his lawyer, Job Harriman, fought extradition efforts by the Mexican government.

In 1911 the Magonistas once again attempted to influence the course of Mexico's political destiny from their haven in Los Angeles. The PLM political activities at the onset of the Mexican Revolution, especially the Socialist invasion of Baja California in 1911, captured local headlines in Los Angeles for nearly half a year. Angelenos learned that the PLM had joined forces with a small army of IWW and Socialist Party members to launch an attack on the principal cities of Baja California.[19] The Mexican Embassy warned the U.S. State Department that press reports in Los Angeles placed IWW leader Simon Berthold in Los Angeles in February 1911, "recruiting adventurers" for forays into Ensenada and Mexicali in Baja California.[20] The Mexican consul in Los Angeles informed the Mexican Secretary of Foreign Affairs two weeks later (March 9, 1911) that Flores Magón was providing arms to the rebels in Baja California and that he possessed at the time at least three cases of arms and munitions.[21]

Once the Socialist rebel army had crossed the border into Baja California, Mexican authorities stepped up efforts to put Flores Magón out of action. Antonio Lozano, the Mexican consul in Los Angeles, obtained the services of a private detective, Fred F. Rico, to whom he assigned the duties of "secret service spy." Following a trip to the border region by Rico, the Mexican consul submitted a report to the Mexican Foreign Affairs Office which clearly implicated Flores Magón as the leader of the Baja California invasion. Lozano advised the ambassador that the "villainous conduct of Ricardo Flores Magón, the 'pseudo-socialist,' had finally managed to awaken the just rage of Mexicans" in his consulate jurisdiction.[22]

Flores Magón did not personally join the rebel forces in Baja California. Instead he remained in Los Angeles in an effort to collect funds and arms. He also prepared a manifesto, published in English and Spanish, which described his ideological stance. In it he acknowledged the role of the PLM in "actual insurrection" in Mexico "with the deliberate and firm purpose of expropriating the land and the means of production and handing them over to the people." Criticizing President Taft for sending twenty thousand soldiers to the Mexican border, the PLM Junta asked that workers awake from their lethargy, calling for "Individual agitation of the class-conscious workers; collective agitation of labor organization and or groups organizing for liberal propaganda: Systematic agitation of the labor press and of free thought; agitation in the street, in the theatre, in the street cars, in meetings . . . in every place where you can find ears disposed to listen, consciences capable of indignation, hearts which are not calloused by injustice."[23]

By 1914, Flores Magón had become one of the principal political organizers in the Mexican communities of southern California. At a Fourth of July gathering he spoke about class divisions and racial injustice in the United States: "Don't you know how many times a Mexican laborer has received a bullet in the middle of his chest when he has gone to pick up his paycheck from a North American boss?"[24] Flores Magón spoke of various incidents of racial nativism directed at the Mexican worker. As Mexicanos, he stated, "You well should know that in this country we are worth nothing!" Reminding the audience of the burning at the stake of Antonio Rodríguez in Rock Springs, Texas, he asked if they had not heard that in Texas and other states it was "prohibited for Mexicans to ride in the train sections of men of white skin. Jim Crow Laws also denied Mexicans admittance to eating places, hotels, barber shops and public beaches."[25]

Finally Flores Magón spoke about the extraordinarily high number of Mexicans sentenced to death. He warned that if the authorities took steps to hang any more Mexicans, "we, the workers, shall put our hands at the throat of the *burgueses*! Now or never! The opportunity presents itself to stop this series of infamous acts that are committed in this country against the people of our race for the only reason that we are Mexican and poor."[26] Flores Magón's passionate orations accurately depicted conditions for most Mexicans in the United States.

Shortly after Flores Magón had given these speeches, a federal grand jury in Los Angeles convened to hear testimony regarding his activities and those of other PLM leaders. They were especially interested in the role of the Magonistas in the capture of Tijuana the previous summer. The grand jury returned indictments against the PLM members, and they were ordered to stand trial for violations of neutrality laws. The court sought to prove that the PLM had conspired to enlist men at their Los Angeles headquarters for the purpose of overthrowing the Mexican government. After a long and boisterous trial in which Magonistas and their supporters packed the courtroom on a daily basis to hear the testimony, the all-White jury found the defendants guilty as charged. Flores Magón was declared guilty on four counts of the charges and sentenced to twenty-three months at the McNeil Island federal prison in Washington.[27]

Mexicans who had moved north across the border and settled in communities like Los Angeles made every effort to keep up with political affairs in their former homeland. Many aspired to assist relatives and friends left behind. They organized community fund drives and collected food and medical supplies for the victims of the Revolution across the border. Former supporters of Díaz, as well as his opponents and followers of other political persuasions, active and passive, resided alongside each other in Los Angeles; bickering among them was not uncommon.[28]

In the years following the outbreak of the Mexican Revolution, most rebel forces maintained some contact with border communities north of the Río Grande. Americans suspected that the revolutionaries depended on the United States for arms and other war supplies. Indeed Francisco (Pancho) Villa sold confiscated herds of cattle to ranchers in South Texas and maintained banking accounts in several U.S. border towns. Provisional President Venustiano Carranza frequented U.S. border cities for the purpose of buying arms and munitions. An arms embargo imposed by President Wilson eventually contributed to the fall of Victoriano Huerta, the successor to Francisco Madero.[29] A sharp limitation on arms sales to Villistas in 1915 caused in part one of Villa's first military setbacks. The constant presence of rebel forces along the international line and reports of battles in the northern region contributed to anxiety among border state residents that the Revolution might spill over onto the American side.

Political activities of PLM members on the Mexican border and a series of articles in Los Angeles' newspapers during the fall of 1913 stirred up unrest and fears of a border invasion. On September 15, the *Los Angeles Times* reported that U.S. cavalrymen had captured several members of a band of Mexican filibusters in Texas. Authorities secured a confession from one of the leaders, Barney Cline, which revealed "the first inkling of a widespread movement to proclaim a new revolution in favor of the Flores Magón branch of Socialists who have their headquarters in Los Angeles." The article left readers unclear as to whether the revolution would occur in the United States or Mexico. Carranzistas who opposed Flores Magón increased their vigiliance in the border region as did military authorities on the U.S. side.[30]

Although the distance from the Mexican border to Los Angeles measured 140 miles, news of border trouble greatly affected the local residents. Following the assassination of Madero, the violence in Mexico took a more pronounced course and the Los Angeles press began to give Mexico and the border region extensive coverage. The

Times of November 9, 1913, commented on the loss of business to Los Angeles industries resulting from the rebellious activities in northern Mexico. Local lumber companies which had supplied the mining communities of Sonora and Sinaloa experienced a severe drop in sales as a result of the Revolution. Another related article appearing the same day reported that the local Carranza Junta based in Los Angeles predicted official recognition by President Wilson of the newly formed Carranza government. Reports that Carranza agent Emiliano Ocampo had circulated "in the Mexican quarters" the previous day in search of recruits for the Carranzistas received press attention.[31]

With few exceptions *Los Angeles Times* news coverage of the Mexican Revolution prior to 1913 had been free of yellow journalism. But beginning in the fall of 1913, the *Times* joined other West Coast newspapers in using the Revolution to promote sales through an appeal to nativistic sentiments. During September, the *Times* reported the experiences of Robert Aylward, a soldier of fortune with service in the Boer War in South Africa. Aylward described the civil war in Mexico as "not war but murder" where neither side took prisoners in this "region of terror." According to Aylward, the retreating armies left their wounded behind "heaped with the dead or cremated."[32]

The *Times* proved no more restrained in describing the Mexican situation in an editorial written on November 16, 1913. Americans living on the border could expect a terrible fate, the paper warned, for "El Paso is practically at the mercy of Villa," who could "loot it and return and entrench his army on Mexican soil" before the United States could respond with "a force adequate to cope with him." As for his rival Carranza, he was "similarly situated" with respect to the border communities of Calexico, El Centro, and San Diego in California and Yuma, Douglas, and Tucson in Arizona. Although the *Times* felt confident that a military force could drive any border invaders back to Mexico, "in the meantime, the mischief would be done; border cities and towns would be looted." The editorial ended with the observation that the Mexican people were a "desperate and despairing" lot who could be swayed "by a prospect of the rich plunder to be obtained by a combined raid upon our border cities."[33] No doubt this type of warning heightened apprehension and increased newspaper sales as well.

The day after the *Times* editorial appeared warning of a border invasion, Los Angeles police began arresting Mexicans, and government agents stepped up their surveillance of the Mexican community. Reports surfaced that "local Carranza sympathizers" were preparing "to take advantage of a possible break between the United States and Mexico." The *Times* referred to Mexicans involved in this scheme as "reds and cholos," commenting for example that the "number of cholos" arrested for carrying concealed weapons had increased by five times.[34] The Mexican consul did little to placate the fears of the nervous officials. Placed there by Carranza's archenemy, President Victoriano Huerta, the consul also expressed some concern over the events of that week, reporting that his office had obtained information "that numerous reds have quit work in the surrounding town and country districts" and were flocking to Los Angeles in "the expectation that something may happen."[35]

Local authorities took the threat seriously, calling in the Justice Department to assist them in the search for revolutionaries. Police officers searched the Santa Monica hills for reported "hidden munitions of war" while "other secret agents" watched suspected leaders of the movement in the city. The *Times*, which had warned two days earlier that rebels were anxious to "plunder" the border towns, again reported that the situation was "due to the efforts of several revolutionaries who spread the news around that there might be a chance to plunder" amid "any confusion that might come from an outbreak of hostilities along the border."[36]

Nativists expressed interest in armed intervention in Mexico two years before Villa's famous 1916 raid on Columbus, New Mexico. Nativists lauded the superiority of U.S. institutions and culture and expected President Wilson to handle the Mexican situation much as McKinley had dealt with Cuba in 1898. West Coast nativists received much of their support from business owners who wished to see their investments safeguarded. Within the Republican Party, nationalist elements argued that only armed intervention by the United States could restore peace and order.[37] U.S. intervention came in April 1914 with the so-called Tampico Incident and the American occupation of Veracruz, Mexico's major port. In the occupation of Veracruz, nineteen Americans lost their lives and there were seventy-one reported injuries. The Mexicans lost nearly two hundred men and at least three hundred were reported wounded, many of them civilians caught in the crossfire.[38]

Angelenos gathered their impressions of Mexicans from the local press, which in 1914 gave extensive coverage to the Revolution. For instance, in the weeks following the Veracruz incident, journalist Arthur Dunn of *Sunset* magazine (published in Los Angeles) traveled to the west coast of Mexico to investigate the situation there.

He began his story with this statement: "It was war in red Mexico." Angelenos curious about the Revolution could learn from Dunn's article that "It is easier to steal and kill if need be, than to work and develop the land." He estimated that half of Mexico was hostile to the United States, "receiving its inspiration from Mexico City and such red governors as he who sits at Colima [a principal state on the west coast]."[39]

The *Los Angeles Times*, which eventually became the leading western advocate of U.S. intervention in Mexico, had demonstrated a measured degree of restraint in earlier years. During the Díaz era, *Times* owner Harrison Gray Otis also served as president of a Los Angeles company which controlled 850,000 acres of land in Mexico. In 1908, Mexico had given Otis an additional 200,000 acres of public land in the Mexican extension of the Imperial Valley.[40] William Randolph Hearst, owner of the *Los Angeles Examiner*, also had land interests in Mexico. They included a cattle ranch in Chihuahua, which up to 1916 had not been broken up by the Mexican revolutionaries.[41] While many western newspapers called for the United States to play a more active role in Mexico, *Times* editorials remained remarkably subdued. On January 11, 1914, for instance, the editors buried the remarks of Benjamin Ide Wheeler, president of the University of California, concerning the Mexican situation. Upon his return from seven months abroad, Wheeler stated that European nations favored U.S. intervention in Mexico. "The foreign powers would be only too glad to have this nation straighten out the difficulties in Mexico."[42] Moreover, on the occupation of Veracruz, the *Times* actually proposed an honorable "withdrawal of our forces" from that region in order to insure that "just claims for injuries to American property and life may be paid." The editors recommended that "we let Mexico alone to frame her own land laws and choose her own rulers."[43]

When the Veracruz affair did not produce the ouster of President Huerta, the call for additional U.S. intervention grew ever louder. Critical of the Mexican government's failure to protect the lives and property of foreign residents, especially U.S. citizens, the *Independent* warned that "the time may come when a strong hand from without must be laid upon the clashing factions that peace may be restored." Reports circulated in Washington that Army and Navy officers expected intervention in Mexico to be "forced on the United States any day."[44] Even Mexican citizens, observed the *Laredo Times*, viewed hostilities between the United States and Mexico as imminent. According to the Laredo paper, "most of the educated Mexicans here and in northern Mexico believe intervention is inevitable, whether started by the hostilities in Mexico or by the humanity of Americans." The border newspaper concluded that the exodus of Americans and Mexican citizens was evidence of the worsening of conditions within Mexico.[45]

Much of the opposition to intervention betrayed nativistic underpinnings. In an article discussing the type of war that Mexico would wage upon the United States in the event of intervention, a journalist warned that a war with Mexico would be unwise because Mexicans would do everything in their power to repel the "gringo invaders" including devastating the country, poisoning it "with plague and pestilence," and "even sacrificing their women folk." Moreover, what would the American soldiers do with the Mexican people, "the nearly 14,000,000 who can neither read nor write, who are of the same class of beings whom Uncle Sam puts on reservations and sets soldiers to guard?"[46]

With the heightening of war sentiments, the Justice Department joined Los Angeles authorities and the Mexican government in monitoring the political activities of PLM members. In 1914, Ricardo Flores Magón spoke at a meeting at the Italian Hall on the east side which attracted between seven hundred and one thousand people, 90 percent of whom were Mexican. One observer of the affair, William W. McEuen, identified the PLM as "an organization of radical Mexicans who are striving to arouse interest in the Mexican Revolution among the Mexicans here emphasizing the social and universal character of that Revolution." Although McEuen could not arrive at an accurate estimate of the party's membership, he conceded that it had a large following, evidenced by the fact that *Regeneración*, the PLM official organ, had a distribution of 10,500 copies. McEuen also said that while partisans of each Mexican leader could be found around the Mexican Plaza of Los Angeles, he had found "little evidence of active assistance of the Revolution by the Mexicans in the city."[47]

Residents of the border region, already rocked by violence and racial discord, learned in the early months of 1915 of a proposed border invasion and insurrection to be led by Mexican Americans and accomplished through the aid of Blacks and Indians. Authorities in Texas uncovered the "Plan de San Diego" in February 1915. By the summer of that year, the national press had given the Plan extensive coverage. The *Chicago Tribune* referred to the possibility of a race war in the Southwest. "Mexican anarchy," the *Tribune* cautioned, "now thrusts its red hand across our border and with an insane insolence attempts to visit upon American citizens in their homes the destruction it has wreaked upon American persons and property abroad."[48]

Angelenos learned about the Mexican plot when the press confirmed that local radical agitators led by Ricardo Flores Magón did indeed have plans for an insurrection in the Southwest. Speaking before a large audience of Mexicans in East Los Angeles on September 19, 1915, Flores Magón allegedly outlined "plans for a general uprising of the Mexican population of Southern California, the seizure and holding of the land by force of arms, following a programme of terrorization by pistol and bomb assassinations, looting and anarchistic demonstrations, together with wholesale jail deliveries."[49] The "red programme" asserted to have been proposed by the Magonistas included the Mexican annexation of Texas and California following the anticipated outbreak of hostilities between the United States and Mexico. A reporter attending Flores Magón's address noted that the meeting attracted a large contingent of women and children as well as men. He commented that frequently the audience compelled the speakers "to stop until the united squalling was appeased by food for that purpose. Annexation was the idea."[50]

Less than two weeks later, Flores Magón published an extensive report on the volatile situation in Texas. He challenged the accuracy of a *Los Angeles Tribune* article of September 7, 1915, which claimed that a territory the size of the state of Illinois had come under siege by rebel forces and that the population had been "overtaken by fear of midnight assaults, burning of ranches and murder." Flores Magón singled out a Texas Ranger report which confirmed the killing of more than 500 Mexicanos along the Texas side of the Río Grande in the previous three weeks. "Justice not bullets is what should be given to the revolutionaries in Texas," Flores Magón proclaimed.[51]

Recruiting and fund-raising activities of the Mexican refugees in Los Angeles increased Anglo anxieties. When burglars committed a rash of robberies in Long Beach, police blamed members of Villa's army. In a December 1915 story headlined "Villa's Men Suspected of Long Beach Crime," law enforcement officers reported that in an attempt to stop the "reign of crime" they had "rounded up" a number of Mexicans seen hanging about the city "believed to have been a part of Villa's army."[52] Such incidents did little to quell the anxieties among Los Angeles citizens that Mexican revolutionaries were now operating north of the border. Angelenos looked upon the local Mexican population with increasing suspicion.

No doubt the political intrigue of Mexican revolutionary factions did spill over to the American side of the border. Under the Carranza government, consuls kept track of anti-Carranza factions. When followers of Villa arrived in Los Angeles in January 1916, Adolfo Carrillo, the Mexican consul, sought to undermine their fund-raising activities through petty harassment and called upon the U.S. Justice Department to investigate their activities in southern California. Carrillo warned that the Villistas gathering in Los Angeles were "not altogether here for their health, as commonly reported." Their presence might not have aroused the attention of the Justice Department had Carillo not cautioned officials that "the exiles are preparing to hatch something, using Southern California as an incubator."[53]

Perhaps no other external event, next to the European war, received more attention in the Los Angeles press during 1916 than the March 9 attack by five hundred Mexican raiders on the border town of Columbus, New Mexico. Although the claim was never decisively proven, observers placed Villa at the head of the raiders, which cost the Mexicans one hundred men and left seventeen Americans dead. National reaction to Villa's raid was almost unanimous in favor of a firm stance.[54]

In Los Angeles, the public expressed rage and alarm at Villa's border raid. Acting on the theory that Villistas had plotted some type of "outbreak," police ordered an extension and reinforcement of a cordon thrown around the Mexican quarters.[55] Four days after the Villista raid, police arrested three Mexican "admitted anarchists" on the charges of carrying concealed weapons. Police officers also arrested W. V. Nicovich, identified as a suspected anarchist, for "attempting to incite Mexicans to attack Americans."[56] Hysteria gripped the community following an announcement by the mayor that he had received an anonymous tip from someone "on the inside" of a plot by local Villistas "to dynamite the federal building, the Courthouse, the power plants and the different newspaper buildings."[57] Chief of Police Snively announced that precautions of a "drastic nature" would be instituted to forestall any outburst on the part of the Villistas. He then placed the following restrictions on the Mexican community: "No liquor will be sold to Mexicans showing the least sign of intoxication. No guns can be sold to Mexicans, and all dealers who have used guns for window display have been ordered to take them from the windows and to show them to no Mexicans until the embargo is lifted."[58]

The day following the local embargo of gun and liquor sales to Mexicans, Chief of Police Snively requested the creation of a special civilian force or militia in anticipation of a possible insurrection by

Villa's supporters. Claiming to have received repeated threats from local Villistas, Snively sent out two thousand recruiting forms for what he termed "special policemen." Meanwhile, in the central Mexican community, referred to as Sonoratown, the chief tripled the patrol and warned that the force in that district might have to be further strengthened.[59]

In light of the extraordinary circumstances, the city's leadership praised the police chief for taking such drastic precautionary steps. The *Times* reported that at least 10 percent of the thirty-five thousand Mexicans in the city were known to the police as "rabid sympathizers with the outlaw, Villa," and many others had spread sufficient inflammatory material "that agitators, given a free hand could stir up to fighting frenzy."[60] Local editorials commended Snively for organizing the special force to keep Mexicans of the city under surveillance. The *Times* warned that "the firebrands—and they are not few—must be watched and snuffed out; the preachers of insurrection must be sequestered and confined."[61]

Prohibition of the sale of guns and liquor to Mexicans and enlistment of special militia made Anglo Angelenos ever more uneasy about the presence of Mexicans in the city and sparked a tense period of nativism and racial discord. It seemed little wonder, therefore, that when the police discovered a "large metal ball" in front of the courthouse steps on March 18, they called in bomb experts and mounted a city-wide search for "two men believed to be Mexicans" seen fleeing the scene minutes after the object was found. Deputies had been alerted to threats of dynamiting public buildings "by Mexicans who were incensed because of the punitive expedition by the United States Army" into Mexico in pursuit of Villa.[62] The police never charged anyone with the "crime," and later issues of the *Times* failed to mention the incident.

During the weeks following Villa's raid, Los Angeles civic leaders entertained numerous suggestions related to easing the tension in the city over Mexican affairs. Some groups favored deporting Mexican radicals, while others recommended that Mexicanos be placed in detention camps. Jim Goodheart, identified as the "famous superintendent of the Sunshine Rescue Mission of Denver," proposed the establishment of a "municipal workhouse and an isolation camp" which he felt would do much "toward solving the Mexican refugee problem." A large percentage of the seventy-five thousand Mexicans in Los Angeles County, Goodheart stated, "are a menace to the health and morals of any community. Afflicted with loathsome and practically incurable diseases, as many of them are, they should be isolated if they cannot be deported."[63]

Less than a month after Villa's raid, Los Angeles County supervisors adopted a resolution requesting federal action in the deportation of "cholos" (lower-working-class Mexicans) likely to become "public charges" and informing the federal authorities "of the dangers existing in further immigration of refugee Mexicans." The supervisors called the attention of the federal government to "the prevalence of disease, poverty, and immorality among these people" and requested "deportation of all undesirables of this class who have come here within the past three years."[64] Federal authorities rejected the request, and Mexicans did not face deportation until after World War I.

During the remaining months of 1916, the campaign against Mexicans in southern California subsided somewhat as Americans gave greater attention to events in Europe.[65] A small number of police officers, however, maintained a vigil on Mexican radicals and revolutionaries. During Cinco de Mayo celebrations in Los Angeles in 1917, the police kept the Mexican Plaza under constant surveillance after rumors circulated that Mexican agitators would make an appearance there.[66]

The celebration, commemorating Mexico's defeat of the French forces at Puebla on May 5, 1862, brought out several thousand Mexicans to the Plaza for a three-day jubilee. Police units reported after the first day that they had "patrolled the Plaza so thoroughly that the loafing Mexicans [presumably PLM members] did not attempt to start trouble."[67] On the second day of the festival, police officers arrested three members of the PLM as they attempted to address a crowd of nearly one thousand. Unable to post bail after their arrest, the three Mexicanos were sent to jail.[68]

Arrest of these three leaders aroused community indignation. A week after the police arrested the "Mexican agitators," a group of Mexicanos distributed a circular calling for the community to unite in securing their release. Rather than advocating rebellion, the circular reflected concern over the safety of the Mexicanos in the city. The arrest of these community members for their political views alarmed some of the activists in the *colonia*. Warning of greater dangers if the community failed to show some unity, the circular accused the police of a "series of abuses" against Mexican laborers of the city. It cautioned that if the Mexican community did not "wish to be victims of greater misbehavior and injustice" by the "dogs who call themselves guardians of public order," it would be necessary to organize an opposition front. Failure of the community to unite might encourage "those savages" to "assassinate us without cause." The *colonia* must demonstrate, the circular concluded, that "we are not disposed to overlook in silence similar abuses" by the police.[69]

Authorities continued to be alarmed by even the slightest political activity within the Mexican community. A few days after the United States declared war on Germany in April 1917, Los Angeles Sheriff John C. Cline noted an unusual disappearance of more than five thousand Mexican workers from the city. He declared that the majority of the workers seemed to be moving toward Baja California. He assumed that they had taken this action "in the belief that with all this preparation going on here trouble between this country and Mexico will follow." The sheriff told southland citizens not to worry, adding, "I have an army here that could lick all Mexico." While his agents reported that "Mexicans are quitting [their jobs] all over the country for no apparent reason, they are not mobilizing . . . The only trouble is the lack of labor."[70] A *Times* investigation into the matter found "no serious organized movement against this part of the country" on the part of Mexicans. "It would be popular with the Mexicans, but they have not the weapons, the commanders, the numbers nor the means of transportation to accomplish it."[71] Somewhat less reassuringly, however, the same investigation resolved that "agitators, mostly of their own race, have been working among the Mexicans hereabouts, urging them to return to Mexico and join her armies."[72] Two residents of Los Angeles recently returned from Mexico proposed an explanation for the exodus of Mexican laborers. They noted that wages for miners in Arizona, Sonora, Sinaloa, and Chihuahua had gone up to $1.75 per day, while the prevailing rate for Mexican labor in and around Los Angeles was $1.25 per day. Another probable reason for the massive flight derived from the announcement that all aliens would be required to register for the U.S. draft and would also be eligible for service in the Allied armed forces. Still, rumors of insurrection and invasion continued to circulate in the Los Angeles area.[73]

Angelenos, like the rest of the American public, had read about German influences in Mexico for several years prior to U.S. entry into World War I. The confrontation at Veracruz in 1914, when American marines and sailors prevented the German ship *Ypiranga* from delivering arms and munitions to the Huertistas, lent credence to the German-Mexican connection. The following year Americans learned of the Plan de San Diego and some American and Mexican authorities blamed it on the work of German agents in Mexico. Historians note that many border residents linked Villa's raid on Columbus, New Mexico, to a larger German plot designed to bring the United States and Mexico into confrontation. A *New York Times* article of June 23, 1916, "German Influence in Mexico," exemplified that argument. The New York newspaper considered the German motive for winning over Carranza as twofold: "Germans might want us [the United States] into war with Mexico in order to leave them a free hand with their U-boats. Moreover, such a war would limit American munition supplies to the Allies and Mexican oil to England."[74]

As the war in Europe took on global proportions, the widespread fear that Mexicans supported German efforts against the Allies and might collaborate with German subversives intensified Anglo hysteria. American suspicion of Mexican-German collusion intensified in 1916, when President Carranza received recognition from the Kaiser and rumors floated around Washington and Mexico City that the Germans intended to establish submarine bases along Mexican shores.[75]

The British informed President Wilson on February 25, 1917, that they had intercepted a telegram from German Foreign Secretary Arthur Zimmermann instructing the German minister in Mexico that in the event of war between the United States and Germany, he was authorized to offer Mexico an alliance.[76] Mexico's support of the Central Powers would be rewarded with the opportunity to recover "her lost territory in New Mexico, Texas and Arizona."[77] (There was no mention of California.) Mexico was also to invite Japan to join the alliance. As Karl M. Schmitt has explained, when the Zimmermann note came to light, Carranza refused to meet Washington's request to repudiate the German offer, but neither did he give the Germans satisfaction. While Carranza did not rebuff the Germans in a blunt manner, it also appears "that he did not entertain serious thoughts of entering into a German alliance."[78]

Meanwhile the *Outlook* of February 21, 1917, had voiced the concern of many Americans when it reported that since the United States broke off relations with Germany, German agents had "been pouring into Mexico" and "anti-German Mexicans are fearful that the Kaiser's agents and his Mexican allies will succeed in embroiling Mexico with the United States by means of German-financed border raids."[79] In April the *Los Angeles Times* carried a speech by Congressman Clarence B. Miller of the House Foreign Relations Committee asserting that "German reservists in the United States" had been flocking to Mexico for the purpose of aiding in the manufacture of arms and serving in the armed forces. Villa, Miller stated, "is now surrounded by a large number of German officers and the Carranza government is largely today in control of Germans."[80]

After Wilson made the Zimmermann note public on March 1, 1917, a wave of anti-German sentiment swept through the nation and was especially strong in the border region. The press and public officials accused German agents not only of stirring up trouble in

Mexico, but also of doing the same among Mexican workers in Los Angeles. The day before President Wilson read his war message to a joint session of Congress, the *Los Angeles Times* warned its readers once again of "German plots" being hatched in the Mexican community:

> If the people of Los Angeles knew what was happening on our border, they would not sleep at night. Sedition, conspiracy, and plots are in the very air. Telegraph lines are tapped, spies come and go at will. German nationals hob-nob with Mexican bandits, Japanese agents, and renegades from this country. Code messages are relayed from place to place along the border, frequently passing through six or eight people from sender to receiver. Los Angeles is the headquarters for this vicious system, and it is there that the deals between German and Mexican representatives are frequently made.[81]

When the United States entered the war in Europe, the supposed German plot in Mexico loomed even larger in scope. In 1917 the American press circulated reports that German officers had taken on training responsibilities for the armies of Obregón and Villa. Ironically, no two armed forces were more at odds than those of these two military leaders. Obregón, a brilliant field general under Carranza, had dealt Villa's forces crippling defeats in 1916. It seemed illogical that by aiding Villa, the Germans could gain favors with Carranza, the man considered by Mexicans at this juncture to be in command of national affairs. Villa adamantly denied the accusations to *Times* reporters, assuring the United States that his army of twenty thousand would cooperate in "ridding Mexico of the German menace."[82] Although Obregón also denied the presence of any German influence in his army, Carranza had more problems convincing the American public of his neutral or pro-Allied position. Carranza, who controlled the oil fields and major ports of Mexico, supplied the British with the majority of their petroleum supplies. However, Mexico also supplied oil to the Germans. The *Los Angeles Times* extended the Mexican-German link, asserting in April 1917 that "German gold made in the United States" had been pouring into Mexico for the purpose of financing the work of German agents among Mexican rebels. Among other things, these "German plotters" had plans to commit acts of sabotage on the rich oil fields of Tampico and Tuxpan. The destruction of these oil fields, the *Times* suggested, would contribute to the collapse of the British mobile forces.[83]

According to the California historian Cornelius C. Smith, Jr., the Justice Department suspected German agents in Los Angeles of recruiting Mexicanos to serve as spies and saboteurs. In his biography of Emilio Kosterlitzky, whom he described as a soldier of fortune and former *rural* (Mexican federal soldier employed in rural areas) under Díaz, Smith briefly discussed Kosterlitzky's role in the Mexican community of Los Angeles during the period 1916–1918. The Justice Department, according to Smith, considered Los Angeles a "hotbed of German intrigue" and recruited Kosterlitzky as a secret agent. They assigned him to monitor the activities of German agents in this area and "to arrest them at the proper moment—not always an easy thing to do." The Justice Department considered the border area between Los Angeles and Tijuana and extending to Mexicali and Tecate as a region vulnerable to German agents. Smith characterized Los Angeles as a "clearinghouse for German agents working to enlist Mexicans in the war against the United States." He believed that men like Kosterlitzky successfully countered such activities.[84]

World War I brought dislocation and instability to the United States in a manner unparalleled since the Civil War. Following the declaration of hostilities between the United States and Germany, the President in rapid succession signed into law the Selective Service Act, the Espionage Act, the Lever Food and Fuel Control Act, and the War Revenue Act. The Selective Service Act required the registration of all men between the ages of eighteen and forty-five, while the Espionage Act provided severe penalties for persons found guilty of aiding the enemy, obstructing recruiting, or causing insubordination, disloyalty, or refusal of duty in the armed services.[85] All of these acts caused considerable confusion in the barrio of Los Angeles and other Mexican communities of the Southwest, since many of the immigrants had not been naturalized. Thousands of Mexicanos joined the armed services, but probably an equal number of them returned to Mexico rather than fight overseas. The Espionage Act, which empowered the Postmaster General to exclude from the mails newspapers, periodicals, and other publications containing materials alleged to be treasonable or seditious, gave government authorities the license to arrest and harass Mexican political refugees, labor organizers, and pacifists. The President also established a Committee on Public Information, for the purpose of uniting the American people behind the war efforts.[86]

In 1917, the California state government took numerous steps designed to calm the fears of Californians worried about a border flare-up. In a speech to a Los Angeles audience on May 1, 1918, Governor William D. Stephens revealed that, at the recommendation of the State Council of the Defense, he would propose the creation of a State Defense Guard. This unit would be "called into existence" in the event that the National Guard had to respond to some danger "beyond the borders of the state." The State Defense Guard "might be called upon at any moment to deal swiftly and decisively with enemy plots anywhere within our state or with disturbances this side of our border line." He concluded his speech by commending the authorities in California cities that had "initiated drastic measures to suppress idleness and seditious disturbances."[87]

The anti-German and anti-radical fear directed against Mexicanos in Los Angeles served as a pretext for neglecting the legitimate complaints of Mexican workers. Industrialists and civic leaders blamed German agents for nearly every labor problem or strike which occurred during the war. In the summer of 1917, the U.S. Department of State asked the Mexican Foreign Office to look into a letter published by a Mexican consul that advised Mexicans to remain out of the United States because "individuals, companies, and even the authorities" subjected them "to outrages and bad treatment." The American Embassy dismissed the validity of the charges, noting that the letter had been published in a "pro-German paper."[88] The war situation forced the American public to grapple with a seemingly apparent contradiction concerning Mexican immigrants. On the one hand, industrialists and agricultural interests considered Mexican labor important to the war effort. On the other hand, nativists had built a public case against the importation of Mexican labor. At the request of southwestern employers, the State Department in 1917 asked the Congress to drop the literacy requirements for Mexican immigrants. This decision temporarily placed the government in favor of Mexican immigration. The State Department obviously regarded efforts by individuals working to lessen Mexican immigration as contrary to the national interest.[89]

During the war years, authorities in Los Angeles labored not only to eliminate the German threat but also to counter any IWW activity among Mexican workers. When two hundred Mexicanos from the Pacific Sewer Pipe Company called a strike on September 21, 1918, law enforcement agents in Los Angeles labeled the strike "German-made." Deputy Sheriff Mauricio L. Reyes, a Mexican American member of the sheriff's department, spoke to the men in Spanish, attempting to convince them that they "had no grievance." Only after Reyes explained the strike as "the work of pro-German agitators" did the men return to work.[90] With similar intentions, in June 1918 Egbert Adams of the Los Angeles Playground Commission had announced the inauguration of weekly programs of speakers at the Mexican Plaza for the purpose of "stamping out I.W.W.ism among the ignorant classes and [putting] Americanism in its place." At one of the programs, the Mexican Vice-Consul, Ramón S. Arriola, informed his audience "of the necessity of cooperation of the Mexican people with America."[91]

While Angelenos were considering the alleged link between pro-German associations and IWW radicalism in the local Mexican community, public leaders were also speaking out against the substitution of Mexican labor for American labor. At the Commonwealth Club in San Francisco, one nativist argued that the Mexican "is dissipated, a trouble maker and has a large camp following that consumes far too much of the products of his labor. Worse than all this, he is an enemy to our country. He is at heart, a German sympathizer and would be at war with us today if he but dared fire the first gun." At the same session, a farmer observed that while a few farmers "favored" Mexican laborers, a Commonwealth Committee had been advised "that German propaganda in the Mexican press" had warned their laborers not to seek work in the United States. The farmer concluded that the committee believed that the Mexican government "had uttered similar warnings" to its people.[92]

Seven days after President Wilson signed the declaration of war, he established the Committee of Public Information (CPI) to educate the American people about the nation's objectives in entering the conflict. By creating a system for voluntary press censorship, the committee assured that only stories which presented the war as a larger goal to promote democracy and freedom throughout the world reached the American public. Under the direction of George Creel, a former journalist, the CPI circulated on a weekly basis some twenty thousand columns of newspaper material dealing with the war.[93]

L. N. Brunswig, a Los Angeles CPI member, personally called on U.S. Secretary of the Interior Franklin K. Lane to ask for his assistance in combatting the "German lies . . . circulated among our Mexicans." In southern California, Brunswig warned Lane, "the government has positive information that Germans attempted to interfere with food crops," and that they "especially tampered" with Mexican labor in the bean and beet fields of the lower counties of California.[94] He suggested that the German agents sought to convince the Mexicans not to raise any more food by arguing that they would only "prolong the war." Brunswig also commented that Spanish-language newspapers would be given "the closest supervision and censorship."[95] Though there was little evidence to support the claims linking the IWW to German national interest, nativists and employer groups effectively utilized patriotic themes to condemn and repress the local labor movement.

The CPI translated stories of war events into several foreign languages in order to reach communities it considered susceptible to German propaganda. Throughout this period of hysteria and accusations of German conspiracies, the largest Spanish-language newspaper in the United States, *La Prensa de Los Angeles*, printed Creel's propaganda and strongly supported the American cause in Europe. In June 1918, *La Prensa* reported action on the battle front in the following partisan manner: "The most horrible killing that has ever been registered in the history of the World accompanies the new offensive of the Huns."[96] In April 1918, in a front-page article headlined "German Spies Conspire against Mexico," *La Prensa* had accused Germany of making substantial efforts to start a war between Mexico and the United States.[97]

The debate concerning Mexico's loyalty to the Allies and suspected cooperation with Germany did not die with the Armistice. Senator Albert Fall opened his Senate "Investigations of Mexican Affairs" in late 1919, and his committee explained the major political events in Mexico during the previous ten years.[98] The *Los Angeles Times* reported the hearings in a manner highly critical of Mexican leaders. For instance, on November 3, 1919, the *Times* published an article alleging a clandestine relationship between President Carranza and Germany: "Carranza's protestations are shown as lies. Alliance with Teutons is shown by letter." Press reports in Los Angeles also claimed that Carranza had allowed Germans to hold official government positions and permitted them to operate wireless stations in Mexico.[99] On November 30, 1919, the *Times* published the full text of the "Plan of San Diego," claiming that it had been definitely linked to the Carranza government.[100]

In the months following the Armistice, nationwide, Americans redirected their anti-German hysteria to political radicalism. Stanley Coben has argued that "opposition to the war by radical groups helped smooth the transition among American nativists from hatred of everything German to fear of radical revolution."[101] During the fall of 1919 and spring of 1920, the nation experienced a "Red Scare" of unprecedented proportions. This hysteria, directed mainly at "radicals and aliens," had characteristics of the "Brown Scare" that swept through Los Angeles over the period 1913–1918.

By the beginning of the 1920s, the Los Angeles *colonia* had felt the impact of nativism, anti-radicalism, and war hysteria. Moreover, nativists in Los Angeles held Mexicanos and other radicals responsible for the rise in irresponsible acts and labor violence. Viewed with fear and contempt by those holding social and political power, physically segregated in housing and in social life, Mexicanos attempted to accommodate to the reality of Los Angeles and face the daily challenge of providing a decent existence for themselves and their families. Their efforts to do so will be considered in Chapter 6.

6 Work and Restlessness

Despite the nativism of the World War I period, as Los Angeles grew, industrialists welcomed Mexican labor and, in many cases, actively recruited workers south of the border. The city's proximity to Mexico provided it with a pool of common labor not available to other industrial regions of the United States. In addition, a large number of migrants of Mexican descent, drawn by job opportunities in industry and agriculture, came to Los Angeles from nearby southwestern states. This chapter summarizes findings concerning occupational and spatial mobility of Mexican workers in Los Angeles between 1918 and 1928.[1]

Like most urban working-class groups, Mexican laborers did not record everyday experiences, and little is known about their adjustment to industrial urban centers such as Los Angeles. Compared to other workers in Los Angeles and Boston, Mexicanos in the Los Angeles work force experienced unusually low occupational mobility. Mexican workers with expectations of entering high blue-collar or white-collar professions during the years 1918 to 1928 were sorely disappointed. Moreover, Mexicanos in Los Angeles changed their place of residence or left the city with far greater frequency than other groups in five other cities over a similar period of time.

Los Angeles marriage records and city directories provided the major sources of data for this chapter. From the 1917 and 1918 city marriage license applications, which furnished the age, occupation, nativity, and religious affiliation of the groom, every man of Mexican ancestry, either born in Mexico or Spanish surnamed, was selected for the sample group.[2] Information about an individual's occupation and residence derived from these records was checked or traced in the 1917, 1918, and 1928 city directories to determine changes in occupational or spatial status of the sample. The information about the nativity of the groom made it possible to determine the occupational status of first-, second-, and third-generation Mexicanos.[3]

The selection of the years 1918–1928 for the analysis of Mexican occupational and spatial mobility in this chapter required special consideration. Most twentieth-century studies on mobility have been based on ten-year periods. Studies of Atlanta, San Antonio, and Boston used the first year of a new decade, such as 1890, 1900, 1910, and 1920, as the starting point for each period.[4] The year 1910 was unacceptable as an initial date for the study of Mexican workers because few Mexicanos lived in Los Angeles at that time. Moreover, that date would necessitate terminating the study in 1920, which would omit the twenties, an era of tremendous industrial activity in the city as well as the decade of the greatest immigration from Mexico in American history. Thus the time period 1918–1928 was selected because it included the twenties, and still excluded the era of the Great Depression, which had an unusual effect on Mexican laborers. Also in 1929 and several years thereafter, thousands of Mexicans were repatriated to Mexico through the efforts of city and county officials,[5] and such unnatural population losses in the Mexican community would have biased the sample.

I

Writers popularized the image of California as the "land of Golden Promise."[6] To hundreds of thousands of immigrants and native midwesterners and easterners, California came to symbolize opportunity and wealth. Southern California businessmen conducted extensive advertising and publicity campaigns designed to lure newcomers to their region. Between the years 1918 and 1930, boosters promoted California as a "Garden of Eden" and a worker's paradise. California was a land "with a climate of semitropical friendliness that robs the mere business of sustaining life of its rigors and leaves human energy free for whatever other tasks the spirit may conceive."[7] No city in California worked harder at attracting migrants, immigrants, and new industries than Los Angeles. Blessed with a year-round pleasant climate and expanding trade due to the opening of the Panama Canal, Los Angeles appealed to both business leaders and workers. Some promoters went so far as to say that climate enhanced employment and social mobility. "The climate is the poor man's benison as well as the rich man's luxury. There is no other place in America where social stratification is so little marked, where all classes do so nearly the same thing at the same time."[8]

Southern California boosterism, which officially began in the late 1880s with the founding of the Los Angeles Chamber of Commerce,[9] reached new proportions after World War I. In Los Angeles, Bruce Bliven wrote in the *New Republic* in 1927, "the first comers, if they can just get their fingers on a little property, are sure to grow rich with unearned increment."[10] Following the recession of 1921, Los Angeles became one of the first industrial centers in the United States to achieve full economic recovery. Industrial output climbed from $800 million in 1921 to $1.2 billion by 1923, and more than 2,400 new industries were established in Los Angeles in the years between 1920 and 1924.[11] For those seeking a new start during the lean months of 1921, James A. B. Scherer recommended Los Angeles, where "every newcomer who's willing to work gets his chance, and gets wholesome sympathy and respect. Climate takes care of the rest."[12]

Promotional campaigns met with striking success as the population of Los Angeles grew from 319,000 to 1,238,000 in the period from 1920 to 1930.[13] The Mexican population in the city also grew in prodigious proportions after 1910. Between 1910 and 1920, the United States census reported that the Mexican population in the city increased from 5,611 to 31,172. By 1930, the Mexican population had more than tripled. Within the city limits of Los Angeles, the Mexican population numbered 97,116, while an additional 70,000 Mexicans resided in Los Angeles County.[14]

Since 1900, Mexicans had worked in agriculture, railroad construction, and mining in the border regions. After the outbreak of World War I, they began to move farther north, filling labor needs created by the war.[15] In 1929, Robert N. McLean, a religious leader in Los Angeles, acknowledged, "In Los Angeles and, indeed, in many communities, it is the Mexican[s] who do the common labor. In fact, we have imported them for that very purpose."[16] Several Los Angeles industrialists explained their preference for Mexican laborers over other workers. For example, A. C. Hardison argued, "There is a certain type of work that the Mexican will do and our experience is that Americans will not do. The American is physically unfitted for certain classes of menial labor that must be done if we are going to preserve our economic position in the world."[17]

Constantly under fire for employing Mexican workers over Anglo workers, industrialists took their case to the public. A. Bent, a Los Angeles contractor, asserted,"I am a construction man, and if we have a job in the Imperial Valley, for instance, to construct water works in those hot regions, I am compelled to use Mexicans. We cannot get our own men to go there to perform that work."[18] Another Californian from the Imperial Valley representing agribusiness put the issue of using Mexican menial labor in this manner: "Mexicans are much preferred to whites. Once fixed, they are permanent and reliable. I do not think that they are good for other types of labor."[19]

Few studies of the period 1900–1930 have closely examined the participation of Mexican immigrants in the Los Angeles labor market. Early publications of Emory S. Bogardus, Jay S. Stowell, and Robert N. McLean briefly discussed urban employment patterns of Mexicans and described the general social and economic experiences of Mexicans in the United States.[20] G. Bromley Oxnam and Charles S. Johnson both utilized sample surveys to estimate the occupational structure of the Mexican community during the 1920s, but, like much other research of that era, Oxnam's and Johnson's studies provide limited data. Using information from jail record files, Oxnam estimated that 72 percent of the Mexicanos in Los Angeles were employed as laborers and another 14 percent held skilled positions.[21] Johnson, who conducted one of the best studies of Blacks in Los Angeles during the 1920s, sampled only a few industries in which Mexicans worked, primarily transportation, building trades, and automobile manufacturing.[22] Very few of those industries, Johnson reported, employed Mexicans, and he found no Mexicans working in the railroad industries. Actually, however, the railroad companies and agricultural groups were among the most active recruiters of Mexican workers, sending their labor agents to numerous border towns in search of laborers. Studies by the United States Department of Labor and data from the United States census indicate that some eleven thousand Mexicanos were employed by the railroad companies in California,[23] and a large percentage of those laborers worked in the numerous railroad yards and camps of Los Angeles.[24]

The major attractions for the Mexican immigrants who settled in the Los Angeles area were economic opportunities in transportation, manufacturing, and agriculture.[25] Most migrants, however, remained in Los Angeles only for a short time. Low wages, a high cost of living, discrimination, and excessive competition for jobs often made life difficult for Mexican laborers and accounted for their exceedingly high turnover.

Industrial establishments with a hundred or more workers on their payrolls employed the majority of Mexican laborers in nonagricultural work in California.[26] Paul Taylor and Emory Bogardus both reported increasing movement of Mexicanos into industrial centers during the 1920s,[27] as did J. B. Gwin, who wrote: "They [Mexicans] have moved into the cities to engage in all kinds of common labor. They replace other laborers, partly because they are working for less wages and partly because they have shown more endurance and strength. They are also more dependable."[28] Governor Clement C. Young's Fact-Finding Committee estimated that the stone, clay, and cement industries employed 40 percent of all the Mexican workers in California during the 1920s.[29] Mexicans were regarded as being among the best tile workers and cement finishers in southern California. The rise in popularity of "Spanish" homes in California during the 1920s created a demand for workers familiar with the construction of tile roofs and floors like those common in Mexico. Metal, wood, food, and clothing industries and public utilities followed the stone and cement industries as the largest employers of Mexicanos in the state between the years 1917 and 1930.[30] New textile factories opened in Los Angeles during the 1920s and employed hundreds of Mexican women and a fair number of Mexican men. The Los Angeles gas company alone employed more than 1,200 Mexican laborers by the mid-1920s.[31] "Los Angeles," wrote Elizabeth Fuller in 1920, "so far has considered the Mexican immigrant chiefly as an industrial asset."[32]

Table 2 indicates that male Mexican workers in Los Angeles in 1917–1918 were much more concentrated in a limited number of industries (most were in blue-collar unskilled positions) than male workers in Boston or native White male workers in Los Angeles.

Table 2. *Occupational Distribution of Male Labor Force in Boston and Los Angeles*

Occupation	Boston: Overall Population, 1920 (%)	Los Angeles: Native Whites, 1920 (%)	Los Angeles: Mexicanos, 1917–1918 (%)
White-collar	32	47.0	6.7
Professional	5	3.9	0.6
Other white-collar	27	43.1	6.1
Blue-collar	68	53.0	91.5
Skilled	27	28.3	15.4
Semiskilled	31	18.7	8.1
Unskilled	10	6.0	68.0

Sources: Thernstrom, *The Other Bostonians: Poverty and Progress in the American Metropolis, 1880–1970* (Cambridge, Mass., 1973), p. 50; U.S. Bureau of the Census, *Fourteenth Census of the United States Taken in the Year 1920*, vol. 4, *Population; Occupations* (Washington, D.C., 1923), pp. 168–172; Data obtained from 1917 and 1918 Los Angeles marriage records.

Table 3. *Occupational Structure of Mexican Men in California, 1930*

Occupation	Number Employed	Percentage Employed	Percentage of Total Mexican Workers
Agriculture	41,455	100.0	37.0
Laborers	40,052	96.6	
Mining	1,660	100.0	1.5
Operatives	1,628	98.1	
Manufacturing	34,858	100.0	31.1
Apprentices	520	1.5	
Carpenters	924	2.7	
Machinists	515	1.5	
Mechanics	861	2.5	
Molders	411	1.2	
Painters	948	2.7	
Plaster-cement	493	1.4	
Tailors	366	1.0	
Clay-glass	431	1.2	
Operatives			
Food	721	2.1	
Iron-steel	858	2.5	
Lumber	357	1.0	
Laborers			
Building	11,698	33.5	
Chemical	1,275	3.7	
Clay-glass	3,192	9.2	
Food	1,520	4.4	
Iron-steel	2,530	7.3	
Lumber	990	2.8	
Transportation	18,878	100.0	16.8
Drivers	1,662	8.8	
Road-street labor	3,362	17.8	
Railroad laborers	11,677	61.9	
Clerks-stores	360	1.9	
Trade	6,079	100.0	5.4
Laborers-porters	1,052	17.3	
Helpers			
Retail	1,391	22.9	
Sales	1,267	20.8	
Public service	856	100.0	0.8
Laborers	641	74.9	
Professional service	1,748	100.0	1.6
Musicians	335	19.2	
Attendants-helpers	451	25.8	

Table 3. *Continued*

Occupation	Number Employed	Percentage Employed	Percentage of Total Mexican Workers
Domestic personnel Service	5,194	100.0	4.6
Barbers	504	9.7	
Janitors	534	10.3	
Labor	314	6.0	
Laundry	512	9.9	
Servants	2,080	40.0	
Clerical	980	100.0	0.9
Clerks	627	64.0	

Total males over ten years old: 143,925
Total number employed: 112,119
Percentage employed: 77.9

Source: Computed from the U.S. Bureau of the Census, *Fifteenth Census of the United States: 1930*, vol. 4, *Population; Occupation* (Washington, D.C., 1932), pp. 86–90. The census lists more than 100 different occupations in which Mexicanos were employed. This table records only the job classifications where 300 or more Mexican workers were employed.

Several thousand Mexican workers in Los Angeles were employed in bakeries, slaughter and packing houses, textile factories, paper and printing establishments, and laundries. Industries employing the majority of Mexican women in Los Angeles were the textile industry, laundries, hotels, wholesale and retail trade establishments, and bakeries.[33] "The secondary recruiters of Mexican labor," wrote Robert McLean, "are the factories and foundries, and construction projects in the great cities. . . . A Mexican, for example, drifts to Los Angeles when the labor demand is at its lowest ebb. He finds employment on a construction gang, and hesitates to leave when the crop which recruited him originally is again calling."[34]

II

Most social scientists agree that one's social position is closely correlated to one's occupation. Peter M. Blau and Otis D. Duncan discussed this relationship in their study, *The American Occupational Structure*. "The occupational structure in modern industrial so-

Table 4. *Occupational Structure of First-, Second-, and Third-Generation Mexicano Men in Los Angeles, 1917–1918*

Occupation	First-Generation (%)	Second-Generation (%)	Third-Generation (%)	Number	Percentage of Total
White-collar	6.6	4.5	9.1	24	6.7
Blue-collar	91.8	95.5	89.0	326	91.6
Student	0.3	0	0	1	0.3
Unknown	1.4	0	2.3	5	1.4
Total				356	100.0
White-collar					
Clerical	3.8	0	9.1	15	4.2
Proprietor	1.4	0	0	4	1.1
Semiprofessional	1.1	0	0	3	0.8
Professional	0.3	4.5	0	2	0.6
Blue-collar					
Unskilled	71.6	59.1	47.7	242	68.0
Semiskilled	7.2	13.7	11.7	29	8.1
Skilled	13.0	22.7	29.6	55	15.4

Source: Data computed from 1917 and 1918 marriage records.

ciety," they stated, "not only constitutes an important foundation for the main dimensions of social stratification but also serves as the connecting link between different institutions and spheres of social life, and therein lies its great significance."[35] In Los Angeles, the occupational structure during the 1920s was closely related to race and ethnic background. Native Whites had positions in the occupational structure substantially higher than even second- and third-generation Mexicanos. As the last column in Table 2 indicates, less than 1 percent of the Mexican men (first-, second-, and third-generations combined) belonged to the professional class. Only 6.7 percent of them held white-collar occupations, as contrasted to 47.0 percent of the native White men. Sixty-eight percent of the male Mexican workers in Los Angeles labored in the unskilled ranks, compared to only 10 percent of the male workers in Boston and 6 percent of the native White male workers in Los Angeles.

As can be seen in Table 4, occupational opportunities for Mexicanos in high blue-collar and all white-collar positions did indeed prove elusive not only for recent immigrants, but for second- and third-generation Mexicanos as well. Among first-generation Mexican men, for instance, nearly 92 percent were employed in blue-collar occupations (unskilled, semiskilled, and skilled workers). Compared to the immigrants, the sons of American-born Mexicanos fared much better in securing semiskilled, skilled, and low white-collar jobs, such as clerical work. Still, few second- and third-generation Mexicanos entered the professional and proprietor classes. As Table 4 indicates, only 6.6 percent of the first generation and 4.5 percent of the second-generation Mexican men held white-collar jobs, although 32 percent of the Boston men (Table 2) held similar positions.

In a survey conducted in 1920 by the Interchurch World Movement in Los Angeles, investigators found that 72 percent of the Mexicans in the city were employed as common laborers, a figure which was amazingly close to the figure of 71.6 percent computed in this study for first-generation unskilled workers (Table 4).[36] Whereas the Interchurch study reported that 7 percent of the Mexicanos were employed in the professions, my findings (see Table 4) indicate that among first-, second-, and third-generation Mexican men, some 6.7 percent worked in white-collar professions, a figure again remarkably close to the earlier estimate. The Interchurch study, unfortunately, did not give a breakdown of the occupational structure of the Mexicanos, nor did it separate American-born Mexicanos from recent immigrants. In my study, evidence showed, most of the white-collar workers were employed in clerical positions and few held jobs in the proprietary, semiprofessional, or professional ranks (Table 4).

The data computed here indicate that second-generation Mexicanos fared only slightly better in employment opportunities than the first generation. Ninety-five percent of the second-generation Mexican men held blue-collar jobs, but a smaller percentage, as compared to those in the first generation, were in unskilled work. In 1929, in the only previous study of second-generation Mexicans in Los Angeles, Emory Bogardus may have shed some light on the reasons for the limited occupational opportunities of Mexicans during the 1920s: "In the occupational field, the second generation Mexicans are beginning to aspire to higher levels. They are seeking entrance into the skilled trades and the professions, but are meeting with rebuffs. Often classed with mulattoes, they have few opportunities and soon grow discouraged and bolshevistic. Their color is one of the main handicaps."[37]

Only a small percentage of the first-, second-, and third-generation Mexicanos found opportunities in the skilled trades and professions. Most surprising of the results of the study was the high participation of third-generation Mexicanos in blue-collar jobs in

1917 and 1918; nearly 90 percent of third-generation Mexicanos were employed as blue-collar workers in Los Angeles during this period (Table 4). Marked differences existed, however, in the numbers of Mexicanos involved in skilled occupations among the first- and third-generation groups. Of the third-generation group, over 29 percent worked in skilled occupations, while no more than 13 percent of the first-generation group held similar positions. Only 47.7 percent of third-generation laborers were unskilled laborers, as compared to 71 percent of the first generation. In comparison, 69.0 percent of non-Mexican men who married Mexican women during the same two-year period worked in blue-collar occupations, a situation similar to the percentage of blue-collar positions held by Boston workers in 1920 (see Tables 5 and 2). These non-Mexican men held significantly more high blue- and white-collar positions than Mexican men. Among these non-Mexicans, mostly Anglo-Americans, 28.9 percent held white-collar positions, generally low-paying clerical and sales jobs. Most of the non-Mexicans were skilled and semi-

Table 5. *Occupational Structure of Non-Mexican Men with Mexican Wives, 1917–1918*

Occupation	Non-Mexican Men (%)	(N)
Blue-collar		
Unskilled	20.6	20
Semiskilled	24.7	24
Skilled	23.7	23
Total	69.1	67
White-collar		
Clerical	18.6	18
Proprietor	6.2	6
Semiprofessional	1.0	1
Professional	3.1	3
Total	28.9	28
Student	1.0	1
Unknown	1.0	1
Total		97

Source: Data computed from 1917 and 1918 marriage records. Significantly, the marriage files indicate that for these two years, at least, the number of Mexican women marrying non-Mexicans was greater than the number of Mexican men marrying outside of their own group.

skilled workers, with only 20.6 percent earning their living as unskilled laborers. Only 3.1 percent of this group could be classified in the professional ranks.

III

In their study *Social Mobility in Industrial Society*, Seymour Martin Lipset and Reinhard Bendix theorized that mobility, "as measured by movement across the manual–non-manual dividing line, has been considerable in many countries of Western Europe as well as in the United States." They concluded that "no known complex society may be correctly described as 'closed or static.'"[38] In agreement with this definition of an "open" society are both Stephan Thernstrom and Michael Hanson, who found that in the period 1910–1920 White workers moved freely from low blue-collar and high blue-collar to white-collar positions.[39] Mexicans in Los Angeles during the 1920s, however, encountered a far more "closed" society; their movements from manual to nonmanual employment categories were almost nonexistent. (See Table 6.)

Among first-, second-, and third-generation semiskilled and unskilled male Mexican laborers in Los Angeles, not a single individual moved upward to a white-collar position during the ten years between 1918 and 1928 (see Table 6).[40] Michael Hanson, in a study of all male Los Angeles workers, noted that during the decade 1910–1920, 20 percent of the unskilled workers moved up to white-collar positions. In a similar study of Boston, Stephan Thernstrom found that 18 percent of the city's unskilled (male) workers moved up to white-collar ranks in the decade 1910–1920. At this time, no occupational-spatial mobility studies are available for the 1920s, and Mexican occupational mobility during the ten-year period 1918–1928 must be compared with studies of other groups reflecting the earlier period, 1910–1920. Although comparisons must be made between different decades, it is doubtful that Mexicans would have had a higher rate of mobility ten years earlier.

The number of white-collar workers among Mexican men in Los Angeles was extremely small, and therefore no generalizations can be made from statistics about this handful of individuals. Only eight Mexicans out of a total of ninety-two, or 8.5 percent, held white-collar positions in 1917–1918.

Mexican skilled workers suffered an unusual downward mobility compared to White workers in both Boston and Los Angeles. Only 2 percent of the skilled workers in Hanson's Los Angeles sur-

Table 6. *Comparison of Male Occupational Mobility in Los Angeles and Boston*

Occupation in 1910	Los Angeles (Overall Population)					
	Occupation in 1920					
	HWC (%)	LWC (%)	S (%)	SS (%)	US (%)	Number
High white-collar (HWC)	88	8	4	0	0	25
Low white-collar (LWC)	7	78	11	3	1	129
Skilled (S)	0	13	79	7	2	61
Semiskilled (SS)	0	21	12	67	0	24
Unskilled (US)	0	20	10	30	40	10

Occupation in 1910	Boston (Overall Population)					
	Occupation in 1920					
	HWC (%)	LWC (%)	S (%)	SS (%)	US (%)	Number
High white-collar	90	7	0	3	0	31
Low white-collar	10	79	2	7	3	134
Skilled	2	21	66	10	1	103
Semiskilled	3	20	5	65	8	106
Unskilled	0	18	8	36	39	39

Occupation in 1917–1918	Los Angeles (First-, Second-, and Third-Generation Mexicanos)						
	Occupation in 1928						
	HWC (%)	LWC (%)	S (%)	SS (%)	US (%)	Unknown (%)	Number
High white-collar	50.0	0	0	0	0	50.0	2
Low white-collar	0	66.6	0	16.6	16.6	0	6
Skilled	4.0	4.0	48.0	12.0	32.0	0	25
Semiskilled	0	0	0	50.0	37.5	12.5	8
Unskilled	0	0	17.6	15.7	64.7	0	51

Sources: Michael Hanson, "Occupational Mobility and Persistence in Los Angeles, 1910–1930" (unpublished paper, University of California, Los Angeles, June 1, 1970); Thernstrom, *The Other Bostonians*, p. 238; data computed from 1917 and 1918 Los Angeles marriage record files and the 1928 city directory.

vey slipped into unskilled positions between 1910 and 1920, whereas among Mexican workers, 32 percent of the 1917–1918 skilled workers held unskilled jobs in 1928. In Boston, Thernstrom found that only 1 percent of the skilled workers in 1910 moved downward to unskilled jobs by 1920. Among semiskilled workers in Boston, 20 percent moved up into low white-collar positions, while 3 percent moved into high white-collar occupations. Similarly, Hanson reported that in Los Angeles 21 percent of the semiskilled workers gained lower white-collar positions, but none reached high white-collar status. In contrast, Mexicans in semiskilled occupations in Los Angeles registered no movement at all into either low white-collar or high white-collar positions between 1917–1918 and 1928; in fact, 37.5 percent moved downward.

IV

The working-class populations of Boston and Los Angeles between 1910 and 1930 were remarkably mobile geographically. In a comparison of six different cities (Boston; Los Angeles; Omaha; Norristown, Pennsylvania; Waltham, Massachusetts; and San Francisco) between the years 1880 and 1968, Thernstrom found a striking consistency in persistence rates of workers (50–60 percent) in all the cities.[41] Unfortunately, since none of the data pertained to persistence rates of ethnic groups at the lower income level, one can only compare the spatial mobility of Mexicanos to that of the overall population in Thernstrom's study. In Los Angeles, as Table 7 demonstrates, first-, second-, and third-generation Mexicanos had comparatively high degrees of spatial mobility, especially among unskilled and semiskilled workers. In Boston, for example, 35 percent of the low blue-collar workers in 1910 could still be found in the city a decade later (Table 7), whereas in Los Angeles, only 15.2 percent of the low blue-collar Mexican workers in 1917–1918 were still in the city a decade later. Hanson found that 58 percent of the low white-collar (clerical and petty proprietor class) workers in 1910 were still in Los Angeles ten years later. Among Mexican low white-collar workers in 1917–1918, only 38.8 percent could still be traced a decade later. Among high white-collar workers (semiprofessional and professional classes) in 1910, Hanson discovered that 72 percent could still be located in Los Angeles a decade later, but among Mexican high white-collar workers in 1917–1918, only 42.6 percent remained in the city for a period of ten years.

Mexicanos seem to have been more spatially mobile than native and foreign Whites for several reasons. No doubt the proximity of Los Angeles to the Mexican border was one of the most important factors. The border was close enough that Mexicanos employed in California could maintain a home in Mexico by working part-time

Table 7. *Persistence Rates for Boston and Los Angeles*

Occupation in 1910	Boston, 1910–1920 Still in City in 1920 (%)
High white-collar	58.0
Low white-collar	50.0
High blue-collar	36.0
Low blue-collar	35.0
Total	41.0

Occupation in 1910	Los Angeles, 1910–1920 Number	Still in City in 1920 (%)
High white-collar	36	72.0
Low white-collar	229	58.0
High blue-collar	137	45.0
Low blue-collar	118	29.0
All white-collar	265	60.0
All blue-collar	255	38.0
Total	520	49.0

Occupation in 1917–1918	First-, Second-, and Third-Generation Mexicanos in Los Angeles, 1917–1918 to 1928 Number	Still in City in 1928 (%)
High white-collar	7	42.6
Low white-collar	18	38.8
High blue-collar	71	35.2
Low blue-collar	322	15.2
All white-collar	25	40.0
All blue-collar	393	18.8
Total	418	29.4

Sources: Data compiled by tracing the names in the 1928 city directory of all the Mexican men who applied for marriage licenses in 1917 and 1918; Thernstrom, *The Other Bostonians*, p. 230; Hanson, "Occupational Mobility and Persistence in Los Angeles."

in the United States. Many preferred to live in Mexico and crossed the border to work only out of economic necessity. Improvements in railroad and highway connections between Los Angeles and Mexico after 1900 added another incentive for Mexicanos to travel back and forth across the border on a regular basis.[42] With little expense and trouble, they traveled to Los Angeles for a season of work and then returned to their homeland. In many instances, barrio residents relocated to other communities within the expansive eastside sector. The eastside neighborhoods appeared to be in a constant state of flux, although, as demographic data indicate, these small sections of the barrio all registered significant growth.[43]

In addition, the nature and location of Los Angeles in relation to the rest of California contributed to high rates of spatial mobility for Mexican workers there during the 1920s. Throughout the period 1910–1930, Los Angeles served as one of the three great clearing centers for Mexican workers. Los Angeles, like San Antonio and El Paso, functioned as a depot or "stepping stone" for Mexican immigrants recruited to work in the Midwest and other areas of the Southwest. Agriculture and railroad industries came to Los Angeles in search of workers for the San Joaquín and Imperial valleys. Helen Walker, a Los Angeles social worker, wrote of the movement of Mexican laborers to other parts of the state: "At certain times in the year when the ranchers of Southern California must have many laborers for a short season to harvest their crops, the employment bureaus are anxious to send out great crews of men to do this work." Mexican labor in southern California, she noted, "migrates up and down the length of the state year around, following the grapes in Fresno; the Valencia oranges, nuts, beets, beans, in Orange County; the navel oranges in Riverside County; the cotton, lettuce, melons, grapefruit in the Imperial Valley; . . . and so on and on."[44]

The unusually high proportion of Mexican laborers who moved in and out of Los Angeles may also be attributed to the fact that high wages were paid in agriculture and railroad construction. These jobs, however, were frequently found outside the city. Jay Stowell reported that some Mexican industrial laborers in Los Angeles actually earned as little as $1.25 per day for a ten- to twelve-hour day.[45] John McDowell of the Home Mission Council in southern California stated that transportation, street paving, and cement companies paid workers "two or three dollars per day."[46] Those industries required day laborers who frequently worked less than six months of the year. Oxnam calculated that in 1920 Mexican workers in Los Angeles earned $2.00 to $3.00 a day and averaged $18.00 per week.[47] For thousands of Mexican workers, the disadvantages of industrial work were the higher costs of housing and food in the city and the ever pressing problem of finding work for younger members of the family.

In agriculture, Mexican workers commonly gained the advantage of combining the earnings of other family members for a more adequate family income. Ethel M. Morrison estimated that during the months of April, July, and October, California agriculture paid an average of $22.50 per week without board, and in other months, a few dollars less per month.[48] Nevertheless, few persons other than agricultural employers have ever suggested that working and living conditions in rural areas were better than those found in the cities, and the latter most frequently were extremely harsh. Reviewing the plight of Mexican workers in the cities during the 1920s, Carleton Beals remarked, "The Mexican workers in our country are more ruthlessly exploited than are other foreigners. They are not absorbed rapidly into autonomous unions in industrial centers and so cannot escape the pitiless exploitation that the 'greener' [immigrant] almost invariably suffers."[49]

Similarly, the presence of negative stereotypes and prejudice stifled the Mexicano's opportunity for upward mobility. During the 1920s, employers stereotyped Mexicanos as menial workers incapable of doing work that required skill or intelligence. Summarizing findings of a 1914 survey, the sociologist William W. McEuen explained the social problems of the Mexican by characterizing him as "a spend-thrift and a born gambler, a happy-go-lucky, careless merry person who seems to have no higher ambition than to live as easily as possible."[50] Los Angeles employers expressed the opinion that "in lines of employment calling for individual judgment and initiative, the Mexican is much inferior to the white."[51] Ernesto Galarza, an economist who only a few years earlier had worked among Mexican laborers in agricultural fields, wrote about the exploitation of Mexicanos in the United States. The Mexican, Galarza stated in 1929, "still feels the burden of old prejudices. Only when there are threats to limit immigration from Mexico is it that a few in America sing the praises of the peon. . . . At other times the sentiments which seem deeply rooted in the American mind are that he is unclean, improvident, indolent, and innately dull."[52]

Finally, in most efforts to improve their socioeconomic status, Mexicanos found that the barriers of overt bigotry were prodigious and steadfast. William McEuen observed racial prejudices in discussions with members of the Los Angeles community. "All other races," he noted, "meet the Mexican[s] with an attitude of contempt and scorn," and generally regard them "as the most degraded race in the city." In the opinion of Emory Bogardus, "color" barred second-generation Mexicanos from the better jobs. In sum, as Ernesto Galarza stressed, in the 1920s the racial prejudice of California employers was to blame for the plight of Mexican families in the United States.[53]

The findings of this study lend little credence to the myth that California was a land of golden opportunity for all. Judging from the low occupational status and limited upward mobility of Mexican workers in Los Angeles, Mexicanos would have been surprised to learn that the 1920s in California was often called the era of the "second gold rush." Data also suggest that the upward mobility of Mexicans in Los Angeles, when compared to that of workers in Los Angeles and Boston, measured unusually low. This low rate of upward mobility among Mexicans may partially explain their high spatial mobility. Mexican laborers who found it difficult to advance in employment status had excellent incentive to leave the area to seek better opportunities. The spatial mobility of low blue-collar Mexican workers was 20 percent higher than that of eastern United States workers during a similar period. The greater geographic mobility of Mexicans in Los Angeles further suggests that they did not remain "trapped" in barrios or slums like the Italians in the East as portrayed by some historians.[54] The barrios of Los Angeles attracted new Mexican immigrants daily, most of whom were common laborers, and the Mexican colonies served as a base for many Mexicans who worked in areas outside of Los Angeles or frequently crossed back into Mexico. Throughout the period 1900–1930, Los Angeles served as a regional distribution center for Mexican workers. Although many of these workers came to Los Angeles on their way to other jobs or as casual laborers, enough of them eventually established their roots in East Los Angeles to make it the "Mexican Capital" of the United States.

7 Reform, Revival, and Socialization

It is commonly perceived that the Mexican residents in the United States have been a "more or less voiceless, expressionless minority."[1] Carey McWilliams and others who place this ethnic group's social and political emergence in the post-1940 period believe that the "Zoot Suit Riots" and the Sleepy Lagoon trials of Los Angeles during the early war years, as well as the experience and training that Mexican Americans received in the armed services, brought them out of their long siesta. More recently, historian Manuel P. Servín has referred to Mexican Americans of the 1925–1965 era as a "nonachieving minority." Mexican Americans, he believes, first gained political consciousness after 1965, when César Chávez and others began challenging their status as second-class citizens.[2] This chapter examines efforts of urban Mexican Americans at institutional building during the formative years 1900–1930, in addition to commenting on the interaction of the first-generation Mexicanos with Anglo society. What is apparent is that a deep gulf separated most Anglos from Mexicanos throughout the first three decades of this century, and frequently the latter group was the victim of racial hostility, especially during the war years, when nativists in the Anglo community attempted (as has been described) to suppress the civil liberties of Mexican residents; nonetheless, the barrio achieved a great deal of social and political maturity during the era. The belief that it remained passive in the face of change and confrontation is erroneous.

In the aftermath of World War I, with the influx of new migrants and improved economic conditions, the Eastside Barrio of Los Angeles became a stable and cohesive community. Its residents came to enjoy a variety of social activities and participated in community institutions. Mexican organizations did not have the sort of political and social impact that Irish, Polish, and Jewish organizations had. Still, political and religious organizations, voluntary associations, social clubs, and to a lesser extent, the Mexican Consulate, did gain acceptance and played an active role in the institutional life of the barrio.

I

Understanding the vibrant external and internal forces that contributed to the cultural, political, and social evolution of the barrio necessitates examining the community's interaction with progressive reformers and religious workers, in addition to the efforts at developing voluntary associations. Over the years between 1910 and 1930, the progressive reformers orchestrated the level of institutional interaction on the east side. While they believed that their impact was minimal, there was more social and cultural interaction between the dominant society and the barrio in the period 1915–1930 than at any other point in the first half of the twentieth century. The relationships developed then by progressive reformers and newly arrived Mexican residents have significant implications. The progressives, who took an interest in municipal reform and meeting the challenge of the rise of socialism, organized labor, and non-Nordic immigration, considered the barrios of Los Angeles an important experimental location for putting their ideals into practice.

Southern California progressives, at both the state and the national level, operated from a position of influence and power. Heavy voter participation in the southern California counties provided the victory margin for Governor Hiram Johnson in 1910 and helped carry the state for President Woodrow Wilson in 1912. Initially brought together by their desire to curb the political influence of the Southern Pacific Railroad, the progressives branched out to other political and social arenas.[3] Often, as a result of their efforts to legislate morality, their programs clashed with the interests of Mexican Americans, the very people that many of them wished to reform. Mexicans, for instance, could never side with those wishing to shut down parochial schools, or step up prosecution of Prohibition violators. The continued support of immigration-restriction laws by progressives—laws especially aimed at immigrants from the non-Nordic countries—won their party few adherents in the barrio. In their efforts to stamp out prostitution, the progressives passed the Red Light Abatement Act in 1913.[4] The result was relocation of the "houses of ill repute" from progressives' own communities or business communities to areas near the Black ghetto and Mexican barrio of Los Angeles. This action served to limit prostitution through zoning laws, an action that barrio residents considered blatantly insensitive to their needs. Progressives also expressed a strong bias against organized labor. *Times* publisher General Harrison Gray Otis, supported by the city's largest employers and managers, waged a thirty-year fight to keep Los Angeles an anti-union town. Rather than side with the workers in their struggle for collective bargaining rights, reformers allied themselves with Otis and big industrialists. At the same time, by keeping Los Angeles an open shop city, the reformers contributed to the forces that attracted Mexican unskilled workers, who, because of their previous working experience, came unprepared to wage the kind of battle needed to win labor organizing fights in the city, and who were not allowed to join the few unions that did exist.

Still, many Californians, especially certain legislators identified with the progressive reform movement, proved sensitive to the plight of the new migrants. In 1913, Progressive Governor Hiram Johnson created the California State Commission on Immigration and Housing (CIH). When the governor signed this bill into law, the state was engaged in an expansive campaign to draw newcomers into its boundaries. It mandated the commission to provide immigrants with information regarding the state's excellent economic climate. The progressive lawmakers desired that the commission give special attention to problems associated with the distribution and assimilation of the immigrants. In its first five years of operation, the agency sent its staff to migratory camps and ethnic enclaves in the urban areas to investigate housing and sanitation conditions. CIH teachers taught the immigrants English, offered classes in the duties of citizenship, and recommended ways by which they could raise their standards of living.[5]

Headed by Simon Lubin, a northern California progressive, the commission collected information concerning the needs and demand for labor in agriculture, industry, and public works. It also made numerous recommendations on the inadequate employment of immigrant labor. During the recession of 1913–1914, the CIH conducted a statewide campaign aimed at creating public works projects for the purpose of lessening the tremendous unemployment crisis. Ironically, Los Angeles, with the largest immigrant population in the state, was the sole city to reject the public works plans as a means of creating employment.[6] Public officials in Los Angeles feared that the public works project would encourage the movement of unemployed laborers into the city. While the CIH had broad investigative powers, including the authority to hold hearings and subpoena witnesses, it lacked the power to force Los Angeles to accept its program. As a result, the unemployed in southern California drifted to other areas of the state in search of work. Nonetheless, the agency proved resourceful in working with officials statewide in the creation of public-sponsored jobs.[7]

Prior to World War I, progressives focused on the housing and living conditions of the immigrant community. Investigators working with the CIH generally criticized employers and landlords for abusing the immigrant. "Bad housing and a bad industrial condition, low wages and unemployment seem to go hand in hand," one report concluded in 1916.[8] Despite the CIH's stated devotion to the migrant class, the "champion" of the immigrants had much to learn about the attributes of and differences among the various ethnic groups. In one instance, the CIH suggested a need to study the "idiosyncrasies" of two groups in particular: "the Italian with his love of industry and frugality, whose adaptability makes him quickly assimilated, and the Mexican with his lack of initiative, whose roving temper increases the difficulty of adjusting him."[9]

Progressive reformers involved with the CIH devoted considerable effort in the early years to the improvement of migratory camps and the distribution of immigrant labor in industrial and agricultural employment; however, during the war period, they focused their energy and attention on the problem of Americanizing the foreign-born. In an informal manner, the CIH became the spearhead of the Americanization movement in 1916, when it began working with the Los Angeles schools in implementing Americanization programs. In a pamphlet issued in 1916 and entitled *Americanization*, the CIH defined its assimilationist objectives. It called for community involvement and promised to provide schools with materials and assistance in carrying out their goals of "good housing, decent working conditions, education, friendly advice when it is needed, real help when trouble comes."[10] A contemporary writer praised Los Angeles' recognition as the "first city where the school training given along the line of Americanization" resulted in a certificate entitling the immigrant to obtain naturalization papers.[11]

At the community level, the progressive educators devised programs in the Americanization experiment that included home teaching, mothers' classes for foreign-born women, special library services for the immigrant, house-to-house visitation by volunteers, poster campaigns, community singing, writing of patriotic essays, production of plays dramatizing the "democratic and cosmopolitan spirit of America," and the development of evening schools in English and citizenship for adult immigrants. The commission also urged church leaders to assist in determining the most efficient ways to enlist religious groups in patriotic work for the immigrant.[12]

Declaring that the problem of immigrant education "is distinctly an adult problem," in 1915 the progressive CIH educators began sending a limited number of "home teachers" to communities with foreign-born residents. In Los Angeles, one home teacher served under the school board, and the other with the Daughters of the American Revolution. The home teacher, one local observer commented, "is really a sympathetic visitor who goes to the home, enters into the problems of the father, mother, and children, assisting them often in the complexities of life in a new and strange city."[13] Suspicious of the home teachers, Mexican women rarely attended the organized sessions at the evening school. As a result, the home teacher found it necessary to arrange visits to each of the homes of the Mexican families for the purpose of recruiting students in English and industrial crafts classes.

Progressives in the educational field believed that the problems associated with immigrant education involved substantially more than teaching English or civics. The CIH gave each home teacher a policy manual which outlined the basic duties, including reporting cases of sickness to relief agencies and visiting employment bureaus and industrial plants to inquire whether they needed workers. Other duties comprised the teaching of sewing, cooking, mending, and shoe repairing. CIH educators also recommended that the overworked and underpaid home teachers devote some time to collecting cast-off clothing and discarded furniture for the purpose of selling them at a "reasonable figure" to the people of the district, either for cash or for labor. The immigrants' task in this arrangement embraced cleaning the facilities and washing and mending clothes to be sold.[14]

During the war years, progressives realized that the problems of the foreign-born community of Los Angeles were far too great for any one social agency to resolve. They directed the immigrants to the various agencies working in this field and encouraged other organizations to give more attention to the foreign-born. In 1916, the CIH commended the efforts of one Los Angeles school to provide the immigrants with many of their essential needs. The Macy Street School, which provided clothing for both children and adults, also offered movies and recreational activities during after-work hours. Occasionally, the school gave beds, stoves, and other furniture to needy immigrant families. Still the problems in this district were enormous. A survey by the CIH in 1916 showed that of 256 men, slightly more than 50 percent were unemployed. The majority of those employed, moreover, held low-paying jobs as laborers.[15]

Los Angeles reformers learned a great deal about the social and economic conditions of the immigrants through the CIH's Bureau of Complaints. The function of this bureau consisted of receiving and diagnosing complaints, steering the complainants to a cooperating agency, and advocating legislative action aimed at protecting and assisting the immigrant population of the state. From the inception of the bureau, Mexicans formed a large share of its complainants. In general, they visited the CIH offices to discuss a wide range of concerns related to work and home. In 1923, a year in which Mexicans led all other groups in filing complaints, 843 of the 2,125 cases represented wage or contract problems.[16] By 1924, Mexicans constituted just over 50 percent of those lodging complaints (1,204 of 2,262 cases); the CIH felt constrained to remark in one of its *Annual Reports* that while "it might appear that the Complaint Department is operated for the benefit of Mexicans," such was not in fact the case.[17]

In the summer of 1917, urban reformers began an assimilation pilot program in Los Angeles for the purpose of promoting the naturalization of barrio residents. The CIH selected a small railroad camp on the east side, housing about forty families. The home teacher sent to the site reported to the commission that year that "upon this group has been heaped all the dislike of a prejudiced American community."[18] For the railroad companies, Americanization programs meant not only combatting unsanitary conditions, but also combatting pro-union sentiment and work stoppages, as well as producing higher employee efficiency through teaching of the English language. The company found the home teachers to have such "productive and concrete" results that it formally requested them for every camp along the line. The company offered in return to furnish a railroad car as a model house for instruction in housekeeping and provided free transportation to the home teacher. According to the superintendent, "this offer was made by the company, not for the love of its Mexican laborers, but because the summer work had proved that it was economically valuable to them." As a result of the program, the company reported that the labor force had become more reliable. Camp conditions improved, according to the superintendent, and "the satisfaction of the workmen was showing itself in the better care of the track."[19]

Governor William D. Stephens, a former president of the Los Angeles Chamber of Commerce, unlike his predecessor, Hiram Johnson, played less than an enthusiastic role in the progressive reform movement. Stephens became governor in March 1917. Among his first acts following the United States' entry into World War I was his mandate that the CIH serve as the Americanization Committee of the state. Acknowledging the "good start" of the CIH in Americanizing the immigrants, Stephens noted that many of the aliens were "at best but imperfectly acquainted either with our language, our institutions, our principles of government, or our reason for being at war." He feared that some might "have their minds permanently poisoned against our government by sowers of discord and treason," and he urged the public to remain vigilant against this possibility. Stephens also praised the American Legion for its work "toward excluding from America all undesirables—unassimilable peoples" (probably a reference to the Asian groups).[20] As governor, he easily dominated the leadership of the Americanization movement in the state. He seemed at ease with the responsibility, declaring in speech after speech such phrases as "America cannot endure half American and half something else" and "We've got to be American first and all the time." His vehement opposition to the immigration of Asians as well as his general distrust of the foreign-born poisoned the good work of many of the progressives of his administration.[21] Like other former progressives, he was swept away with the emotional wave of Americanism. The tolerance and sensitivity that the progressives had demonstrated toward immigrants through programs such as the CIH suffered during the war years as they too became entangled in the currents of anti-alien hysteria, such as the "Brown Scare" described in Chapter 5.

The leadership and energy expended by progressive civic reformers in the barrio of East Los Angeles had little impact on the social and political structure of the community. The progressives, many of them associated with agencies like the CIH, were too few in number to accomplish the broad objectives of the movement. The CIH, which had limited state financing, also suffered when the legislators linked it to the Americanization movement. One major factor for this failure was that, with the exception of teaching the immigrants English, there seemed to be little agreement on the objectives and goals of the Americanization movement or the means of achieving them.[22] The progressives' goals of assimilating a first-generation immigrant group proved too ambitious. When the progressives sided with the restrictionist forces in Congress during the early 1920s, many of the progressives and the programs that they inaugurated lost credibility in the barrio. Indeed, when the CIH called for a termination of unrestricted immigration from Mexico in the 1920s based on the assumption that immigrants "were causing an immense social problem in our charities, schools and health departments," it became apparent that the CIH was no longer the professed "champion of the immigrants."[23]

II

One of the first cooperative ventures between the American pioneer settlers and the vanquished southern Californios following the end of the Mexican-American War was the creation of public schools. The first school ordinance in 1851 provided "that all the rudiments of the English and Spanish languages should be taught therein."[24] Los Angeles Mayor Antonio Coronel, who presided over the establishment of the Los Angeles School Board and served as county superintendent of schools between the years 1850 and 1855, appointed Manuel Requena to one of the three posts for board trustees in 1854. Fifteen years later, rancher Vicente Lugo vacated his town house and presented it to the Catholic diocese, which in turn created on the premises Saint Vincent College, a boys' school.[25] Over the years many of the wealthy Mexican families would send their sons to Saint Vincent's. Indeed, it wasn't until 1872 that Los Angeles opened its first high school. Although Los Angeles was "half Mexican" in 1875, of the first six seniors to complete public high school that year, not a single one was of Mexican ancestry.[26]

Beginning with the establishment of a kindergarten program in 1889, Los Angeles assumed a leading role in California in reforming the schools along progressive educational ideals. It started night and evening classes in 1887, including a course of study that offered adults an elementary education. Ten years later, Los Angeles incorporated vocational classes and the study of domestic sciences, courses which were very popular with progressive educators at that time, and also began experimenting with "ungraded" classes in 1900. By 1905, Los Angeles had pioneered classes for deaf and blind children. Influenced by successful programs in eastern cities through the efforts of settlement workers, the school district offered day nurseries for working mothers as well as home teaching opportunities for mothers who did not work outside the home. Similarly, Los Angeles sponsored mothers' clubs and parent-teacher organizations, two projects long lobbied for by progressive educators.[27]

The new generation of Mexican immigrants who began flocking to Los Angeles in the unsettling period of 1900–1930 were introduced to a school system undergoing dramatic transformation. It was in this era that progressive educators, especially those who followed the lead of John Dewey, began to challenge the traditional methods of educating the masses, and particularly the immigrant groups. Progressive educators envisioned the schools as institutions where individuals could prepare themselves for the real world. Dewey, who placed great faith in the scientific method, argued that educational programs should reflect the life of the larger society. In a modern industrial society, such preparation included vocational training and lessons in citizenship and morals. Such change became evident when the Los Angeles schools extended manual training classes to elementary schools in 1910. This followed Dewey's contention that "whereas formerly the child participated in the industrial activities of the household, he now participated in the industrial activities of the school, with artisans, nurses, gardeners, lunchroom supervisors, and accountants taking the place of father, mother, and older siblings in the older agrarian home."[28] Over the years the vocational classes would become the principal course of study in the working-class communities of the Spanish-speaking and Black residents of the city.

For progressives, compulsory education provided the issues and a crucial opportunity to institute reform. The very existence of compulsory education, according to Lawrence A. Cremin, "inexorably conditioned every attempt at educational innovation during the decades preceding World War I."[29] This fact was best exemplified by California's efforts to educate non-English-speaking immigrants. Armed with data from intelligence tests, generally administered in English, the teachers looked for the "illiterate" and docile student. "Our task," said the dean of the School of Education at Stanford, Ellwood P. Cubberley, "is to assimilate and amalgamate these people as a part of our American race, and to implant in their children, so far as can be done, the Anglo-Saxon conception of righteousness, law and order . . . and to awaken in them a reverence for our democratic institutions."[30] The opinions of many of these progressive educators revealed a strong bias against the foreign-born. An example of this tendency to stereotype the immigrant child is apparent in state educator Helen Heffernan's statement that "Our Mexican population had leisureliness; gay, lighthearted enjoyment of the present; a spirituality and quiet devotion; a passionate love of color, music, and dancing."[31] In Heffernan's judgment, the school had a responsibility to teach cleanliness "to these little foreign children, many of whom have had no opportunity for warm water, soap, or a comb at home, with the added fact that no one cared whether they were clean or dirty."[32]

The clamor for broad educational reform during the progressive era came not only from businesses and labor unions demanding that

the schools assume the major responsibility for vocational appren-
ticeship, but also from settlement workers and municipal reformers
who vigorously urged instruction in hygiene, domestic science, manual arts, and child care. Then, of course, there were the patriots of
every political persuasion who insisted on adding Americanization
to the school curriculum. When the United States entered the war in
Europe, Los Angeles Superintendent of Schools Dr. Albert Shields
directed the establishment of the manual training department for
the purpose of "revealing young men and women who were fitted to
assist in actual work" in the defense industries.[33]

The Mexican *colonia* had an ambivalent relationship with the
public schools. Mexicans enrolled their children in the schools and
viewed the learning opportunities as superior to those they had
known at home but remained troubled by the segregation policies
and the degrading experiences forced upon their children.[34] Throughout the period 1915–1930 the issue of numbers became prominent
in public debates as the enrollment of Mexican children in the Los
Angeles schools more than doubled. The Los Angeles Chamber of
Commerce estimated an enrollment of 15,499 Mexican students in
1920, while the U.S. Census for that year arrived at a figure of
21,598. By 1930, Mexican students in Los Angeles numbered 55,005
according to the census for that year, or approximately 14.2 percent
of the total school population.[35] Superintendent of Schools Susan B.
Dorsey addressed the issue of increased Mexican enrollment when
she complained to a meeting of principals: "It is unfortunate and unfair for Los Angeles, the third largest Mexican city in the world, to
bear the burdens of taking care educationally of this enormous
group. We do have to bear a spiritual burden quite disproportionate
to the return from having this great number of aliens in our midst.
This burden comes to us merely because we are near the border."[36]

Many educators completely ignored the Mexican community or
assumed that Mexicans did not place a high value on education.
Helen Heffernan in a "Guide for Teachers of Beginning Non-English
Speaking Children," aimed primarily at Mexicans, concluded that
foreign groups generally lacked initiative and teachers should "make
a conscious effort to develop it from the beginning of school life."
Joseph M. Santos, a Mexican American researcher working on a sociology degree in California during the late 1920s, observed an opposition among "many Americans" to educating Mexicans "because
it makes them [Mexicans] dissatisfied with their lot and makes
them look upon farm labor as menial." Santos also encountered a
strong belief that Mexicans lacked the intellect, instinct, or energy
to acquire the things deemed essential to an American standard of

living. "Thus education can only bring them unhappiness." David A. Bridge, a progressive educator who examined the Americanization efforts of the Los Angeles schools during the 1920s, however, found a strong interest among Mexican Americans in schooling. He conducted a house-to-house survey in the northeast section of the Mexican *colonia* and discovered 94.4 percent of the Mexican children of elementary school age enrolled in classes. Indeed, the Italian children of the district registered a lower attendance rate, 89.7 percent.[37]

The Los Angeles School District maintained separate schools for Mexicans based on the premise that Mexicans had special needs, an idea that progressive educators did not challenge. Very often the rationale given for establishing segregated schools for Mexicans rested on the conviction that Mexicans exhibited "different mental characteristics" from Anglos. Mexican children, according to one stereotypic assessment, "showed a stronger sense of rhythm" than Anglos, and unlike Anglo children they "are primarily interested in action and emotion but grow listless under purely mental effort." In a mixed school, Mexicans are said to be "handicapped by the lack of home training, by shyness, and by an emotional nature all of which interfere with their progress in the conventional course of study."[38] Santos, however, found the reasons for segregation more closely allied to the fear that Mexicans introduced diseases to the schools, as well as a consciousness of racial differences on the part of the Anglos, in addition to the desire by Mexican families "of protecting Mexican children from the social prejudice of the Americans." He found that the most common method of segregating Mexican children "was accomplished by drawing the boundaries of a school around a Mexican colony and providing a school therein."[39]

The obvious contradictions of establishing segregated schools for the purpose of assimilating Mexican children seem to have escaped the progressive reformers. Segregation was a fact of life in Los Angeles during this period. The segregation of Mexican American children, writes Meyer Weinberg, was "widespread" in all of California, not just Los Angeles. In eight of the largest counties, there were 64 schools with an enrollment of 90–100 percent Mexican children.[40] The personal cruelties inherent in official segregation, Weinberg writes, were felt in many ways. School officials required Mexican children in one part of Los Angeles to have separate graduation ceremonies from Anglos attending the same school. In another county school district, when school officials were unable to provide separate buildings for the Mexicans, they simply assigned Mexican children to separate classrooms.[41]

Progressive educators justified segregation on the basis that children were given a better chance to learn. The Los Angeles schools segregated children through an "ability-grouping three-track plan." One writer described the process as a "scientific treatment" where "each child under this system who fails to fit in with the school's scheme of work is taken out of the regular grade and put in a special grade in a room sometimes called an 'opportunity' room, for here the backward child, the timid child, or the child who is developing along one line and not another, may be brought into normality."[42] The sociologist Emory Bogardus, who visited the schools, observed that "in the non-segregated schools, the Mexican children are often at a disadvantage. They arrive at school age with little or no knowledge of English, and hence do poorly until they learn English." He favored segregated schools because there Mexicans did not have to suffer through "invidious comparisons with Anglo students."[43]

During the war years and continuing into the 1920s, the Los Angeles schools adopted the ideal of Americanization as a means of preparing Mexican students for adulthood. In 1919, progressive legislators at the state capital in Sacramento helped pass Section 1702 of the state educational code, which mandated the teachers to teach "the principles of morality, truth, justice, and patriotism" as well as to impress upon the students the evils of "idleness, profanity, and falsehood," while at the same time instructing them in the "comprehension of the rights, duties, and dignity of American citizenship."[44] Later, as an aid in establishing Americanization programs in Spanish-speaking communities, Pearl Ellis wrote *Americanization through Homemaking*. Published in Los Angeles in 1929, the book outlined specific reasons for promoting Americanization among Mexicanos: to "raise their standard of living, improve sanitation, and control disease," and to have them in return "adopt our customs, our ideals, and our country."[45] A principal objective of the book appeared to be the teaching of skills to Mexican women so as to aid them in earning a living. Since 1916 home teachers had taught sewing, weaving, and millinery to the immigrant women. Ellis proposed a continuation of this type of instruction. "Mexican girls are very fond of sewing," she maintained. "Since only about five percent of Mexican girls who graduate from the eighth grade enter the high school, their ability as seamstresses must be developed in the elementary schools." Thus Ellis saw Americanization not only as conformity to Anglo models but also as vocational instruction and supply of labor skills to local industries.[46]

Inherent in progressive educational curriculum reforms was the view that the schools should give less attention to traditional goals and instead prepare students for a modern industrial world. Indeed,

John Dewey believed that vocational training in the poorer communities enabled "the child to pick up the thread of life in his own community by giving him an understanding of the elements of the occupations that supply man's daily needs . . ."[47] Few programs better reflected this idea than the Maple Avenue Evening High School located in the Mexican American barrio. The unique feature of this program was that the students met for their evening classes at the Los Angeles Labor Temple. Progressive educators viewed this concession by the schools as a major triumph considering the strong anti-union sentiments of the Los Angeles business community. Attendance in the regular evening classes had fallen short of expectations, and something different had to be tried. The program at the Labor Temple offered the Mexican American *colonia* a variety of courses which included electricity, mechanical drawing, plumbing, sheet metal work, power machine operation, vulcanizing, and welding, in addition to art, Americanization, and music. The course of study in these evening schools, one visitor commented, was "necessarily simple and elastic, adapted to the foreigner who does not speak English nor understands the laws of his adopted country."[48]

That progressive education had a profound impact on the barrio schools of Los Angeles is evident from the description of the Amelia Street School provided by state Bureau of Education specialist Emeline Whitcomb. The instruction, all of which took place in a segregated setting, essentially revolved around the learning of American values and tradition. But the teachers also set aside ample time for classes in the domestic sciences. The foreign-born, Whitcomb reported, spent most of their day in a "modern two-story building" separated from the regular classrooms.[49] There the girls prepared the school luncheon, washed and ironed clothing belonging to the day nursery, and learned about taking care of preschool children. The curriculum also included instruction in arts and crafts and home interior arrangement. Visitors, Whitcomb wrote, are favorably impressed with the "training which develops worth-while Americans."[50]

The home teachers involved in Americanization classes had little success in the socialization aspect of the Americanization programs. Few Mexicans living in Los Angeles seemed inclined to file citizenship papers during this period. A West Los Angeles evening school teacher, having gained the confidence of several of her students from Mexico, received various responses when she questioned why so few Mexicanos applied for citizenship. "Well, what good would it do us?" asked one student. "The Americans wouldn't treat us any better if we did. They say we are black, they call us Indians,

Greasers, Cholos, and getting naturalized wouldn't make us any different."[51] Another student explained that the reluctance among Mexicanos to become citizens was due to the allegiance to the old country. "Mexicanos are very patriotic," the student explained. "They love their own birthplace, their own land, better than anything else. A Mexican who becomes an American citizen is looked upon as a renegade, a traitor; and since the Americans also look down upon him, he is like a 'man without a country.'" The same student lamented that Europeans "are treated more like equals. To the Americans, a Mexican is always inferior, and in some places they will not allow us in theaters, barber shops and other public places. Does treatment like that make us want to be citizens?"[52]

The teaching of English and the problem of language loyalty emerged as one of the principal issues among progressive educators, who tended to ignore numerous factors related to the difficulty of converting Mexican children to monolingual English-speakers. Mexicans reasoned that Los Angeles, like other southwestern border areas, was simply a geographic extension of the homeland. It was only natural that the Spanish-speakers would have an easier task than European immigrants when it came to language maintenance. Mexicans were no doubt encouraged by the survival in this area of thousands of Spanish place names and streets as well as by the persistence of Mexican culture. Mexican parents also recognized that the preservation of certain traditional cultural patterns could only be accomplished by the teaching of the mother tongue at home.[53] Finally, many of the Mexican immigrants were influenced by certain historical experiences and realities that generated negative feelings toward learning English. Foremost among those feelings was the belief that learning the host language implied a "direct and immediate submission to a foreign culture and frame of reference." Speaking in English was viewed by many in the *colonia* as tantamount to acceptance of Anglo mores and society. Mexican parents ideally hoped that their children could grow up bilingual and learn to appreciate both Mexican and American culture.[54]

III

The growing response to the cause of social justice was evident in the development of progressive education and the rise of public and social reform organizations, as discussed above, as well as in the ascent of the Social Gospel movement. A national spokesman for this movement wrote that the chief purpose of the Christian Church had shifted from the salvation of individuals to making over "an anti-quated and immoral economic system . . . to create just and broth-erly relations between great groups and classes of society; and thus to lay a social foundation on which modern men individually can live and work in a fashion that will not outrage all the better ele-ments in them."[55] Likewise southern California ministers associ-ated with the Social Gospel pleaded for better treatment of the Mex-ican immigrants. They spoke the language of the progressive reformer as they exposed injustices such as that of the employers in the rural communities near Los Angeles who allowed exploitation of Mexican migrant workers. Los Angeles religious leader Robert McLean voiced such a concern when he wrote about one of the mi-grant camps inspected by the State Housing Bureau. Much like a muckraking journalist, he noted that "moral conditions were be-yond description: Bootleggers, gamblers, and vicious women preyed throughout the camp, carrying off the ready money which found its way into the pockets of the laborers after the debts were paid at the commissary. Babies were being born in tents where there were nei-ther beds nor mattresses. . . ."[56]

Throughout the 1910s and 1920s the progressive spirit within the Christian Church influenced the religious activities in the barrio. While the vast majority of Mexicans believed in Catholicism, church leaders from this denomination and Protestant sects as well felt challenged by the apparent weak bonds between the community and Roman Catholic parishes. Unlike Irish and Polish immigrants in eastern cities, Mexicans made only limited economic sacrifices to-ward the building of local parishes. There were two principal rea-sons for this. First, many of the immigrants anticipated returning to Mexico and saw little reason to build God's Kingdom in East Los Angeles. Second, many Mexicans possessed a strong anticlerical phi-losophy nurtured by anticlerical sentiments in Mexico during and after the Mexican Revolution. When Mexicans began moving to the east side of Los Angeles, the initial settlement occurred in areas for-merly occupied by Italian and Polish families. Mexicans saw little reason for establishing their own ethnic churches, and likewise, the Roman Catholic Church seemed reluctant to expend funds for new facilities.

A serious problem faced by the Catholic and Protestant churches was the shortage of Spanish-speaking personnel. In one Catholic church offering sermons in Spanish, "over 20,000 people" heard mass on Sunday mornings. Linna E. Bresette reported that the church held eight masses on Sundays with 2,500 to 3,000 people at each mass. At Venice Beach in West Los Angeles, the missionary

Brother Isaias, a popular Evangelical "prophet" among the Spanish-speaking population of the city, attracted 3,000 persons to an outdoor speaking engagement arranged to seat 600. Bresette, a Catholic layperson hired to examine the impact of religious work among the Mexicans in the United States, recommended that the church make greater use of refugee priests and nuns in the Mexican communities. In Los Angeles she reported some success in several of the churches and parochial schools where refugee nuns accepted work in teaching regular classes, giving Spanish lessons and operating day nurseries.[57]

Although Catholic and Protestant denominations in Los Angeles appeared inspired by the Social Gospel movement, they committed only limited funds and programs to the barrio over the period 1900–1930. In the western portion of Belvedere, the Catholic diocese maintained only one church for an estimated Mexican population of 10,000, and many church-going members of the community had to attend services in other areas. Protestant denominations in Belvedere accounted for a total of six churches, including two Pentecostal facilities. The one Baptist church in the barrio admitted that its facilities could not meet the needs of the increasing number of Mexicanos turning to that sect.[58]

In the eastern sector of Belvedere (known as Maravilla Park), Mexicanos had even fewer religious facilities than in the western part of that community. Although an estimated 8,000 to 10,000 Mexicanos made their homes in Maravilla Park in the mid-1920s, only three churches served the entire community, and only one of them had a Mexican pastor. In addition, the three churches extended only a minimum of social activities.

During the 1920s, when many middle- and upper-class Mexican families resided in Boyle Heights, religious and social welfare experts considered the facilities in that community among the best in the city, certainly better than those in Belvedere and Maravilla Park. In a sociological study, Samuel Maldonado Ortegón surveyed the quality of services provided for Mexicanos by the churches in Los Angeles and concluded that Boyle Heights offered the best facilities. Large homes dotted the hillsides of that community, and the high number of Italians there as well as the wealth of the district may have accounted for the excellent religious facilities available. By the end of the 1920s, thirteen churches served the residents of Boyle Heights.[59]

By contrast, in "Sonoratown," only two churches, the Plaza Methodist-Episcopal Church and the Catholic Church Nuestra Señora la Reina de los Angeles, attended to the religious needs of the

Mexican *colonia*. This district consisted predominantly of working-class Mexican residents, many of them boarders in the rooming houses and hotels around the Plaza center. To meet the tremendous social and religious needs of these newer immigrants, the Plaza Methodist-Episcopal Church, headed by the Mexican-born and -educated Dr. E. M. Sein, established the most extensive social program for Mexican immigrants in the city. The influences of the Social Gospel and social work were strongly evident in this center. Started in 1915 by Catherine B. Higgins of Chicago, the Methodist-Episcopal social service center received national acclaim for its work among Mexican immigrants. The center offered legal aid; employment, naturalization, and "deportation" services; and relief and rehabilitation programs. As an added assistance to the poor Plaza *colonia*, the church provided a well-equipped medical clinic staffed by trained personnel.[60]

Three main Catholic organizations devoted their energies to working with the Mexican population of Los Angeles: the National Catholic War Council, the National Catholic Welfare Council, and the Catholic Council of Women. The Catholic Council of Women directed community activities and took responsibility for implementing programs such as citizenship instruction.[61] It also promoted athletic teams, especially baseball, home classes for mothers, and sewing classes and picnics for young girls. The Mexican Committee of the Knights of Columbus assisted the National Catholic Welfare Council in publishing a Spanish-language *Civics Catechism* which discussed the rights and duties of citizens. The book received praise from some for doing much "to educate the Mexican to the consciousness that he has rights in America."[62] The local churches also distributed free copies of its two newspapers, *La Revista Católica* and *La Propagandista*. The church well knew of the tremendous work to be done in the Mexican communities. Still, Catholic leaders did not always demonstrate an empathy with the immigrants. At the Catholic Conference in Los Angeles in 1927, a "Catholic authority" on the Mexican population stated that "the greatest missionary problem" is that of "the incoming hordes of our Mexican brothers." He urged Catholics at all levels to take on this work as a "patriotic duty."[63]

Like the progressive educators, Social Gospel ministers considered assimilation as a first step toward Christian responsibility. Protestant churches hoped to integrate Mexican immigrants by promoting American values and customs through classes and informal social and educational activities. Most churches and missions in Los Angeles sponsored recreational activities that emphasized American traditions. For instance, Mexican children were taught to play popular American sports such as basketball, baseball, and American football, and they were discouraged from engaging in traditional Mexican sports such as boxing, billiards, and soccer. Some church leaders got carried away with the whole idea of assimilation and conversion to fundamental religion. Baptist pastor Edwin R. Brown, for example, observed that "without the moral restraints of evangelical Christianity the Mexican in our midst is a menace and a liability." However, once converted, Brown argued, the Mexican could become an asset "socially, politically and economically for even from the standpoint of patriotism, we can do no greater service to our country than to evangelize the Mexican migrant."[64]

Church leaders, taking the Social Gospel to heart, aimed other religious activities at raising the standard of living for the Mexican family. McLean reported that nearly every church began its ministry through night schools, clinics, boys' and girls' clubs, and diversified activities. Jay S. Stowell confirmed that the Americanization programs offered at the missions or neighborhood church resembled those instituted at the local schools to bring about assimilation. These programs, according to Stowell, included instruction in English, Spanish, music, electronics, practical nursing, health, sanitation, sewing, and cooking.[65]

To complement the work of progressive schools in the barrio, religious organizations, principally Catholic and Protestant denominations, thus took an active role in attempting to Americanize the Mexican immigrants. The program, with an ultimate goal of stripping the immigrants of their old homeland attachments and making them over, appealed to adherents of the Social Gospel. Further, they considered the overall goals of Americanization as consistent with their own ideals. Religious leaders understood that their work of spreading the gospel among the newcomers would be significantly easier if the foreign-born learned English and accepted American values.

To some Protestant workers, the task of assimilating the Mexican immigrants extended beyond civic training, English instruction, and advice in proper health and sanitation. The newcomers, if they were to succeed in American society, had to do nothing less than to shed all of their old-world habits, including Catholicism. Los Angeles pastor Charles A. Thomson implied as much when he wrote that, while "nominally Roman Catholic, a large proportion of the Mexicans are religiously adrift and are not served effectively by any church."[66] Jay Stowell was one of the most strident anti-Catholics. He believed that the time had arrived "for the Roman

Catholic Church to frankly acknowledge her shortcomings in the past and to embark upon an educational campaign designed to substitute a religion of enlightenment for a religion of superstition; a religion of service for one of moral and financial exploitation."[67] Many Catholic observers were well aware of the campaign to discredit their work done among the Mexican immigrants. Catholic priests also accused Protestants of engaging in deceptive schemes for the purpose of winning converts. A Catholic layman reported witnessing Mexican women in one Protestant church engaged in saying the rosary. When the action was commented on, the minister responded: "We can't take everything away from them at once."[68]

The outcome of the Americanization efforts and proselyting activity during the period of the Social Gospel movement varied with the community. Some new sections of the Mexican *colonia* realized few benefits from the social arm of the Christian churches. In some cases religious leaders duplicated their efforts in offering social services. Ortegón estimated that at least forty churches provided social and religious services to the Mexican *colonia* of Los Angeles in the 1920s.[69] The impact of Americanization programs generated through the church, although popular with many of the Protestant ministers, had a limited appeal and received criticism from some quarters. A Los Angeles priest, for instance, responded in anger to a question regarding the success rate of Americanizing Mexicans. Other than the Christian activities of the church, he found only "anti-Americanization here and there and everywhere." He reasoned that as long as "Americans treated Mexicans as an inferior race," undervalued their work, paid them low wages, and mistreated them in general, Mexicans would show little interest in becoming U.S. citizens. In his opinion it was no wonder that "they do not care a bit for this thing called 'Americanization.'"[70]

In the twenties, as progressives became involved with the issue of immigration restriction, local religious leaders also rallied behind the quota system. Reverend Robert N. McLean of the Spanish Speaking Works, Board of National Works, of the Presbyterian Church's National Missions, in Los Angeles, however, came to the defense of the Mexicans during this period of nativist awakening. McLean wrote several books and numerous articles praising the contribution of Mexicans to the southwestern economy, claiming that negative stereotypes resulted from racial and class prejudice. The Mexican worker, McLean wrote, "is here to stay, and inevitably he will make his contribution to our national life." McLean worked with Mexicans on Los Angeles' east side as well as with the rural migratory workers who picked crops in the region between Los Angeles and the Salinas Valley. He criticized those who accused the Mexican of "being a rover." The Mexican's "habits are not migratory, but the habits of the industries which furnish him a livelihood most certainly are."[71]

Religious centers with facilities such as the Plaza Methodist-Episcopal Church complemented the services offered by voluntary organizations. Unfortunately for the Mexican *colonia*, many of the projects catering to the ideals of the Social Gospel never succeeded beyond the planning phases or were only in the initial stages of development when the Great Depression hit in 1929. Most religious groups provided only minimum funds for assisting Mexicanos in Los Angeles throughout the 1900–1930 period and extending into the Depression years. Furthermore, few had Spanish-speaking staff members. Contemporary studies by Manuel Gamio, Evangeline Hymer, and Samuel Ortegón suggest that the social activities sponsored by the various religious denominations in Los Angeles, although in some cases useful and entertaining, were not as actively attended as were those activities sponsored by the Mexicanos' own community organizations.[72] Although the churches were one of the few formal institutions reaching out to meet the needs of the Mexican immigrants, the majority of the religious groups had become interested in working with Mexicanos in Los Angeles only during the post–World War I era. In the short span of a decade, few religious centers achieved the goals that they had envisioned.

IV

When the Mexican *colonia* began to spread eastward in the post–World War I years, it acquired a new cohesiveness. In the Plaza area, Mexicanos mingled with Europeans and sections of the neighborhood crossed into Chinatown and the Black community. On the east side, by contrast, the barrio had more clearly defined boundaries that gave the community an insulated character. Sociologists of that era considered the segregated features of the Mexican *colonia* an inevitable consequence of American racism. Mexicans recognized that the narrow range of choices for housing was determined by racial factors, but they also moved in great numbers to the east side for the opportunity to maintain the social relationships that made their transitions to American life easier. In the *colonias* they found Spanish spoken in the stores and churches, and there they could expect to receive credit and meet with others from their village or homeland. The social world of the Mexican immigrant in Los Angeles depended on the primacy of personal relationships. In the *colonia*, Mexicans could expect their neighbors to understand Mexican values and customs. On the east side, moreover, Mexican nationalism and cultural consciousness found fertile soil, and sentiments influenced the character of voluntary institutions.

The barrio associations that emerged in Los Angeles after 1918 had three basic functions: meeting the immediate needs of the immigrant family worker, especially in housing, employment, and health care; maintaining the traditional culture and values of the homeland through the promotion of patriotic and religious festivals and raising both the ethnic and the class consciousness of the community; improving the status of the immigrant community and individuals by challenging unjust laws, exploitation, and deprivation of civil rights.[73]

The majority of the membership rolls of these community organizations have not survived, and therefore we do not have an accurate profile of the members or their level of participation. Since over 90 percent of the Mexican community worked in low-skilled or unskilled blue-collar occupations and earned wages far below those of the average Anglo American worker, it can be assumed that most who did join the barrio's associations were from a low socioeconomic status.

Since the majority of the Mexican immigrants in Los Angeles probably considered the possibility of eventually returning to Mexico, many of their activities in the United States involved maintaining Mexican patriotism. One organization, Club Independencia, began in Los Angeles in 1920 "with the patriotic objective of making some propaganda against [U.S.] intervention in Mexico and for the protection of the rights of Mexicanos" in the United States. The association also promised to "work actively toward lessening the slander which certain elements of bad faith had directed at our country." The president of the club, Luis G. Franco, noted that the club sought the unification of Mexican political parties and would "preoccupy itself in the defense of the interests of *La Patria* [the homeland] without mixing in the politics of this country"[74] Some of the Mexican *colonia's* strongest and most effective leaders lent their efforts to political and social issues related to Mexico. This strong concern with affairs in the homeland frequently diluted the political strength that Mexican immigrants could have commanded in the Los Angeles community.

Another organization, Comisión Honorífica, which was similar to Club Independencia, also functioned as a patriotic club for Mexican migrants. The Comisión pledged to represent all the Mexicanos of the city and to "guard with zeal the dignity of *La Nación* [Mexico]."[75] In Los Angeles, as in other cities with a Mexican Embassy, the Comisión had as its president the Mexican consul or vice consul. In most areas where Comisión Honorífica existed, local community leaders and other voluntary associations worked under its direction to plan the annual commemoration of the Mexican festivals of May 5 and September 16.

The fiestas gave new immigrants an opportunity to demonstrate group consciousness. For the most part, the festivities called for a parade down Spring and Broadway streets followed by a dance and beauty contest in the evening. *La Prensa* and *El Heraldo* generally provided extensive coverage of the two celebrations and used the occasion to remind Mexicanos of their "glorious heritage" and patriotic duty to the homeland. Despite the strong Mexican nationalism exhibited in these festivals, the membership of the patriotic clubs well understood the political realities of their new environment. For instance, the sponsors of the festivities always invited a distinguished member of the Anglo community, usually the mayor or a high-ranking city official, to give the keynote speech. In 1919 the committee invited General Frank C. Prescott, who tactlessly told the crowd of five thousand that "if the leaders of Mexico failed to get together [resolve the Revolutionary fighting], the United States would be forced to intervene militarily."[76] The following year the fiesta committee chose a less controversial speaker who urged the audience to enroll in Americanization programs and "to take advantage of the education afforded by the public schools."[77]

The decade of the 1920s also brought commercialization and expanded entrepreneurship to the fiestas. For example, during the years 1919–1921, "Las Fiestas Patrias," which had been organized by a number of Mexican voluntary associations under the direction of the Comisión Honorífica, came under the influence and partial control of several enterprising Latin American associations. The main interests of those groups seemed to be in profiting from the celebrations, and increasingly after World War I an atmosphere of a county fair dominated the events as sponsors capitalized on the commercial potential of the Mexican holidays. More than five thousand persons attended the 16th of September celebration in 1919 at Lincoln Park, where the *Los Angeles Times* noted that the biggest attraction was the merry-go-round.[78] The large attendance at the 1919 celebrations apparently encouraged a group of ambitious persons not associated with the Mexican planning committee to introduce several new commercial events in the fiestas in 1920. That year promoters increased the number of concession stands and sold tickets to a wrestling exhibition.[79]

Organizers of the festivals of 1921 and 1922 received adverse publicity following the cancellation of a scheduled bullfight at Praeger Park during the Cinco de Mayo celebration in 1922. This publicity convinced most Mexicanos in Los Angeles that the fiestas had indeed fallen to crass commercialization. After a large number had paid admission to enter the arena, the announcer informed them that the Society for the Prevention of Cruelty to Animals had succeeded in canceling the show. The sponsors, the Sociedad Hispano Americano, refused to refund the $1 admission price to the disappointed audience.[80] Further bad publicity followed in the next few days, when the *Los Angeles Times* reported that Pedro Espejo, the contracted bullfighter, had filed a suit against the Sociedad for failing to pay the $400 promised to him.[81]

After this incident, the Confederated Mexican Societies of California filed a suit against the Sociedad in an effort to "halt further asserted 'exploitation' of the public." The petition read: "Year by year a group of individuals sheltered under the name of Spanish American Societies takes advantage of our national festivities to exploit the good faith and high patriotic sentiments of the Mexican colony in this city, organizing festivities which have no other object than profit of a small number of persons."[82] In 1924, members of the Mexican American press, the Mexican consul, and a group of leaders from the voluntary associations met to resolve the problem by designating a special commission, the Unión Mexicana de Periodistas, to make all arrangements for that year's fiestas.[83]

The selection of Unión Mexicana, which refused to cooperate with the Latin American voluntary associations, demonstrated yet another feature of Mexican nationalism. For several months following the creation of the Unión Mexicana, dozens of letters appeared in *El Heraldo* defending and attacking the new organizational structure because it left the Central Americans of Los Angeles out of the planning of the Mexican celebrations.[84] The discussion no longer centered only on the question of exploitation and commercialization but also directly on a controversy over celebrating Mexican and Central American Independence on the same day, since anniversaries of both holidays occurred in September. Mexican association leaders successfully resisted the idea of joint celebrations because of earlier problems with the 1921 and 1922 festivals. The idea of "Latin unity" seemed stillborn.

Another organization, La Alianza Hispano Americana, one of

the most popular Mexican voluntary associations in Los Angeles and throughout the Southwest, fell under severe criticism during the mid-1920s for failing to give greater attention to the social needs of the Mexican community.[85] Founded in 1894 through the efforts of Carlos Velasco, a wealthy member of the Arizona oligarchy, and Manuel Samaniego, a Tucson businessman, the Alianza expanded rapidly to other areas of the Southwest. According to one of its founders, Ignacio Calvillo, they launched the Alianza to "protect and fight for the rights of Spanish-Americans in Tucson, for at that time there was a lot of strife and ill-feeling between us and the Anglo-Saxon element caused in great part by prejudice, misunderstanding and ignorance."[86]

By 1917 the Alianza had eighty-five chapters in New Mexico, Arizona, California, Nevada, and Chihuahua, Mexico.[87] Although the association had built a reputation by providing fraternal and insurance benefits to all classes of Mexicans in the Southwest, in the 1920s its leadership became complacent and organized little besides social dances and conventions. Seldom did La Alianza in Los Angeles contribute to any charitable causes or assist, as did some of the other organizations, in efforts to provide for the welfare and education of the most recent immigrants.

During the Alianza's thirty-third annual convention in Los Angeles in 1927, editors of *El Heraldo* took the association to task for giving too much attention to selfish material ends and for having too many Anglo-Americans on the national and local boards of directors.[88] In reality, *El Heraldo* noted, "*La Alianza* is only an insurance company which offers services inferior to other companies."[89] Second, its critics asserted, the association needed to "Mexicanize" the leadership. "Surely," one editorial writer asked, "among 9,000 members of *La Alianza* there are *Mexicanos* capable of directing the association."[90]

Other questions posed by *El Heraldo* indicated the increasing concern among leaders of the Mexican community in Los Angeles for the working-class Mexicano. The editors of the community newspaper pressed La Alianza to initiate a program that would assist Mexican immigrants troubled with employment problems. Mexican workers, *El Heraldo* reminded the convention delegates, "had come to this country in search of a better life, but had been enslaved, and treated as if they were inferior and [now] had been completely abandoned." La Alianza, continuing to hold its convention, paid little attention to the criticism; no commitment was made on the part of either the membership or the delegates. According to Manuel P. Servín, membership of La Alianza increased during the late 1920s, and the organization persisted at least into the Depression as one of the most powerful associations of Mexicanos in the country. Its success was due principally to its low-cost insurance program and the fact it gave many immigrants a rare opportunity to belong to something resembling an "exclusive" fraternal order. One of the unique features of the organization was the establishment of branches in Mexico, for few other organizations of Mexicanos in the United States expanded into the immigrants' homeland.[91]

Women also played a significant role in the institutional life of the barrio. Fortunately for the community, Mexican women did not limit their participation to the organizations founded for their gender, but instead worked in various capacities in numerous organizations. Many of the Mexican fraternal clubs and political organizations excluded women from their membership and/or restricted their involvement to a subordinate or auxiliary status, but nonetheless it is apparent that by the 1920s women worked actively in social and political causes, and the community accepted in general their dedication to volunteer work.

Few community organizers matched the dedication and accomplishments of Elena de la Ilata, head of Cruz Azul (Blue Cross). Cruz Azul was formed in 1920 and, according to one press article, it was "sanctioned" by the Mexican government and approved by the Mexican vice consul of the city.[92] Mainly through the efforts of de la Ilata's leadership, Cruz Azul emerged in the early 1920s as one of the most active and successful of the numerous charity associations in the city. When a sudden storm left hundreds of Mexicans homeless in San Gabriel in 1921, Cruz Azul worked around the clock for two days to find temporary housing and provide hot meals for the victims. De la Ilata also assumed the task of writing to the local newspapers requesting additional assistance in relocating the flood victims. Later that year, Cruz Azul organized a circus benefit for the unemployed in the barrio. For more than a week, both afternoons and evenings, circus performers entertained the Mexican community. Organizers from other clubs marveled at the successful operation, a result of de la Ilata's energy and the enlistment of fifty young women to assist in ticket sales and ushering.[93]

Other activities of Cruz Azul included fundraisers for medical needs and assistance to families in emergencies. One such instance came in 1921, when the organization, with the cooperation of the Mexican government, assisted a group of destitute Mexican immigrants who wished to return to Mexico.[94] The Mexican government chartered one of its passenger ships to take the 1,500 unemployed Mexicanos and their families back to Mexico, and Cruz Azul of Los

Angeles assumed responsibility for feeding the emigrants as they waited for the ship at San Pedro Harbor. For two days before the ship arrived, hundreds of Mexicanos camped at the loading docks, many without sufficient funds to buy a hot meal.[95] Adding to the plight of the *repatriados* were the extended visitations on the docks of friends and family who had come to see their departure. Several other organizations under the direction of Cruz Azul worked long hours to feed the multitude and see the returning Mexicans safely to the ship.[96]

Only rarely did the older generation of American-born Mexicanos—or Californios, as some preferred to call themselves—labor toward establishing an organization dedicated primarily to mobilizing the immigrant class in any way. In 1918, R. F. del Valle made such a gesture when he announced the formation of La Liga Américo-Latina. Del Valle was a descendent of an old Spanish Californio family who had held numerous public offices in California. The purpose of La Liga was threefold: (1) to educate the employers of Mexicanos for the purpose of enhancing "better understanding between the laborers and their bosses," (2) to develop projects that would serve "to better the conditions and lives of the Mexican workers," and (3) to create means of generating accurate information about Mexicanos in the United States and Mexico itself.[97] Ultimately La Liga hoped to insure that Mexicanos could improve their social status and receive the benefits of American schools. La Liga stressed the importance of learning English. La Liga appears to have been a product of the war years, and it had a very limited impact on the Los Angeles community.[98] Given the strong ethnic consciousness of the barrio, it may have been that the average Mexican laborer was suspicious of an organization that included four Anglos in a steering committee of six.[99]

Mexican voluntary associations also played a major role in the formation of trade unions among Mexicanos of Los Angeles. In 1927, a committee of individuals involved in voluntary organizations met and "adopted a resolution calling upon the mutual and benefit societies . . . to lend their support to the cause of organizing trade unions of Mexican workers." Among those at the first meeting were Pedro M. Salinas, president of the Asociación Cooperativa de Belvedere, a voluntary association of workers in that community, and F. Alfonso Pesqueira, the Mexican consul.[100] As a result of several meetings, a committee of workers formed a local union calling itself the Confederación de Uniones Obreras Mexicanas (CUOM). The CUOM modeled its constitution after that of the Confederación Regional de Obreros Mexicanos (CROM).[101] The CUOM constitution expressed numerous radical perspectives, as exemplified by Article I of the Declaration of Principles: "That the exploited class, the greater part of which is made up of manual labor, is right in establishing a class struggle in order to effect an economic and moral betterment of its conditions and at last its complete freedom from capitalistic tyranny."[102]

One of the aims of CUOM, as listed in Article 18 of its constitution, was the limitation of immigration from Mexico, while another goal stated by the members called upon the Mexican government to "offer colonization opportunities to those Mexicans who find it difficult to make a living in California because of lack of employment." The confederation pledged "to establish solid ties with organized labor of Mexico [CROM] and to try to stop the immigration of unorganized labor into the United States," since they considered such immigration harmful to the working classes of both countries.[103]

V

While voluntary associations afforded opportunities for social interaction and provided mutual benefits, they lacked the resources to cope with all problems faced by the new immigrants. In addition, not all immigrants belonged to voluntary associations. The Mexican consulate, although its influence varied with the competency and dedication of the consul and his staff, functioned as the one formal organization primarily responsible for the Mexican population in the United States. The consulate operated year-round and, more importantly, had a Spanish-speaking staff. Since few of the Mexicanos in Los Angeles had citizenship papers, the immigrants looked to the consulate to protect their rights in the United States. The sociologist Emory Bogardus, noting the tendency of Americans to consider Americans of Mexican descent as second-class citizens, suggested that Mexicanos preferred to remain Mexican citizens, for "by remaining a citizen of Mexico and by calling on the Mexican consul for assistance the Mexican can secure justice, whereas if he becomes an American citizen, he feels helpless. He does not understand our courts and is not able to secure as adequate a hearing as if he remains a Mexican citizen."[104]

The role of the Mexican consulate in Los Angeles was not well defined and was often misunderstood by Mexicanos and Americans alike. While the consuls assisted Mexicanos in numerous situations and even supported unpopular causes such as the formation of a Mexican trade union, the community generally viewed the consulates as public relations agencies for the Mexican government. Robert McLean, for example, commented that the role of the Mexican consulate was one of simply "maintaining the spirit and patriotism" of Mexican nationals in the United States. Bogardus observed that while the consuls knew about the hardships of Mexican workers in the United States and secured redress for wrongs inflicted on Mexican laborers, they were naturally loath to take part in the economic or social life of the United States. Nevertheless, the consulate kept in close touch with Mexican immigrants who got into trouble in the United States and often helped them.[105]

Mexicanos in Los Angeles thought no problem too small or too complicated to bring before the consul. They ranged from a painter looking for work to a man sentenced to die in the gas chamber who asked the consul to intervene in his behalf for a last-minute pardon from the governor of California. Mexicanos also depended upon the consulate to assist them in civil suits and legal matters. For example, when the Fullerton School District offered Jacinto García only $2,000 for his property instead of the $3,000 he believed the property to be worth, he petitioned the Mexican consulate in Los Angeles for assistance. In such cases, the consulate could only encourage an individual like García to seek the advice of a lawyer or to find proper documentation which would support his case.[106]

Because of political instability during the Revolutionary period in Mexico, the consulates in Los Angeles and throughout the Southwest operated under noticeable strain. The Mexican government's insistence on subjecting the position of consul to a game of political musical chairs undermined the consulate's efficiency. During a nine-year period in Los Angeles, some thirteen consuls received appointments from Mexico. Soon after the May 1920 departure of Consul José Garza Zertuche from Los Angeles, the arrival of Lino B. Rochín prompted the *Los Angeles Times* to comment: "Following the appointment of five separate consular agents in Los Angeles since December, 1918, resulting from political upheavals and reorganization of the government in Mexico, the office of Mexican consul in this city was yesterday 'permanently filled.'"[107]

The most difficult assignment assumed by the Mexican consulate in Los Angeles during the 1920s involved the painful process of repatriating Mexicanos unable to find employment in the area. In May 1921, the consulate informed Mexicanos in southern California that President Alvaro Obregón had asked Mexicanos without means of supporting themselves to return to Mexico. A commission in the Mexican government monitored the unemployment problem in the United States and its effect on Mexican workers, and a committee of Mexican workers in Los Angeles visited Mexico City in an effort to find out what the Mexican government intended to do about those workers who wished to return to their homeland.[108]

Although the repatriation program in 1921 lasted only one year and affected only several thousand Mexicanos in Los Angeles, Mexican community leaders sought means of assisting those forced to leave the United States. Local voluntary associations and Mexican charity groups in the community provided for some of the expenses of those returning to Mexico. The Mexican government allocated a small amount of money for transportation costs, but only from the Mexican border to the interior states of the Republic. All in all, neither the consulates nor the Mexican government handled the repatriation program effectively. *La Prensa de Los Angeles* had correctly cautioned in 1920: "The repatriation of Mexican workers [remains] one of the most serious problems which the Mexican government has to resolve."[109]

The Mexican consulate in Los Angeles served southern California from Ventura to the Mexican border, an area that included more than a quarter of a million Mexicanos by the mid-1920s. The responsibility for such a vast area and the large number of Mexican immigrants made it all but impossible for the consulate to minister effectively to the community's needs. In the mid-1920s, the Mexican government gave the consul in Los Angeles permission to hire American lawyers to assist in handling immigrants' problems, but the budget allocated remained pitifully small compared to the number of cases handled by the Mexican office. The processing of petitions often took months, and frequently even the simplest request became entangled for weeks in bureaucratic procedures.[110]

In addition, misunderstandings between the consulate and its constituents commonly arose either because the immigrants misperceived the power of the consul or because the consul misrepresented the extent of his influence and authority. It was one thing to expect the consul to protect the immigrant from unscrupulous employers and landlords but another to expect him to take part in a decision involving U.S. legal proceedings. When a California state law prohibiting foreigners from carrying guns passed in 1923, for instance, many immigrants called upon the consul for the repeal of the law.[111] On October 6, 1923, the consul voiced an official protest over the passage of the Foreign Gun Law. Since a large proportion of the foreigners in California were of Mexican descent, he suggested that the law affected Mexicanos more severely than any other ethnic group.[112] A week later, the consul dropped his protest and agreed to cooperate with U.S. authorities. He advised Mexicanos to bring their guns to the consular office in Los Angeles to be surrendered to local authorities. Thus the consul, within the short span of a week, reversed his position from one of protest to one of compliance and cooperation. The haste with which the Mexican consul retreated on the issue of repealing the law disappointed many Mexicanos and demonstrated his powerlessness to intervene in matters of U.S. law and policy.[113]

On several occasions during the 1920s the consulate, the voluntary associations, and the Spanish-language press combined in efforts to deal with important community issues. In few instances in the 1920s, however, did the Mexican community of Los Angeles expend more energy than it did in behalf of Aurelio Pompa, a man who for Mexicanos in southern California and in other parts of the Southwest became a symbol of the immigrant victimized by injustice. The campaign to save Aurelio Pompa's life began when he went to trial in 1923 for killing an Anglo American coworker in Los Angeles. Because the community believed the killing had been in self-defense and felt that a Mexican could not get a fair trial in the United States, they organized a national campaign in his behalf. Community leaders, who refused to wait for the Mexican consul to sanction the campaign, raised $3,000 in a matter of weeks and hired a prominent Los Angeles Mexican American attorney, Frank Domínguez, to defend Pompa.[114] While voluntary associations sent out appeals to lodges and friends throughout the Southwest, the press wrote editorial accounts of the trial. The consulate, meanwhile, kept a low profile in the case, apparently uncertain about the steps it could or should take in favor of Pompa. As the defendant came to trial, *El Heraldo* emerged as his most persistent supporter, while the consulate gave only lukewarm support to the campaign. Only after Pompa had been sentenced to death and transferred to the facilities at San Quentin did the Mexican consul in Los Angeles issue his first public statement on the condemned man's behalf.[115]

The editor of *El Heraldo*, Juan de Heras, stepped up the campaign to free Pompa, organizing a statewide petition drive in his behalf. In Los Angeles, some supporters criticized the plan, arguing that only the personal intervention of President Obregón of Mexico would save Pompa. La Sociedad Melchor Ocampo, a Mexican voluntary association in Los Angeles, pressured the consulate in an effort to obtain Obregón's support. During the last week of January 1924, President Obregón appealed to Governor Friend W. Richardson of California to pardon Pompa—a request many Mexicanos believed was the only hope for saving his life.[116] While Governor Richardson studied the appeal, *El Heraldo* reported to its readers that 12,915 names had been collected on a petition to be delivered to the governor on Pompa's behalf. As community leaders in Los Angeles prepared to deliver the appeal, they learned that Pompa had been executed.[117] The shock of the news of the execution was tremendous, given the excitement and optimism following President Obregón's intervention and the tremendous success of the petition drive. Governor Richardson's denial of a stay of execution did not reach the editors of *El Heraldo* in time for publication, and Pompa's death took the community by surprise.

Pompa's death angered Mexicanos throughout the state, and his supporters naturally felt a sense of betrayal. When his body was brought to Los Angeles, thousands gathered to bid farewell.[118] In a *corrido* (ballad) composed shortly after his death, these words were attributed to the young Mexican:

> Farewell, my friends, farewell my village:
> Dear Mother, cry no more.
> Tell my race not to come here,
> For here they will suffer:
> There is no pity here.[119]

VI

The role of immigrant organizations in American communities has been examined from various perspectives by scholars over the past century. Recent studies suggest that the immigrant mutual aid societies and voluntary associations actually aided rather than hindered assimilation. Those who follow this line of thought argue, essentially, that the ethnic organizations made it possible for the immigrants to adjust more easily to their new environment. The history of numerous organizations of this sort in the Mexican community of Los Angeles does not, however, conform to this interpretation. The organizations appear to have played an insignificant role in assimilation over the period 1900–1930. The few early studies concerned with twentieth-century Mexican residents confirmed the low assimilation of this group as judged by intermarriage, naturalization, and apparent cohesiveness of their ethnic communities. Emory Bogardus, Manuel Gamio, and Paul S. Taylor concluded that the rate of integration in both rural and urban areas during the second and third decades of this century was significantly lower among Mexicanos than among Europeans.[120]

In his seminal study of assimilation in American society, Milton M. Gordon studied Blacks, Jews, Catholics, and White Protestants. While he excluded Mexicans from his overall analysis, he made a brief reference to them suggesting that a number of factors made the process of acculturation unique for Blacks, Indians, and Mexicans. For Blacks and Mexicans moving into urban areas, Gordon noted, the acculturation process was retarded "because of the massive size and strength of the prejudice and consequent discrimination" directed toward them. For the Mexican and sometimes the Indian, he noted, language difference accounted for additional problems.[121]

An examination of the naturalization and intermarriage rate for Mexican immigrants in Los Angeles during the period 1917–1930 provides some insight into their level of assimilation. The 1920 census shows that among all ethnic groups in California, Mexicans had the lowest rate of naturalization. Out of a total of 60,546 foreign-born Mexicans living in the state, 88.9 percent had kept their alien status. Only 5 percent (3,008) had become American citizens by 1920, while less than 1 percent (471) had received First Papers. Italian immigrants, on the other hand, numbered 80,179 in 1920, and their naturalization rate was significantly higher than that of Mexicans. Slightly over a quarter of them had become American citizens, while another tenth had taken out First Papers.[122] A study commissioned by California Governor C. C. Young in 1930 reported that while Los Angeles led the state with 149 naturalized citizens of Mexican ancestry, the average number of years in residence before application was 14.8. Nationwide, only 3.3 percent of the Mexicans twenty-one years of age and older had become naturalized, compared to 47.8 percent of all the foreign-born in this country. Indeed, 47.2 percent of the foreign-born of all ages and both sexes had taken out naturalization papers by 1920.[123]

Pastor G. Bromley Oxnam of the Church of All Nations of Los Angeles conducted a survey in 1920 and uncovered a naturalization rate of 23.0 percent among the Mexicans. While the 23 percent figure was substantially higher than that found by census takers for the same year, these figures, Oxnam concluded, still "indicate that the Mexican is not interested in becoming a citizen."[124]

The Commission of Naturalization of the United States Department of Labor made still other investigations of the naturalization rate in 1923 and again in 1928. Their figures for 1928 show that only 0.1 percent, or 497 Mexicans, had been admitted to U.S. citizenship over the previous five years. Over the same period, 179,699 Italians became citizens. Even immigrants from Central and South America, who made up a much lower proportion of the Latin American immigration, became United States citizens in greater numbers than the Mexicans. During the period 1923–1928, some 1,307 foreign-born immigrants from those regions applied and received U.S. naturalization papers. The evidence clearly demonstrates in the period before 1930 Mexicans fell significantly below other groups in attaining American citizenship.[125]

Another important indicator of assimilation suggested by social scientists is intermarriage. If this index is valid, then the process of integration had begun for Mexicans by 1917, although it had yet to achieve significant proportions. Constantine Panunzio, an economics professor with the University of California, carried out the most extensive research examining the rate of intermarriage in Los Angeles during the 1920s. Panunzio and his assistants examined Los Angeles marriage licenses for the period 1924–1933, working with a total of 170,636 applications. Panunzio was interested in the intermarriage rates of Whites, Asians, Mexicans, and Blacks. Mexicans constituted the largest of the county's ethnic groups, accounting for 167,024 persons, or 76 per thousand of the population of the county. Out of a total of 11,016 marriages involving at least one Mexican mate, he found intermarriage between Mexicans and Whites at a level of 116 per thousand.[126]

A study of the marriage records for the years 1917 and 1918 reveals a somewhat higher level of exogamy. The total number of individuals who were married in those two years was lower than the average yearly number for the Panunzio study, perhaps as a result of the high proportion of men serving in the armed services at that time. Still, for the two years, a total of 14,951 individuals obtained marriage licenses. Mexicans accounted for 660 of this group. A total of 50 of these marriages were between Mexican men and non-Mexican women. Thus out of a total of 660 marriages, 147 were mixed, or 222 per thousand.[127]

The ethnic cohesiveness of the Mexican community also illustrated the slow rate of assimilation of this group. Contemporary observers and scholars interested in the Mexican *colonia* all spoke about the persistence of Mexican culture and tradition in the barrios of Los Angeles. In a survey by Evangeline Hymer, 55 percent of the Mexicans questioned stated that they considered it a "duty to remain loyal to Mexico, while less than a third responded that they expected to live permanently in the United States."[128] Indeed, the very presence of the *colonia* in Los Angeles during the 1920s at a time when other ethnic colonies were disappearing or losing their ethnic characteristics suggests the strong residue of ethnic solidarity. The slow entry of Mexicans into the "great melting pot" prompted one scholar to write: "It is commonly stated that the Mexican is the hardest to assimilate of any racial group, and it is true that he naturalizes the least often and keeps apart from Americans."[129] Thus, as their *colonia* on the east side grew, the need for Mexicanos to interact with Anglo residents of the city lessened or diminished. The *colonia* quickly became socially and culturally insulated, and the opportunity increased for Mexicanos to live out their lives with only minimal association with American institutions.

The slow assimilation of Mexicans in Los Angeles, as demonstrated by the low naturalization rates, eventually came to haunt the community. When the Great Depression hit the United States, California, already one of the most populous states in the union, was drastically affected. Initially, public officials incorrectly diagnosed the problem and dealt with the symptoms rather than with the causes of the Depression. President Hoover blamed Mexicans for the high unemployment, holding them responsible for taking jobs away from Americans.[130] The unemployment crisis drove dustbowl migrants to California, creating additional burdens on the labor pool. Panic gripped the Los Angeles *colonia*, which by 1930 had become the unofficial Mexican capital of the United States. Mexicanos, poorly organized politically, highly visible in segregated communities, and misunderstood socially and culturally, became the target for immigration raids that touched the lives of at least one of every three Mexican families.[131] Although the deportation of Mexicans occurred in numerous cities, Los Angeles became the first city to employ local and federal tax funds for the purpose of repatriating Mexicans.[132] By 1935, some 500,000 had been repatriated nationwide; the largest share of those deported had resided in the "City of Angels." For a class of immigrants who had been welcomed only a decade earlier by city industrialists, an era had ended.

8 Afterword—East Los Angeles since 1930

The 150th anniversary of the founding of Los Angeles in September 1931 was marked by festivities planned by the Chamber of Commerce and the movie industry and opened by a papal emissary. For a few days, at least, the activities succeeded, as one broadcaster noted, in showing "the country that we in southern California refuse to acknowledge that there is any depression."[1] The festivities, however, were but a warm-up for a more elaborate demonstration of civic pride, the 1932 Olympic Games.

The successful staging of these events, however, did not diminish the impact of the Depression on Los Angeles. There had been some early signs of the coming economic debacle with the collapse in 1925 of the real estate boom in the new westside shopping and business districts.[2] Journalist James H. Collins conceded in 1930 that "jobs are rare and eagerly sought." Nonetheless, he concluded that if a newcomer "cannot get a job in a factory, he readily turns his hand to a trade. He will transform himself into a fair carpenter, or drive a motortruck, or pump gasoline at a service station."[3] Collins was a bit optimistic, for even those jobs were hard to come by in Los Angeles.

Promoting Los Angeles to the rest of the nation had appealed to city officials in the twenties, but, as industrial production continued to fall and plants closed their doors by the hundreds, southern Californians grew less enthusiastic about further in-migration. Indeed, they even took steps to encourage out-migration.

During the 1920s, private citizens and public officials had waged a national campaign in the press and in the Congress against the utilization of Mexican immigrant labor. Even southern Californians, who for years had welcomed Mexican labor, began to lose their enthusiasm as economic paralysis struck the region. Scholars, union leaders, social workers, and religious leaders debated the issue of Mexican immigration during the late 1920s and early 1930s. Influential members of the Commonwealth Club of San Francisco heard speakers characterize Mexican labor as a danger to the health standards of the state. Mexicans now seemed racially unacceptable and were said to pose a serious threat to the nation's democratic values. Samuel J. Holmes, a zoologist at the University of California, Berkeley, articulated the anti-Mexican feelings when he noted that Mexicans represented a population of a "low social and economic and intellectual level, thus a menace from the standpoint of public health." To allow unrestricted immigration to continue, he warned, "will undoubtedly be to force the native American labor in the west out of industry after industry."[4] In the decade of the Depression, this attitude would lead to plans to cut off Mexican immigration and to remove those Mexican migrants already in Los Angeles.

As many citizens saw it, the Mexican's principal value had been as cheap labor. With the Depression, the pool of jobs dried up, and employers no longer needed unskilled laborers. By 1930 thousands of Mexicans had left Los Angeles for Mexico or other regions in search of work. Mexican consular inspector Enrique A. González visited the area in 1931 to evaluate the consequences of the Depression on Mexican families. In every district, González noted high unemployment, ranging from 20 to 50 percent, "with the latter percentage being the most common."[5] Harold Fields, writing for *Social Forces*, noted that Californians employed "social pressure and threats of violence" against employers "who hired Mexicans rather than unemployed Americans."[6] Out of work or underemployed, eastside Mexicans faced a difficult economic and social situation during the 1930s. At soup kitchens and charity houses, they encountered hostile looks and rejection.

Angelenos attempted to resolve the unemployment problems through a deportation program designed to return unemployed Mexicans to their homeland. The Los Angeles Chamber of Commerce, which had praised the Mexicans throughout the teens and twenties, urged that immigration officials undertake an aggressive "deportation drive and even offered to pay the cost of passage back to the border."[7] Expressing concern over the repatriation program, Carey McWilliams wrote: "One wonders what has happened to all the Americanization programs of yesteryear. The Chamber of Commerce has been forced to issue a statement assuring the Mexican authorities that the community is in no sense unfriendly to Mexican labor and that repatriation is a policy designed solely for the relief of the destitute."[8] Los Angeles officials made arrangement with the Southern Pacific "to ship Mexicans back to Mexico at a wholesale per capita rate of $14.70."[9] Charles Visel, Coordinator for the Los

Angeles Citizens Committee on Coordination of Unemployment Relief, praised the federal immigration authorities for their "efficiency, aggressiveness and resourcefulness" in handling the deportation of Mexicans who had violated American laws.[10] Recognizing that many of the Mexicans had entered the United States legally and that their unemployment itself did not put them in violation of any law, Los Angeles officials and the press "played up the government's deportation efforts" prompting a Los Angeles district director of immigration to note that thousands of Mexicans "have been literally scared out of southern California."[11] Overall, nearly 500,000 Mexicanos, most born in Mexico, but many of them born in the United States, left for Mexico during the 1930s.[12]

World War II, however, revolutionized many aspects of social and economic life in East Los Angeles. By the summer of 1942, many barrio homes displayed American flags in their front windows, a symbol that a member of the family was in uniform. An estimated 400,000–500,000 Mexicanos from across the nation joined the armed forces during the war, with Los Angeles contributing the largest percentage of any one community.[13] The participation of the majority of the male labor force of the eastside community opened new job opportunities for women in the war industries, especially in textile, aircraft, ship-building, and food-processing plants. Women also contributed to the military effort by planting "victory gardens" and handling all of the family responsibilities. Writers and scientists researching the East Los Angeles barrio during the early war years applied a new classification to the group: Mexican American.[14] Educated in the United States, the second generation spoke English better than Spanish. Overall, they considered themselves Mexican Americans rather than Mexicans, although there was a small group that objected to both terms.

If the barrio appeared to have the characteristics of a giant train depot during the war years, it was largely because the Navy and Marines stationed thousands of new recruits in a camp in Chávez Ravine, adjacent to the east side. The internment of Japanese Americans in 1942 produced additional movement of people. Many of the Japanese Americans forced to dispose of their homes, sell their belongings, and board trains at the nearby depots were neighbors of barrio residents. As a result of a 1942 agreement between Mexico and the United States, more than 100,000 Braceros also came into California to fill the labor vacuum created by the exodus of Mexican American field hands and Japanese American laborers. During the first full year of the Bracero Program, 73 percent of all the Braceros contracted to work in the United States worked in California.[15] Los

Angeles became a major destination and distribution point for the Braceros, many of whom became railway workers.

A nation at war is capable both of ignoring domestic issues, and of exhibiting intolerance toward nontraditional behavior. Such was the case in East Los Angeles, where a quiet rebellion against American values and lifestyles surfaced during the late 1930s and early 1940s. Youthful members of the second generation, the principal figures in this rebellion, expressed their estrangement from American society by forming cliques or gangs. Carey McWilliams, noted author and attorney, remarked that these individuals, "rebuffed in the schools and in the community," have "been made to feel that they do not belong, that they are Mexicans, not Americans, and that they will never be accepted as equals."[16] Poor schooling and problems with the law kept many of them out of the armed services, and prejudice denied them equal opportunity in the work sector. The early gang members from this era were recognizable by their dress styles, use of English and Spanish slang words or a combination of both, and tattoo marks on their hands and arms. In the early 1940s they began to sport zoot suits, long ducktail haircuts, and pointed shoes. Many of them hung around pool halls and gathered on the weekends at local dance halls. They called themselves "Chucos," short for the word *Pachuco*. The police and the press preferred to call them hoodlums or "zoot suiters."[17]

Relations between young men from the Eastside Barrio and police authorities had been poor long before the body of José Díaz was found on August 2, 1942, at a barrio swimming hole popularly known as "Sleepy Lagoon." Although the exact cause of death was never determined, members of the 38th Street gang had been reported in the vicinity on the night of Díaz' death. The police arrested twenty-two members of the gang, charging all of them with conspiracy to commit murder. The mass trial which followed, unprecedented in U.S. judicial history, gained national attention and provoked new anti-Mexican sentiments in the Los Angeles community. Captain Ed Durán Ayres of the Foreign Relations Bureau of the Los Angeles Police Department testified that "while Anglos fought with the fists, Mexicans generally preferred to kill, or at least let blood." The court found three defendants guilty of first-degree murder and sentenced them to San Quentin Prison for varying terms. Nine more defendants were found guilty of second-degree murder and two counts of assault. Five were convicted of lesser offenses, and some of these served time in the Los Angeles County Jail. Five were acquitted on all counts. The East Los Angeles community organized the Sleepy

Lagoon Defense Committee, and the convictions were appealed. The District Court of Appeals found the trial judge biased against the defendants and overturned the convictions. On October 4, 1944, all the defendants who remained in jail were freed as a result of the appeals court's reversal of the guilty verdicts.[18]

The rejoicing that followed lasted but a short time, as youths from the east side soon fell into conflict with soldiers and sailors stationed in the city. The origins of the "zoot suit riots" which occurred in Los Angeles during the first week of June 1943 have never been clear. Young Mexican Americans had clashed with members of the armed services on numerous occasions in the downtown section of Los Angeles; the press had been virulent in its presentation of Mexican American gang activity.[19] Enlisted men from the camps considered the youngsters from the barrio as draft dodgers. Mexican Americans resented the constant traffic of soldiers and sailors in their community. A major confrontation began on the evening of June 3, 1943, when sailors looking for a fight with Mexican gang members attacked several of them near a dance hall in Venice. Rumors that Mexican hoodlums had started the fight brought hundreds of marines and sailors into the barrio and downtown section of Los Angeles that evening. Over the next few days, more fights followed. Mexican Americans wearing zoot suits were stripped of their clothing and beaten. The mob, which grew larger every night, marched through the downtown area in search of Mexican zoot suiters, but Blacks and Filipinos were also attacked. At one theatre, the mob stormed into the building, switched the lights on, and dragged out persons they considered zoot suiters. The riots stopped when the commanding officers of the local bases placed the downtown section and the barrio off limits. This was done only after the Mexican government put pressure on officials in Washington to quell the disturbances, and the State Department, which was aware of the negative international attention that the riots were receiving, ordered the Navy and Marine Corps to act since it appeared that local Los Angeles officials would not.[20]

Mexican Americans accounted for one-fifth of the total casualties from Los Angeles in World War II, although they comprised only one-tenth of the city's population. Some of the GIs returned as heroes to the barrio. Private José Martínez, who died in the Philippines, had a local post of the American Legion in Los Angeles named after him. Nationwide, Mexican Americans returned as the most decorated ethnic group in the armed services, winning seventeen Medals of Honor.[21] Those who did not receive Medals of Honor often gained in other ways from their experiences in the service. Many soon applied the skills that they learned while in uniform to civilian life.

When Mexican American servicemen returned, they discovered that the east side had undergone profound changes. The Sleepy Lagoon case and the "zoot suit riots" were still fresh in the minds of most residents, as was the internment of Japanese Americans from the neighboring communities. The defense of the Mexican American youths involved in the Sleepy Lagoon case had unleashed a new political awareness among eastside residents. This new political stirring was apparent when thirty residents of East Los Angeles organized the Community Service Organization (CSO). Unlike the mutual aid or voluntary associations of the previous generation, the CSO claimed no allegiance to Mexico, nor did its members assign a leadership role to the local Mexican consul. One of its early leaders was Edward Roybal, a college graduate and veteran of World War II.[22]

Unquestionably, the Mexican American veterans gave the eastside community a new political profile in the immediate postwar years. The old political climate began to change with the veterans' persistent challenging of Jim Crow laws and discriminatory practices. In Los Angeles as well as across the Southwest, when a Mexican American veteran or war hero was denied service in a restaurant or burial in the local cemetery, there was likely to be some press coverage. Veterans became indignant over these occurrences; they felt they deserved better treatment for having served in defense of their country. In East Los Angeles some of the veterans formed a chapter of the American GI Forum, a Mexican American organization founded in Texas by World War II veterans.[23]

In the League of United Latin American Citizens (LULAC), the barrio residents of Los Angeles and surrounding communities found an ally in challenging the segregation of children in the public schools. Parents from several southern California communities banded together in 1945 to sue the Westminster School District for placing their children in segregated classrooms. The Mexican American parents won their case in the courts and gained an additional victory on June 14, 1946, when Governor Earl Warren signed into law a repeal of the last remaining school segregation statutes in California's Educational Code.[24] Although the case would set an important precedent in other states, the court ruling still had limitations, since it did not affect de facto segregation which prevailed in barrio communities such as East Los Angeles. Nonetheless, it was an important first step for Mexican Americans.

The postwar years were also marked by increased political activism aimed at obtaining local political representation, metropolitan services and improvements, and equity in the judicial system. In a 1946 city council race, Edward Roybal campaigned for better streets, community recreational facilities, and an end to police harassment of juveniles. He lost the race, but the experience prepared him for the 1949 campaign, which he won. His victory made him the first Mexican American to serve in City Hall since 1881. Other returning veterans such as Julian Nava, who later became the first Mexican American to serve as Ambassador to Mexico, also attended colleges under the GI Bill. Nava, whose parents had barely escaped repatriation during the 1930s, began his college career at nearby Pomona College and eventually earned a doctorate in history from Harvard. From this generation of Mexican American veterans came a new class of college-educated professionals, including lawyers, teachers, parole officers, and doctors.[25]

Most second-generation Mexican Americans, either by choice or as a result of exclusion from Anglo communities, lived on the east side by 1950. Although the state of California outlawed restrictive covenants in 1948, real estate agents, developers, and lending institutions found ways to keep Mexicanos out of the Anglo neighborhoods. A study by Eshref Shevky and Molly Levine completed in 1949 confirmed the residential concentration of Mexican Americans. Nearly 75 percent of the Mexican Americans, the study showed, lived in three of southern California's twenty-nine census tracts. Almost half of them lived in East Los Angeles, especially Belvedere, Boyle Heights, Chávez Ravine, and Lincoln Heights, the population core of the east side.[26] When Mexican Americans moved outside the core of the east side, they frequently went farther east into communities such as Monterrey Park, Azusa, and Alhambra.

Barrio residents faced two major problems during the 1950s: discrimination in housing and employment and the intrusion of freeways and public structures upon their community. Under the auspices of Urban Renewal, giant earth movers began carving up East Los Angeles in the mid-1950s. The old barrio of Chávez Ravine had already disappeared, a victim of the construction of a new home for the Los Angeles Dodgers. Angry homeowners had taken the city of Los Angeles to court in a futile attempt to keep the Dodger organization from destroying their neighborhood.[27] The displaced homeowners eventually left the Ravine, with its splendid view of City Hall and downtown, for the crowded east side. Their move to the east side coincided with the influx of thousands of new migrants from Mexico. Pulled to southern California by economic forces and aided in their journey by the continuing Bracero Program, these new migrants represented the first postwar migration wave from Mexico.

In the late 1950s the massive construction of freeways linking the Anglo suburban communities with the central business core began. High overpasses and expansive six-lane freeways crisscrossed the east side. Thousands of residents from Boyle Heights, Lincoln Heights, City Terrace, and surrounding neighborhoods were relocated.[28] The freeways divided the neighborhoods without consideration for the residents' loyalties to churches, schools, businesses, or family. Residents, especially the young and the aged, became increasingly isolated from other areas of town as the massive layers of grey concrete and asphalt eliminated the trolley lines and disrupted public transit service. The daily trek of hundreds of thousands of autos left a gloomy grey cloud of smog hanging over the east side. Only on a rare day could the eastsiders catch a glimpse of the nearby mountains or downtown skyline.

With the massive migration of Mexicans into southern California during the 1950s and 1960s, Los Angeles solidified its position as the Mexican capital of the United States. Many of the migrants who settled in Los Angeles entered the Golden State destined for the agricultural fields of the Imperial Valley or the San Joaquín Valley. Los Angeles' remarkable industrial and commercial growth demanded a steady supply of unskilled, semiskilled, and service workers. By the 1960s, "Los Angeles had become the major destination for Mexican immigrants and Mexican in-migrants from other areas of the southwest."[29] While many were attracted to the metropolis by the prospect of steady work, others came because of the high wages paid in Los Angeles. The city ranked among the top five cities in the Southwest in terms of family income.[30] In the crowded east side, the newcomers found inexpensive housing, businesses where Spanish was spoken, and restaurants that appealed to their appetites.

New windows were opened into East Los Angeles during the late 1960s and early 1970s as a result of protest movements among high school students, antiwar demonstrations, and picketing of area supermarkets by members of the United Farmworkers Union. Between 1967 and 1972, rallies featuring César Chávez, land grant leader Reies López Tijerina, and Black Power activists became common in the community. A Chicano antiwar movement mobilized thousands of citizens to protest the war during the early 1970s. This social and political activity gave birth to a Chicano Movement, which attempted, with considerable success, to instill ethnic pride, call attention to inequities in the judicial system, and give rise to new political consciousness. From this movement also emerged La Raza Unida Party and Chicano Studies programs in colleges and high schools throughout the city. Chicanismo found expression not only in the political arena, but also in the mural art, music, and literature of the people of Mexican origin.

In Los Angeles, "the capital of MexAmerica," the question of "limits" isn't important, according to Joel Garreau, author of *The Nine Nations of North America*. "After all," writes Garreau, "seven million people demonstrably can live in a Los Angeles Basin which God saw fit to endow with the resources to support only two hundred thousand."[31] However, the question of limits has eastsiders concerned. Over the past twenty years, the Mexican population of East Los Angeles has grown from one million to nearly two million.

The crucial question, of course, is that of the quality of life. On the east side, where there is a serious housing shortage and many of the existing houses are of substandard construction, where the schools are overcrowded and the children often poorly educated, where traffic congestion has become a way of life, where smog alerts are still too common, and where residents have but little command over their economic and political destiny, the problems of urban growth are ever present in residents' minds. Lacking ethnic political representation in city and county elected offices, eastsiders have had difficulty in presenting their views on the type of community that their children will inherit. The emergence of United Neighborhood Organizations (UNO), a highly successful grass-roots organization which recently has won some important municipal battles, has raised the hopes of many citizens that they can influence the direction of social, economic, and political development.

The "city within a city" has changed to a "metropolis within a megalopolis" in the post–World War II years, and eastsiders have demonstrated a renewed pride in living east of the Los Angeles River—a pride largely based on the knowledge that they, Los Mexicanos, have had an important role in creating one of the great ethnic marvels of urban America.

Notes

1. Introduction

1. In 1930 the U.S. Bureau of the Census estimated the Mexican population of the city at 97,116 and the number of Mexicans in the county at 167,000 (*Fifteenth Census of the United States: 1930, Population*, vol. 2, pp. 266–267, 287). Hazel D. Santiago, a social worker, estimated that the enrollment of 35,921 Mexican children in the Los Angeles public schools in 1928 suggested a Mexican population in the city of 190,000 ("Mexican Influence in Southern California," *Sociology and Social Research* 16 [September 1931]: 69–73). Another social worker, Linna E. Bresette, who interviewed church officials concerning religious services to Mexicans during the late 1920s, believed that perhaps 250,000 came closer to a true figure (*Mexicans in the United States: A Report of a Brief Survey to the Catholic Welfare Conference* [Washington, D.C., 1929], p. 8).

2. Stephan Thernstrom, *The Other Bostonians: Poverty and Progress in the American Metropolis, 1880–1970* (Cambridge, Mass.: Harvard Univ. Press, 1973); idem, *Poverty and Progress: Social Mobility in a Nineteenth Century City* (New York: Atheneum, 1971; 1st ed., Cambridge, Mass.: Harvard Univ. Press, 1964). See also Leo F. Schnore, ed., *The New Urban History: Quantitative Explorations by American Historians* (Princeton: Princeton Univ. Press, 1975); William O. Aydelotte, Allan G. Bogue, and Robert W. Fogel, *The Dimensions of Quantitative Research in History* (Princeton: Princeton Univ. Press, 1972).

3. See, for instance, Thomas Kessner, *The Golden Door: Italian and Jewish Immigrant Mobility in New York City, 1880–1915* (New York: Oxford Univ. Press, 1977); Peter R. Knight, *The Plain People of Boston, 1830–1860* (New York: Oxford Univ. Press, 1971); and Humberto Nelli, *The Italians in Chicago, 1880–1930: A Study in Ethnic Mobility* (New York: Oxford Univ. Press, 1970). The recent publication of Albert Camarillo, *Chicanos in a Changing Society: From Mexican Pueblos to American Barrios in Santa Barbara and Southern California, 1848–1930* (Cambridge, Mass.: Harvard Univ. Press, 1979), is principally devoted to Mexicans in Santa Barbara. See also Mario García, *Desert Immigrants: The Mexicans of El Paso, 1880–1920* (New Haven: Yale Univ.

Press, 1981), and Richard Griswold del Castillo, *The Los Angeles Barrio, 1850–1890: A Social History* (Berkeley: Univ. of California Press, 1979).

4. Gunther Barth, *Instant Cities: Urbanization and the Rise of San Francisco and Denver* (New York: Oxford Univ. Press, 1975); Frederick Jackson Turner, *The Frontier in American History* (New York: Holt, Rinehart and Winston, 1962; 1st ed., 1920); and Gerald D. Nash, *The American West in the Twentieth Century: A Short History of an Urban Oasis* (Englewood Cliffs, N.J.: Prentice-Hall, 1973).

5. U.S. Bureau of the Census, *Fifteenth Census, 1930, Population*, vol. 1, Table 23.

6. For an economic and social profile of early nineteenth-century Los Angeles, see, for example: Jackson Alpheus Graves, *My Seventy Years in California, 1857–1927* (Los Angeles: Times-Mirror Press, 1927); James Miller Guinn, *Los Angeles and Environs* (Los Angeles: Historic Record Co., 1915); W. W. Robinson, *Ranchos Become Cities* (Pasadena: San Pasqual Press, 1939); Harris Newmark, *Sixty Years in Southern California, 1853–1913*, ed. Maurice H. Newmark and Marco R. Newmark (New York: Knickerbocker Press, 1916); and Boyle Workman, *The City That Grew*, ed. Caroline Walker (Los Angeles: Southland Publishing Co., 1935).

7. David J. Weber, *Foreigners in Their Native Land: Historical Roots of the Mexican Americans* (Albuquerque: Univ. of New Mexico Press, 1973), p. 151; Rodolfo Acuña, *Occupied America: The Chicano Struggle for Liberation* (San Francisco: Canfield Press, 1972), pp. 108–118.

8. Leonard Pitt, *The Decline of the Californios: A Social History of the Spanish-Speaking Californians, 1846–1890* (Berkeley and Los Angeles: Univ. of California Press, 1966), pp. 149, 263; Griswold del Castillo, *The Los Angeles Barrio.*

9. Earl Pomeroy, *The Pacific Slope: A History of California, Oregon, Washington, Idaho, Utah, and Nevada* (Seattle: Univ. of Washington Press, 1965), pp. 107, 141; Carey McWilliams, *Southern California: An Island on the Land* (New York: Duell, Sloan, and Pearce, 1946), pp. 125–127; Walton E. Bean, *California: An Interpretive History* (New York: McGraw-Hill, 1973), p. 277.

10. See, for example, Joseph Hergesheimer, "The Magnetic West," *Saturday Evening Post* 195 (January 6, 1923): 32, 35, 36, 38; James H. Collins, "Los Angeles Grows by a Formula," *Southern California Business* 12 (September 1933): 18–19; Garet Garrett, "Los Angeles in Fact and Dream," *Saturday Evening Post* 203 (October 18, 1930): 7, 134ff.

11. U.S. Bureau of the Census, *Thirteenth Census of the United States Taken in the Year 1910*, vol. 1, *Population*, pp. 854–855; *Fourteenth Census of the United States Taken in the Year 1920*, vol. 4, *Population*, pp. 729–731; and *Fifteenth Census, 1930, Population*, vol. 1, pp. 248–250.

12. Bruce Bliven, "Los Angeles: The City That Is Bacchanalian—in a Nice

Way," *New Republic* 51 (July 13, 1927): 198–199; Shannon Crandall, "Industrial Los Angeles County," *Southern California Business* 8 (June 1928): 9–11. An excellent analysis of Los Angeles' rise to metropolitan status is provided by Stephan Thernstrom, *The Growth of Los Angeles in Historical Perspective: Myth and Reality* (Los Angeles: Institute of Government and Public Affairs, Univ. of California, Los Angeles, 1970).

13. Maldwyn A. Jones, *Destination America* (New York: Holt, Rinehart and Winston, 1976), p. 225.

14. Mark Reisler, *By the Sweat of Their Brow: Mexican Immigrant Labor in the United States, 1900–1940* (Westport, Conn.: Greenwood Press, 1976), pp. 26–28.

15. Charles S. Johnson found employers prejudiced against both Blacks and Mexicans in his unpublished "Industrial Survey of the Negro Population of Los Angeles, California" (National Urban League, 1926). Details of Johnson's survey were made available to me by the National Urban League office in New York City through Professor Emory Tolbert.

16. See, for example, Emory S. Bogardus, "The Mexican Immigrant and Segregation," *American Journal of Sociology* 36 (July 1930): 74–80; Harvey A. Levenstein, "The AFL and Mexican Immigration in the 1920s: An Experiment in Labor Diplomacy," *Hispanic American Historical Review* 48 (May 1968): 206–219; Eva Frank, "The Mexican 'Just Won't Work,'" *Nation* 125 (August 17, 1927): 155–157; Ernesto Galarza, "Without Benefit of Lobby," *Survey Graphic* 66 (May 1, 1931): 181; Carl L. May, "Our Anti-Social Mexican Population," *Los Angeles County Employee* 2 (1929): 12–13.

17. Robert Fogelson, *The Fragmented Metropolis: Los Angeles, 1850–1930*. (Cambridge, Mass.: Harvard Univ. Press, 1967), p. 188.

18. See Ricardo Romo, "The Urbanization of Southwestern Chicanos in the Early Twentieth Century," *New Scholar* 6 (1977): 185.

19. Nash, *The American West in the Twentieth Century*, p. 11.

20. Fogelson, *The Fragmented Metropolis*, pp. 138, 187, 188.

21. Ralph Thomlinson, *Urban Structure: The Social and Spatial Character of Cities* (New York: Random House, 1969), p. 194. For an expression of this theory, see Robert E. Park, "Human Migration and the Marginal Man," *American Journal of Sociology* 33 (May 1928): 881–893; and Robert E. Park and Ernest W. Burgess, *The City* (Chicago: Univ. of Chicago Press, 1925).

22. Manuel Gamio, *Mexican Immigration to the United States: A Study of Human Migration and Adjustment* (Chicago: Univ. of Chicago Press, 1930), p. 73.

23. Carey McWilliams, *North from Mexico: The Spanish-Speaking People of the United States* (Philadelphia: J. B. Lippincott, 1949), pp. 212–213.

24. David R. Hunter, *The Slums: Challenge and Response* (New York: Free Press, 1968), p. 59.

25. Sam Bass Warner, Jr., and Colin B. Burke, "Cultural Change and the Ghetto," *Journal of Contemporary History* 4 (1969): 187.
26. Sam Bass Warner, Jr., *The Urban Wilderness* (New York: Harper and Row, 1972), p. 107.
27. J. Lilly, "Metropolis of the West," *North American Review* 232 (September 1931): 240.
28. U.S. Bureau of the Census, *Thirteenth Census, 1910,* vol. 2, *Population,* pp. 180, 185; *Fourteenth Census, 1920,* vol. 2, *Population,* p. 125; *Fifteenth Census, 1930, Population,* vol. 2, pp. 73–78.
29. Leo Grebler, Joan W. Moore, and Ralph C. Guzman, *The Mexican-American People: The Nation's Second Largest Minority* (New York: Free Press, 1970), p. 301.
30. Robert A. Divine, *American Immigration Policy, 1924–1952* (New Haven: Yale Univ. Press, 1957); Emory S. Bogardus, "The Mexican Immigrant and the Quota," *Sociology and Social Research* 12 (March–April 1928): 371–378.
31. Some of the characteristics of that new urban Mexican American culture are reflected in the composition of *corridos* (ballads). See for example, "El Radio y Chicanos" (1926), discussed in Ricardo Romo, "Los Chicanos del Oeste en el Siglo XX," *Las culturas hispánicas en los estados unidos de América* (Madrid: Asociación Cultural Hispano Norteamericana, 1978), p. 43.
32. For a fuller discussion of the persistence of their native language among the Spanish-speaking immigrants, see Joshua A. Fishman, *Language and Loyalty in the United States: The Maintenance and Perpetuation of Non-English Mother Tongues by American Ethnic and Religious Groups* (The Hague: Mouton, 1966), pp. 280–317.

2. Prelude to the Barrio

1. See. W. W. Robinson, "Story of Ord's Survey As Disclosed by the Los Angeles Archives," *Historical Society of Southern California Quarterly (HSSCQ)* 19 (September–December 1937): 121; Carl I. Wheat, ed., "The Ord Maps of Southern California," *HSSCQ* 18 (March 1936): 20.
2. "Diary of Juan Crespi," in Herbert E. Bolton, *Fray Juan Crespi, Missionary Explorer* (Berkeley: Univ. of California Press, 1927), pp. 146–154. See also John and LaRee Caughey, *Los Angeles: Biography of a City* (Berkeley and Los Angeles: Univ. of California Press, 1976), p. 50.
3. Quoted by Donald C. Cutter, "Report on Rancho El Encino," *HSSCQ* 43 (June 1961): 201. See also Francisco Palou, *Historical Memoirs of New California,* trans. and ed. Herbert E. Bolton, 4 vols. (Berkeley: Univ. of California Press, 1926), 2: 137–138; and Pedro Fages, *A Historical, Political and Natural Description of California,* trans. and ed. Herbert I. Priestly (Berkeley: Univ. of California Press, 1937).
4. "Neve's Instruction to Fages, His Successor," in Edwin A. Beilharz, *Felipe de Neve: First Governor of California* (San Francisco: California

Historical Society, 1971), p. 165; "Translation of Portion of Order of Governor Felipe de Neve for Founding of Los Angeles," *Historical Society of Southern California Annual Publications* 15, Part 2 (1931): 154–155.

5. See Walton E. Bean, *California: An Interpretive History* (New York: McGraw-Hill, 1973), pp. 46–47; R. F. Heizer and M. A. Whipple, eds., *The California Indians: A Source Book* (Berkeley: Univ. of California Press, 1971), pp. 71, 119–120, 238. General studies of early Los Angeles include: John Steven McGroarty, *Los Angeles from the Mountains to the Sea*, 3 vols. (Chicago: American Historical Society, 1921); Morrow Mayo, *Los Angeles* (New York: Knopf, 1933); Remi A. Nadeau, *Los Angeles: From Mission to Modern City* (New York: Longmans, Green and Co., 1960); Harry Carr, *Los Angeles: City of Dreams* (New York: Grosset and Dunlap, 1935); and James Miller Guinn, *Los Angeles and Environs* (Los Angeles: Historic Record Co., 1915).

6. Theodoro de Croix, "Instructions for the Recruitment of the Original Settlers of the Pueblo of Los Angeles," trans. Marion Parks, *Historical Society of Southern California Annual Publications* 15, Part 1 (1931): 135; Fray Zephyrin Engelhardt, *The Missions and Missionaries of California*, vol. 2, *Upper California* (Santa Barbara, 1930), p. 368.

7. Thomas Workman Temple II, "First Census of Los Angeles," *Historical Society of Southern California Annual Publications* 15 (1931): 148–149. See also "Translation of Portion of Order of Governor Felipe de Neve for Founding of Los Angeles," *Historical Society of Southern California Annual Publications* 15, Part 2 (1931): 154–155.

8. Beilharz, *Felipe de Neve*, p. 165. For a similar viewpoint, see Nellie Van de Grift Sánchez, *Spanish Arcadia* (San Francisco: Powell Publishing Co., 1929), p. 9.

9. C. Alan Hutchinson, *Frontier Settlement in Mexican California: The Hijar-Padres Colony and Its Origin, 1789–1835* (New Haven: Yale Univ. Press, 1969), p. 61; Jack D. Forbes, "Black Pioneers: The Spanish-Speaking Afroamericans of the Southwest," in George E. Frakes and Curtis B. Solberg, eds., *Minorities in California History* (New York: Random House, 1971), p. 24.

10. Forbes, "Black Pioneers," pp. 20–33; Temple, "First Census of Los Angeles"; J. Gregg Layne, "The First Census of the Los Angeles District," *HSSCQ* 18 (June 1936): 99–105.

11. Caughey and Caughey, *Los Angeles*, p. 75; W. W. Robinson, "The Domínguez Rancho," *HSSCQ* 35 (December 1953): 343–346; "The Domínguez Family, 1791–1956," *HSSCQ* 38 (December 1956): 366–372. The remarks of Fray Vicente Santa María are cited by Caughey and Caughey, *Los Angeles*, p. 76.

12. Hubert Howe Bancroft, *History of California* (San Francisco: A. L. Bancroft, 1884–1890), 19: 175.

13. Ibid., 20: 643; 19: 354–356. The early history of Mission San Gabriel is discussed in John S. McGroarty, *California: Its History and Romance* (Los Angeles, 1911), pp. 77–78, 95, 167; see also Fray Zephyrin En-

gelhardt, *San Gabriel Mission and the Beginnings of Los Angeles* (San Gabriel: Franciscan Herald Press, 1927).

14. José del Carmen Lugo, "Life of a Rancher," *HSSCQ* 32 (September 1950): 185–236.

15. Robert F. Heizer and Alan F. Almquist, *The Other Californians: Prejudice and Discrimination under Spain, Mexico and the United States to 1920* (Berkeley: Univ. of California Press, 1971), p. 6.

16. Ibid., p. 7. See also Tomás Almaguer, *Interpreting Chicano History: The "World System" Approach to 19th Century California* (Berkeley: Institute for the Study of Social Change, 1977), pp. 17–20.

17. Bancroft, *History of California,* 19: 355.

18. Cited by Robert G. Cleland, *From Wilderness to Empire* (New York: Macmillan, 1922), p. 78.

19. The Bancroft Library at the University of California, Berkeley, has the best collection of documents pertaining to the Californios. See, for example: José del Carmen Lugo, "Vida de un ranchero . . ." (1877; translated as "Life of a Rancher,"—see note 14 above); Mariano Guadalupe Vallejo, "Documentos para la historia de California" (1874): Thomas Savage, "Documentos para la historia de California" (1876– 1879).
Two interesting biographies dealing with ranch work are Arnold R. Rojas, *The Vaquero* (Charlotte, N.C.: McNally and Loftin, 1964); and Joseph J. Mora, *Californios: The Saga of the Hardriding Vaqueros* (Garden City, N.Y.: Doubleday and Co., 1949).

20. Lugo, "Life of a Rancher," pp. 215–216. For additional insights, see J. N. Bowman, "Prominent Women of Provincial California," *HSSCQ* 39 (June 1957): 159; and Terry E. Stephenson, *Don Bernardo Yorba* (Los Angeles: Glen Dawson, 1941).

21. Mariano Guadalupe Vallejo, "Ranch and Mission Days in Alta California," *Century Magazine* 41 (December 1890): 183.

22. Clarice Bennett, "A History of Rancho La Brea to 1900" (Master's thesis, Univ. of Southern California, 1938), p. 3.

23. LeRoy R. Hafen and Carl C. Rister, *Western America* (Englewood Cliffs, N.J.: Prentice-Hall, 1950), p. 222; John G. Neihardt, *The Splendid Wayfaring* (Lincoln: Univ. of Nebraska Press, 1971), pp. 239, 258.

24. Bancroft, *History of California,* 20: 393; Iris Higbie Wilson, *William Wolfskill, 1798–1866: Frontier Trapper to California Ranchero* (Glendale, Calif.: Arthur H. Clark Co., 1965), p. 78.

25. Marie E. Northrop, ed., "The Los Angeles Padron As Copied from the Los Angeles City Archives," *HSSCQ* 42 (December 1960): 360–422.

26. Alfred Robinson, *Life in California* (Santa Barbara: Peregrine Press, 1970), p. 44 (originally published in 1846). Robinson, a native of Massachusetts and an adoptive Californian from 1829, married into an influential California family by his union with Ana María de la Guerra y Noriega in 1837.

27. Leonard Pitt, *The Decline of the Californios: A Social History of the Spanish-Speaking Californians, 1846–1890* (Berkeley and Los Angeles: Univ. of California Press, 1966), pp. 120–130; David J. Weber,

ed., *Foreigners in Their Native Land: Historical Roots of the Mexican Americans* (Albuquerque: Univ. of New Mexico Press, 1973), pp. 209–210.

28. George Tays, ed and trans., "Pio Pico's Correspondence with the Mexican Government, 1846–1848," *California Historical Quarterly* 13 (June 1934): 148–149; Helen Tyler, "The Family of Pico," *HSSCQ* 35 (September 1953): 221–238.

29. E. Gould Buffum, *Six Months in the Gold Mines* (Philadelphia, 1850), quoted by Caughey and Caughey, *Los Angeles*, p. 120.

30. John A. Hawgood, "The Pattern of Yankee Infiltration in Mexican Alta California, 1821–1846," *Pacific Historical Review* 27 (February 1958): 27–37.

31. Stephen Clark Foster, *El Quacheno: How I Want to Help Make the Constitution of California* (Los Angeles: Dawson's Book Shop, 1949), p. 7.

32. Bancroft, *History of California*, 20: 745.

33. M. Colette Standart, "The Sonora Migration to California, 1848–1856: A Study in Prejudice," *HSSCQ* 58 (Fall 1976): 334.

34. "Los Angeles in 1849: A Letter from John S. Griffin, M.D., to Col. J. D. Stevenson March 11, 1849," in Carlos Cortés, ed., *Mexicans in California* (New York: Arno Press, 1976), p. 9.

35. Antonio Franco Coronel, "Cosas de California," in Richard Morefield, *The Mexican Adaptation in American California, 1846–1875* (San Francisco: RCE Publishers, 1971), pp. 140–186. See also José Fernández, "A Californian's View of the Gold Rush" in John Caughey, *California Heritage* (Los Angeles: Ward Ritchie Press, 1962), pp. 218–225.

36. *Alta Californian*, March 1851; Standart, "The Sonora Migration to California," p. 348. J. R. Scott, Justice of the Peace, reported an 1850 population of 1,610 inhabitants "exclusive of non–tax paying Indians and living in two hundred and seventy-four dwellings" (Marco R. Newmark, comp., "Ordinances and Regulations of Los Angeles, 1832–1888," *HSSCQ* 30 (March 1948): 34.

37. Cleland, *From Wilderness to Empire*, p. 255; Gunther Barth, *Instant Cities: Urbanization and the Rise of San Francisco and Denver* (New York: Oxford Univ. Press, 1975), p. 121.

38. Robert G. Cleland, *A History of California: The American Period* (New York: Macmillan, 1922), pp. 303–321; James M. Guinn, "The Passing of the Cattle Barons of California," *Historical Society of Southern California Annual Publications* 1 (1890): 33–39.

39. W. W. Robinson, *Ranchos Become Cities* (Pasadena: San Pasqual Press, 1939), p. 100; see also Standart, "The Sonora Migration to California," p. 348.

40. Morefield, *The Mexican Adaptation*, p. 31.

41. Coronel's political career is discussed in "Las Familias de California: Antonio Franco Coronel," *HSSCQ* 43 (March 1961): 102. See also Newmark, comp., "Ordinances and Regulations of Los Angeles," p. 36; Marco R. Newmark, "Antonio Franco Coronel," *HSSCQ* 36 (1954):

161–162; "Antonio Franco Coronel," *HSSCQ* 43 (March 1961): 102; *Los Angeles Star*, May 14, 1853; Harris Newmark, *Sixty Years in Southern California, 1853–1913*, ed. Maurice H. Newmark and Marco R. Newmark (New York: Knickerbocker Press, 1916).

42. Henry Winfred Splitter, "Education in Los Angeles: 1850–1900," *HSSCQ* 33 (June 1951): 104, 105.

43. Ibid., pp. 101, 103, 104.

44. Richard Griswold del Castillo, "Myth and Reality: Chicano Economic Mobility in Los Angeles, 1850–1880," *Aztlán* 6 (1975): 153–154.

45. Pitt, *The Decline of the Californios*, p. 183. See also Maymie R. Krythe, "Daily Life in Early Los Angeles," *HSSCQ* 36 (March 1954): 28–39.

46. *El Clamor Público*, March 1, 1856.

47. *El Clamor Público*, July 26, 1856. For an excellent discussion of Ramírez' career, see Pitt, *The Decline of the Californios*, Chapter 11, pp. 181–194; Rodolfo Acuña, *Occupied America: A History of Chicanos* (New York: Harper and Row, 1981), pp. 109–117.

48. James M. Guinn, "Exceptional Years: A History of California Floods and Droughts," *Historical Society of Southern California Annual Publications 1 (1890): 36.

49. Pitt, *The Decline of the Californios*, pp. 246–248.

50. Ibid., p. 252. According to Iris H. Wilson, William Wolfskill's ledger book contained the accounts of many pueblo citizens. During the late 1840s and in 1850, Wolfskill lent money to such prominent citizens as Pico, Castro, Sepúlveda, Bandini, Stearns, Carrillo, Lugo, Vallego, Yorba, Olivera, Alvarado, and Figueroa. He lent in amounts from $300 to $10,000, at an interest rate of 1–2 percent per month (Wilson, *William Wolfskill*, p. 196).

51. "The Domínguez Family, 1791–1956," *HSSCQ* 38 (December 1956): 370.

52. Tyler, "The Family of Pico," pp. 228–238.

53. Newmark, *Sixty Years in Southern California*, p. 396. One of the city's most notable adobes, that of José Antonio Carrillo, was razed in order to make way for Pico's eighty-room hotel. See also Oscar Lawler, "The Pico House," *HSSCQ* 35 (December 1953): 335–342; Frank B. Putnam, "Pico's Building: Its Genealogy and Biography," *HSSCQ* 39 (March 1957): 74–89.

54. Cited by Richard Reinhart, "On the Brink of the Boom: Southern California in 1877, As Witnessed by Mrs. Frank Leslie," *California Historical Quarterly* 52 (Spring 1973): 65–66.

55. Cited by Earl Pomeroy, *The Pacific Slope: A History of California, Oregon, Washington, Idaho, Utah, and Nevada* (Seattle, Univ. of Washington Press; 1965), p. 141. See also Henry W. Splitter, "Los Angeles As Described by Contemporaries, 1850–1890," *HSSCQ* 37 (June 1955): 125–138.

56. Pomeroy, *The Pacific Slope*, p. 143.

57. Glenn S. Dumke, *The Boom of the Eighties in Southern California*,

4th ed. (San Marino, Calif.: Huntington Library, 1955); Newmark, *Sixty Years in Southern California*, p. 572.

58. Sister Clementia Marie, "The First Families of La Ballona Valley," *HSSCQ* 37 (March 1955): 48.
59. Newmark, *Sixty Years in Southern California*, p. 581.
60. Henry Huntington's efforts to build a major harbor in Santa Monica are discussed by Charles D. Willard, *The Free Harbor Contest at Los Angeles* (Los Angeles: Kingsley-Barnes and Neuner Co., 1899).
61. Pitt, *The Decline of the Californios*, p. 253; Helen Hunt Jackson, *Ramona: A Story* (Boston: Roberts Brothers, 1887).
62. Newmark, *Sixty Years in Southern California*, pp. 605–607; Boyle Workman, *The City That Grew*, ed. Caroline Walker (Los Angeles: Southland Publishing Co., 1935), p. 261. Charles F. Lummis' works include *The Land of Poco Tiempo* (New York: Scribner's, 1893). Lummis is said to have been the first scholar to label the region bordering Mexico the Southwest. See also Christina Weilus Mead, "Las Fiestas de Los Angeles," *HSSCQ* 31 (1949): 61–113.
63. U.S. Bureau of the Census, *Thirteenth Census of the United States Taken in the Year 1910*, vol. 1, *Population*, pp. 207–213.

3. From Homeland to Barrio

1. Donald Fleming and Bernard Bailyn, "Dislocation and Emigration: The Social Background of American Immigration," *Perspectives in American History* 7 (1973): vi.
2. Maldwyn A. Jones, "The Background to Emigration from Great Britain in the Nineteenth Century," *Perspectives in American History* 7 (1973): 3–4.
3. Matías Romero, *Geographical and Statistical Notes on Mexico* (New York: G. P. Putnam's Sons, 1898), p. 1; *Southern Pacific Bulletin*, December 1967, pp. 23–24; Alfredo B. Cuéllar, *La situación financiera de los ferrocarriles nacionales de México con relación* (Mexico City: Universidad Nacional Autónoma de México, 1935), pp. 1–24; Francisco R. Calderón, "Los ferrocarriles," in Daniel Cosío Villegas, ed., *Historia moderna de México*, vol. 1, *El porfiriato: La vida económica* (Mexico City: Editorial Hermes, 1965), pp. 483–491; Frederick C. Turner, *The Dynamic of Mexican Nationalism* (Chapel Hill: Univ. of North Carolina Press, 1968), pp. 95–96.
4. Manuel Gamio, *Mexican Immigration to the United States: A Study of Human Migration and Adjustment* (Chicago: Univ. of Chicago Press, 1930), p. 13. See also idem, *Quantitative Estimate: Sources and Distribution of Mexican Immigration into the United States* (Mexico City, 1930).
5. Paul S. Taylor, *Mexican Labor in the United States: Chicago and the Calumet Region*, Univ. of California Publications in Economics 7, no. 2 (Berkeley, 1932), p. 49.
6. Anna Christine Lofstedt, "A Study of the Mexican Population in Pas-

adena, California" (Master's thesis, Univ. of Southern California, 1922), p. 3.

7. Romero, *Geographical and Statistical Notes on Mexico*, pp. 28, 254; Robert Glass Cleland, *The Mexican Year Book* (Los Angeles: Mexican Year Book Publishing Co., 1922), p. 201.

8. Percy F. Martin, *Mexico of the Twentieth Century* vol. 2 (London: E. Arnold, 1907). See Chapter 45, "State of Nuevo Leon," pp. 81–90.

9. Friedrich Katz, "Labor Conditions on Haciendas in Porfirian Mexico: Some Trends and Tendencies," *Hispanic American Historical Review* 54 (February 1974): 33; Florence C. Lister and Robert H. Lister, *Chihuahua, Storehouse of Storms* (Albuquerque: Univ. of New Mexico Press, 1966), p. 177; Fernando Rosenzweig, "El desarrollo económico de México de 1877 a 1911," *El Trimestre Económico* 33 (July–September 1965): 450.

10. Katz, "Labor Conditions," p. 33.

11. Paul Eiser-Viafora, "Durango and the Mexican Revolution," *New Mexico Historical Quarterly* 49 (1974): 221, 225. For a brief discussion of the mining situation in the northern states, see Stanton Davis Kirkham, *Mexican Trails: A Record of Travel in Mexico, 1904–1907* (New York: G. P. Putnam's Sons, 1909), pp. 273–284.

12. Durango's agrarian production and industries are discussed in Herman Schnitzler, ed., *The Republic of Mexico: Its Agriculture, Commerce and Industries* (New York: N. L. Brown, 1924), pp. 21–22, 84–88, 182–183, 222–224, 312–314, 353–354, 468–469.

13. Colegio de México, *Estadísticas económicas del porfiriato: Fuerza de trabajo y actividad económica por sectores* (Mexico City, n.d.), pp. 30–31; Schnitzler, ed., *The Republic of Mexico*, pp. 84–88.

14. Colegio de México, *Estadísticas*, pp. 38–44, 147; W. E. Weyl, "Labor Conditions in Mexico," *United States Bureau of Labor Bulletin* 7 (January 1902): 1–94. See also John H. Coatsworth, "Railroad, Agrarian Protest, and the Concentration of Landholding in the Early Porfiriato," *Hispanic American Historical Review* 54 (1974): 48–71.

15. Manuel Gamio, *The Life Story of the Mexican Immigrant* (Chicago: Univ. of Chicago Press, 1931), p. 145.

16. Albert Alexander Graham, *Mexico with Comparisons and Conclusions* (Topeka: Crane and Co., 1907), p. 58.

17. Moisés González Navarro, *México: El capitalismo nacionalista* (Mexico City: B. Costa Amic, 1970), pp. 26–27.

18. N. O. Winter, *Mexico and Her People of To-day* (Boston: L. C. Page, 1907), pp. 194–195.

19. George McCutchen McBride, *The Land Systems of Mexico* (New York: American Geographical Society, 1923), p. 155.

20. For an insightful analysis of prerevolutionary economic conditions, see T. Esquivel Obregón, "Factors in the Historical Evolution of Mexico," *Hispanic American Historical Review* 2 (May 1919): 135–172; "The Mexico of 1909," *American Review of Reviews* 40 (1909): 492–493.

21. McBride, *The Land Systems*, pp. 154–155.

22. John Womack, Jr., *Zapata and the Mexican Revolution* (New York:

Knopf, 1968), pp. 42–43; Carlos B. Gil, ed., *The Age of Porfirio Díaz* (Albuquerque: Univ. of New Mexico Press, 1977).

23. Katz, "Labor Conditions," pp. 24, 44; Roger D. Hansen, *The Politics of Mexican Development* (Baltimore: Johns Hopkins Univ. Press, 1971), p. 23.

24. Gamio, *The Life Story of the Mexican Immigrant*, p. 149.

25. Cleland, *The Mexican Year Book*, p. 248.

26. México, Dirección General de Estadística, *Censo general de la población: Resumen 1930*, p. 33.

27. Katz, "Labor Conditions," p. 28.

28. México, Dirección General de Estadística, *Anuario estadístico, 1930*, p. 155.

29. Nathan L. Whetten, *Rural Mexico* (Chicago: Univ. of Chicago Press, 1948), Table 50, p. 261.

30. Colegio de México, *Estadísticas*, pp. 52, 57; John H. Coatsworth, "Anotaciones sobre la production de alimentos durante el porfiriato," *Historia Mexicana* 26 (October–December 1976): 167–187.

31. For contemporary perspectives on American foreign investments in Mexico, see Edward M. Conley, "The Americanization of Mexico," *American Review of Reviews* 32 (December 1905): 724–725; Elisha Hollingsworth Talbot, "The American Invasion of Mexico," *World's Work* 17 (February 1909): 11,274–11,278; David Pletcher, *Rail, Mines, and Progress: Seven American Promoters in Mexico, 1867–1911* (Ithaca: Cornell Univ. Press, 1958).

32. México, Dirección General de Estadística, *Quinto censo de población, 1930*, p. 72. The harsh working conditions in this industry are described by H. A. Franck, "Working in a Mexican Mine," *Century Magazine* 92 (September 1916): 673–683.

33. México, Dirección General de Estadística, *Quinto censo de población, 1930*, p. 72; Colegio de México, *Estadísticas*, p. 32. Although the mining industries suffered from boom-and-bust cycles, the number of mining titles registered with the government averaged 9,000 in the years 1898 and 1899 and soared to more than 30,000 in 1909, with a ten-year high of 32,251 in 1908 (Colegio de México, *Estadísticas*, p. 126).

34. Colegio de México, *Estadísticas*, pp. 106, 108, 48, 113, 119.

35. Ibid., pp. 71 (cotton production), 124 (sugar). A discussion of Mexico's industrial production level is briefly analyzed in "The Mexico of 1909," *American Review of Reviews* 40 (1909): 492–493.

36. Quoted by Gamio, *The Life Story of the Mexican Immigrant*, p. 45.

37. A useful discussion of the workers' situation during the Porfiriato is found in Rodney D. Anderson, "Mexican Workers and the Politics of Revolution, 1906–1911," *Hispanic American Historical Review* 54 (February 1974): 112–114. See also Colegio de México, *Estadísticas*, pp. 45–47.

38. Martin, *Mexico of the Twentieth Century*, 2: 214–215.

39. Interview with Ramón Lizárraga, April 10, 1972, Los Angeles; interview with Abundio Chacón, August 15, 1972, Los Angeles.

40. Graham, *Mexico with Comparisons and Conclusions*, p. 61.

41. Rafael de Zayas Enriques, *Porfirio Díaz*, as quoted in a review in the *Outlook*, December 12, 1908, p. 837.
42. F. León de la Barra, "Present Conditions in Mexico," *Independent* 70 (1911): 545–546.
43. Charles C. Cumberland, *Mexican Revolution: Genesis under Madero* (Austin: Univ. of Texas Press, 1952), pp. 117–119. For a look at the activities of Mexican exiles in the United States during Díaz' last few years in power, see, for instance, James D. Cockcroft, *Intellectual Precursors of the Mexican Revolution, 1900–1913* (Austin: Univ. of Texas Press, 1971), esp. pp. 40, 69, 176; and John M. Hart, *Anarchism and the Mexican Working Class, 1860–1931* (Austin: Univ. of Texas Press, 1978), esp. pp. 88–89.
44. An excellent treatment of the revolutionary period is found in John Womack, Jr., "The Mexican Economy during the Revolution, 1910–1920: Historiography and Analysis," *Marxist Perspectives* (Winter 1978). For a perceptive analysis of the period 1895–1929, see also Arnoldo Córdova, *La ideología de la Revolución Mexicana: La formación del nuevo régimen* (Mexico City, 1973); and James W. Wilkie, *The Mexican Revolution: Federal Expenditure and Social Change since 1910* (Berkeley: Univ. of California Press, 1967).
45. Mexican refugees apparently had no problems crossing into the United States during the Revolution. A few studies documenting this immigration include: Andrés Landa y Piña, *El servicio de migración en México* (Mexico City: Talleres Gráficos de la Nación, 1930); Gamio, *Mexican Immigration to the United States*; Enrique Santibáñez, *Ensayo acerca de la imigración mexicana en los Estados Unidos* (San Antonio: Clegg Co., 1930); John Martínez, "Mexican Emigration to the United States, 1910–1930" (Ph.D. dissertation, Univ. of California, Berkeley, 1957).
46. Patrick O'Bannon, "Railroad Construction in the Twentieth Century: The San Diego and Arizona Railway" (unpublished paper, 1977; Univ. of California, San Diego, Special Collections Central Library), pp. 20, 25.
47. "Exiles Long for Home," *Los Angeles Times*, March 27, 1914; "Refugees Rush Back to Mexico," ibid., January 2, 1916; "Missing Mexicans a Remarkable Mystery: Five Thousand Quit Work and Disappear from Los Angeles County," ibid., April 1, 1917.
48. Margaret L. Holbrook Smith, "The Capture of Tia Juana," *Overland Monthly* 58 (July 1911): 4–5. For other examples, see George Marvin, "The Quick and Dead on the Border," *World's Work* 33 (January 1917): 297–302.
49. Oscar J. Martínez, *Border Boom Town: Ciudad Juárez since 1848* (Austin: Univ. of Texas Press, 1978), pp. 38–56. See also James Hopper, "Twin Towns of the Border," *Collier's* 57 (August 19, 1916): 5–7.
50. "Troops Massed on the Mexican Border," *Independent* 70 (March 16, 1911): 537.
51. Marion Ethel Hamilton, "Insurrecto Prisoners Captured by Uncle Sam," *Overland Monthly* 62 (November 1913): 432–433.

52. "Exiles Long for Home," *Los Angeles Times*, March 27, 1914.

53. Gamio, *The Life Story of the Mexican Immigrant*, p. 49.

54. George Edward Hyde, "A Plain Tale from Mexico," *New Republic* 2 (February 13, 1915): 38.

55. David Lawrence, "Mexico Rebuilding," *Independent* 91 (July 28, 1917): 126–127.

56. "Three Years of Revolution in Mexico," *Outlook*, December 2, 1914, p. 759.

57. Edwin Walter Kemmerer, *Inflation and Revolution: Mexico's Experience of 1912–1917* (Princeton, 1940), pp. 48–49; Francisco Bulnes, *The Whole Truth about Mexico: President Wilson's Responsibility* (New York: M. Bulnes Book Co., 1916), p. 312.

58. Thomas Edward Gibbon, *Mexico under Carranza* (Garden City, N.Y.: Doubleday, Page, 1919), p. 8. The idea of offering asylum in neutral territories within the Republic was suggested by some international observers. See "The Mexican War: Prisoners and Refugees," *Outlook*, January 24, 1914, p. 147.

59. Charles C. Cumberland, *Mexican Revolution: The Constitutionalist Years* (Austin: Univ. of Texas Press, 1972), p. 139.

60. H. Hamilton Fyfe, *The Real Mexico: A Study on the Spot* (London: Heinemann, 1914), p. 5. See also "Three Years of Revolution in Mexico," *Outlook*, December 2, 1914, pp. 759–761.

61. Fyfe, *The Real Mexico*, p. 53. For a description of the war in the western region, see Arthur Dunn, "War on the West Coast," *Sunset* 33 (July 1914): 145–151.

62. "The Situation in Mexico," *Outlook*, August 30, 1913, pp. 1003–1004.

63. Ibid., p. 1004. See also Clarence Senior, *Land Reform and Democracy* (Gainesville: Univ. of Florida Press, 1958), p. 49.

64. Interview with Enrique Félix Vásquez, February 1, 1972, Los Angeles.

65. The midwestern repatriation program is discussed by Neil Betten and Raymund A. Mohl, "From Discrimination to Repatriation: Mexican Life in Gary, Indiana, during the Great Depression," in Norris Hundley, ed., *The Chicano* (Santa Barbara, Calif.: Clio Books, 1975), pp. 124–143.

66. Paul S. Taylor, *A Spanish-Mexican Peasant Community: Arandas in Jalisco, Mexico* (Berkeley: Univ. of California Press, 1933), p. 36.

67. Ernesto Galarza, *Barrio Boy* (Notre Dame: Univ. of Notre Dame Press, 1971), p. 99.

68. "Mexican Invaders Relieving Our Farm-Labor Shortage," *Literary Digest* 66 (July 17, 1920): 54.

69. E. D. Trowbridge, *Mexico To-day and To-morrow* (New York: Macmillan, 1920), p. 169; Taylor, *A Spanish-Mexican Peasant Community*, p. 24; Bulnes, *The Whole Truth*, p. 312.

70. Fyfe, *The Real Mexico*, pp. 67–68. See also "The Mexican Invaders of El Paso," *Survey* 36 (July 8, 1916): 380–381.

71. Interview with Jesús Moreno, November 15, 1972, Los Angeles. American businessmen in Mexico reported in May 1924 that north of Mex-

ico City Mexicans earned from $1.50 to $2.00 (U.S.) per day "and just across the border in the United States wages are about double what they are in Northern Mexico." See "Mexican Labor and Foreign Capital," *Independent* 112 (May 24, 1924): 276.

72. Manuel Gamio, *Forjando patria*, 2d ed. (Mexico City: Porrúa, 1960), p. 147 (originally published in 1916). Carranza's struggles for internal stability are discussed by Douglas W. Richmond, "El nacionalismo de Carranza y los cambios socioeconomicos—1915–1920," *Historia Mexicana* 26 (July–September 1976): 107–131.

73. *La Prensa de Los Angeles*, February 23, 1928.

74. "For a Pan American Movement," *Survey* 36 (July 15, 1916): 402–404; "Mexican Labor Conference in Washington," *Survey* 36 (July 8, 1916): 382. Gompers noted that, in the Arizona mining strikes of 1915, American and Mexican miners had "stood shoulder-to-shoulder" and that he wished to see this type of cooperation extended to both sides of the border ("For a Pan American Movement," p. 402). For a fuller discussion of this interaction, see Ricardo Romo, "Responses to Mexican Immigration, 1910–1930," *Aztlán: International Journal of Chicano Studies Research* 6 (1975): 173–194.

75. Gibbon, *Mexico under Carranza*, p. 31.

76. "The Present State of Mexico," *American Review of Reviews* 56 (September 1917): 281.

77. Ibid.

78. Charles C. Cumberland, *Mexico: The Struggle for Modernity* (New York: Oxford Univ. Press, 1968), p. 372.

79. Chester Lloyd Jones, *Mexico and Its Reconstruction* (New York: D. Appleton and Co., 1921), pp. 206–208. See oil production figures as representative indices of economic growth in Wilkie, *The Mexican Revolution*, p. 197.

80. Cleland, *The Mexican Year Book*, p. 242; Schnitzler, ed., *The Republic of Mexico*, pp. 63, 145, 167; Kemmerer, *Inflation and Revolution*, p. 41.

81. Wayne A. Cornelius, *Mexican Migration to the United States: Causes, Consequences, and U.S. Responses* (Cambridge, Mass.: Center for International Studies, M.I.T., 1978), pp. 13–18. See also Samuel Taylor Moore, "Smuggled Aliens," *Independent* 112 (May 24, 1924): 273–274, 296.

82. Ramón Eduardo Ruiz, *Labor and the Ambivalent Revolutionaries: Mexico, 1911–1923* (Baltimore: Johns Hopkins Univ. Press, 1976), p. 31.

83. From a collection of Calles' speeches published in Plutarco Elías Calles, *Mexico before the World* (New York: New York Academy Press, 1927), p. 59.

84. Whetten, *Rural Mexico*, p. 261; Taylor, *A Spanish-Mexican Peasant Community*, p. 24. Mexicans also encountered difficult times in the United States during the early twenties. See, for example, Lawrence A. Cardoso, "La repatriación de braceros en época de Obregón—1920–

1923," *Historia Mexicana* 26 (April–June 1977): 576–595.

85. Ernest H. Gruening, *Mexico and Its Heritage* (New York: Century Co., 1928), p. 347.

86. Interview with José Novoa, September 8, 1972, Los Angeles.

87. Gamio, *The Life Story of the Mexican Immigrant*, pp. 87–88.

88. Marcelo Villegas, "The Soviet System, Mexican Style: The Red Thread in the Mexican Maze," *Outlook*, October 17, 1928, p. 969.

89. México, Dirección General de Estadística, *Quinto censo de población, 1930*, p. 33.

90. Gamio, *The Life Story of the Mexican Immigrant*, p. 159.

91. Moisés Sáenz and Herbert I. Priestley, *Some Mexican Problems* (Chicago: Univ. of Chicago Press, 1926), pp. 44, 50.

92. Ruiz, *Labor*, p. 94.

93. William English Walling, *The Mexican Question* (New York: Robin Press, 1927), p. 69; see also Rafael Nieto, "Mexico Yesterday and Today," *Living Age* 326 (July 4, 1925): 7–11.

94. Robert E. Quirk, *The Mexican Revolution and the Catholic Church, 1910–1929* (Bloomington: Indiana Univ. Press, 1973), p. 176.

95. Charles W. Hackett, "Mexican President Accused of Bolshevism by Church," *Current History* 25 (October 1926): 120, 121. See also, idem, "Mexican Government Frees Imprisoned Catholics," *Current History* 26 (September 1927): 958–960. In Los Angeles, former Provisional President Adolfo de la Huerta issued a statement on May 15, 1927, that there were more than 30,000 men under arms fighting against the Calles government ("Mexico," *Current History* 26 [July 1927]: 637).

96. Hackett, "Mexican President Accused," p. 121.

97. Carleton Beals, "Civil War in Mexico," *New Republic* 51 (July 6, 1927): 166. See also "Mexico and Central America," *Current History* 26 (May 1927): 310.

98. Taylor, *A Spanish-Mexican Peasant Community*, p. 39.

99. Quirk, *The Mexican Revolution*, p. 208. See also Victor Alba, *The Mexicans: The Making of a Nation* (New York: Praeger, 1967), pp. 161–162; and David C. Bailey, *¡Viva Cristo Rey! The Cristero Rebellion and the Church-State Conflict in Mexico* (Austin: Univ. of Texas Press, 1974), pp. 141–142.

100. Calles, *Mexico before the World*, p. 125. On the agrarian question, see Ricardo J. Zevada, *Calles el presidente* (Mexico City: Nuestro Tiempo, 1971), esp. Chapters 6 and 7; and Frank Tannenbaum, *Peace by Revolution: An Interpretation of Mexico* (New York: Columbia Univ. Press, 1933), pp. 187–257.

101. Sáenz and Priestley, *Some Mexican Problems*, p. 123.

102. Frank Tannenbaum, "Making Mexico Over," *New Republic* 55 (July 18, 1928): 216.

103. Eyler Simpson, *The Ejido, Mexico's Way Out* (Chapel Hill: Univ. of North Carolina Press, 1937), pp. 34–35; Frank R. Brandenburg, *The Making of Modern Mexico* (Englewood Cliffs, N.J.: Prentice-Hall, 1964), p. 69.

104. Calles, *Mexico before the World*, p. 58. A foreign analysis of Mexico's problems with land distribution can be found in "Mexico's Land Problem," *Outlook*, August 20, 1924, pp. 592–593.

105. Interview with Ramón García, October 15, 1972, Los Angeles.

106. "Mexican Labor and Foreign Capital," *Independent* 112 (May 24, 1924): 276.

107. Computed from México, Dirección General de Estadística, *Quinto censo de población, 1930*, p. 3; and México, Dirección General de Estadística, *Anuario estadístico, 1930*, pp. 34, 50–52.

108. Interview with Manuel Terrazas, November 10, 1972, Los Angeles.

109. México, Dirección General de Estadística, *Anuario estadístico, 1942*, p. 321.

110. U.S. Bureau of the Census, *Fifteenth Census of the United States: 1930, Abstract of the Census*, p. 130; Lawrence A. Cardoso, *Mexican Emigration to the United States, 1897–1931: Socio-Economic Patterns* (Tucson: Univ. of Arizona Press, 1980), pp. 53, 94.

4. Creating the Eastside Barrio

1. U.S. Congress, House Committee on Immigration and Naturalization, *Hearings on Seasonal Agricultural Laborers from Mexico*, 69th Cong., 1st sess. (1925–1926), p. 128.

2. Garet Garrett, "Los Angeles in Fact and Dream," *Saturday Evening Post* 203 (October 18, 1930): 142.

3. U.S. Bureau of the Census, *Thirteenth Census of the United States Taken in the Year 1910, Abstract of the Census*, pp. 211, 602; *Fourteenth Census of the United States Taken in the Year 1920*, vol. 2, *Population*, pp. 123–125; *Fifteenth Census of the United States: 1930, Population*, vol. 1, p. 67.

4. William J. Dunkerley, *Know Los Angeles County* (Los Angeles: County Board of Supervisors, 1930), pp. 74–75.

5. U.S. Census Office, *Report on Population of the United States at the Eleventh Census: 1890*, Part 1, pp. 580–583; U.S. Bureau of the Census, *Thirteenth Census, 1910*, vol. 2, *Population*, pp. 180, 185; *Fourteenth Census, 1920*, vol. 2, *Population*, p. 125; *Fifteenth Census, 1930, Population*, vol. 3, p. 287; Oscar O. Winther, "The Rise of Metropolitan Los Angeles, 1870–1900," *Huntington Library Quarterly* 10 (August 1947): 391–405.

6. Carey McWilliams, *Southern California: An Island on the Land* (New York: Duell, Sloan, and Pearce), pp. 165–182.

7. Leo Grebler, *Mexican Immigration to the United States: The Record and Its Implications*, Advance Report 2, Mexican American Study Project (Los Angeles: Graduate School of Business Administration, UCLA, 1966), computed from Table 5, p. 45. See also T. Wilson Longmore and Homer L. Hitt, "A Demographic Analysis of First and Second Generation Mexican Population of the United States: 1930," *Southwestern Social Science Quarterly* 24 (September 1943): 138–149.

8. Edgar Lloyd Hampton, "Los Angeles, a Miracle City," *Current History* 24 (April 1926): 42.

9. Lawrence B. de Graaf, "The City of Black Angels: Emergence of the Los Angeles Ghetto, 1890–1930," *Pacific Historical Review* 39 (1970): 323–326; Charles Wollenberg, "Working on El Traque: The Pacific Electric Strike of 1903," in Norris Hundley, ed., *The Chicano* (Santa Barbara: Clio Books, 1975), p. 103; U.S. Bureau of the Census, *Thirteenth Census, 1910*, vol. 1, *Population*, pp. 854–855; *Fourteenth Census, 1920*, vol. 4, *Population*, pp. 729–731; *Fifteenth Census, 1930, Population*, vol. 2, pp. 248–250.

10. Max J. Bond, "The Negro in Los Angeles" (Ph.D. dissertation, Univ. of Southern California, 1936), p. 34.

11. Lawrence Brooks de Graaf, "Negro Migration to Los Angeles, 1930–1950" (Ph.D. dissertation, Univ. of California, Los Angeles, 1962), p. 19; James McFarline Ervin, "The Participation of the Negro in the Community Life of Los Angeles" (Master's thesis, Univ. of Southern California, 1931), pp. 13–14, 40.

12. Ervin, "The Participation of the Negro," p. 40.

13. Ibid. Charles S. Johnson found similar attitudes among White employers. See his essay, "Negro Workers in Los Angeles Industries," *Opportunity: A Journal of Negro Life* 6 (August 1928): 234–240.

14. Max Vorspan and Lloyd Gartner, *History of the Jews and Los Angeles* (San Marino, Calif.: Huntington Library, 1970), p. 117.

15. U.S. Bureau of the Census, *Fourteenth Census, 1920*, vol. 3, *Population*, p. 125; Carey McWilliams, *Brothers under the Skin* (Boston: Little, Brown and Co., 1944), pp. 280, 290; Harris Newmark, *Sixty Years in Southern California, 1853–1913*, ed. Maurice H. Newmark and Marco R. Newmark (New York: Knickerbocker Press, 1916), pp. 396, 608, 618, 643, 644.

16. Vorspan and Gartner, *History of the Jews of Los Angeles*, pp. 118, 203; U.S. Bureau of the Census, *Fifteenth Census, 1930, Population*, vol., 3, Part 1, pp. 267–269.

17. George M. Day, "Races and Cultural Oases," *Sociology and Social Research* 18 (March–April 1934): 334.

18. Pauline V. Young, "Russian Molokan Community in Los Angeles," *American Journal of Sociology* 35 (1929): 395.

19. Pauline V. Young, *Pilgrims of Russian-Town* (Chicago: Univ. of Chicago, 1932), p. 19.

20. Lillian Sokoloff, "The Russians in Los Angeles," *Sociology Monograph* 3, no. 11 (March 1918): 10. See also Young, "Russian Molokan Community," pp. 393–402.

21. Sokoloff, "The Russians in Los Angeles," p. 6.

22. Day, "Races and Cultural Oases," p. 333. See also George M. Day, "The Russian Colony in Hollywood" (Ph.D. dissertation, Univ. of Southern California, 1930).

23. Religious leader Robert N. McLean reported the arrival of Mexican

families in these communities as early as 1916, but attributed a "mass movement" to the area in 1922 (quoted by Mabelle Ginn, "Social Implication of the Living Conditions of a Selected Number of Families Participating in the Cleland House Program" [Master's thesis, Univ. of Southern California, 1947], p. 17).

24. Spencer Crump, *Ride the Big Red Cars: How Trolleys Helped Build Southern California* (Los Angeles: Trans-Anglo Books, 1962), p. 149.

25. Rufus Steele, "The Red Cars of Empire," *Sunset* 31 (October 1913): 710–717.

26. Crump, *Ride the Big Red Cars*, p. 235; J. Lilly, "Metropolis of the West," *North American Review* 232 (September 1931): 239–245; James H. Collins, "Los Angeles: Ex-Crossroads Town," *World's Work* 59 (August 1930): 53–56.

27. Samuel Bryan, "Mexican Immigrants in the United States," *Survey* 7 (September 1912): 728; Victor S. Clark, "Mexican Labor in the United States," *U.S. Bureau of Labor Statistics Bulletin* 78 (September 1908): 478.

28. For a brief discussion of the satellite barrios, see Christine Lofstedt, "The Mexican Population of Pasadena, California," *Journal of Applied Sociology* 7 (May–June 1923): 260–268; Samuel Maldonado Ortegón, "The Religious Status of the Mexican Population of Los Angeles" (Master's thesis, Univ. of Southern California, 1932); and Helen Walker, "The Conflict of Cultures in First Generation Mexicans in Santa Ana, California" (Master's thesis, Univ. of Southern California, 1928).

29. Clara G. Smith, "The Development of the Mexican People in the Community of Watts, California" (Master's thesis, Univ. of Southern California, 1933), p. 7.

30. Ibid., p. 37.

31. John Emmanuel Kienle, "Housing Conditions among the Mexican Population of Los Angeles" (Master's thesis, Univ. of Southern California, 1912).

32. C. G. Smith, "The Development of the Mexican People," p. 8.

33. Bertha H. Smith, "Dollar Down Can Build a Town," *Sunset* 36 (March 1916): 37.

34. Bond, "The Negro in Los Angeles," p. 44.

35. C. G. Smith, "The Development of the Mexican People," p. 41.

36. Olive P. Kirschner, "The Italian in Los Angeles" (Master's thesis, Univ. of Southern California, 1920), p. 7.

37. Data computed from 1917 and 1918 marriage license applications of the city of Los Angeles. The data are taken from a total sample of 406 marriage applications of Mexican residents in the city.

38. Ibid.

39. William W. McEuen, "A Survey of the Mexican in Los Angeles (1910–1914)" (Master's thesis, Univ. of Southern California, 1914), pp. 73–75.

40. George William Baist, *Baist's Real Estate Atlas of Surveys of Los Angeles* (Philadelphia, 1905), plates 5–12. See also Eshref Shevky and

Marilyn Williams, *The Social Areas of Los Angeles: Analysis and Typology* (Berkeley: Univ. of California Press, 1949), pp. 23–25.

41. G. Bromley Oxnam, "The Mexican in Los Angeles from the Standpoint of the Religious Forces of the City," *Annals of the American Academy of Political and Social Science* 93 (January 1921): 131.
42. Kienle, "Housing Conditions," p. 11.
43. Emory S. Bogardus, *The Mexican in the United States* (Los Angeles: Univ. of Southern California Press, 1934), p. 37.
44. McEuen, "A Survey of the Mexican in Los Angeles," pp. 12–15, 62–63; Emory S. Bogardus, "House-Court Problem," *American Journal of Sociology* 22 (November 1916): 391–399; Elizabeth Fuller, *The Mexican Housing Problem in Los Angeles*, Studies in Sociology Sociological Monograph, no. 17, vol. 5 (November, 1920), p. 3.
45. William H. Matthews, "The House Courts of Los Angeles," *Survey* 5 (July 5, 1913): 461.
46. McEuen, "A Survey of the Mexican in Los Angeles," p. 62.
47. Matthews, "The House Courts of Los Angeles," pp. 462–463.
48. Bogardus, "House-Court Problem."
49. Fuller, *The Mexican Housing Problem*, pp. 3–4.
50. California, Commission of Immigration and Housing (CIH), *Second Annual Report* (Sacramento, 1916), pp. 252–254.
51. Ibid., pp. 259–261.
52. John McDowell, *A Study of Social and Economic Factors Relating to Spanish-Speaking People of the United States* (Philadelphia: Home Missions Council, 1927), p. 16. Oxnam found that prior to the war Mexican laborers earned from $1.60 to $2.80 a day. After the war he placed their average daily salary at $3.45 ("The Mexican in Los Angeles," p. 14). McEuen surveyed sixty-three Mexican workers in five house courts and noted that forty-five earned between $1.75 and $2.25 daily in 1914 ("A Survey of the Mexican in Los Angeles," p. 26).
53. C. G. Smith, "The Development of the Mexican People," p. 41; G. Bromley Oxnam, *The Mexican in Los Angeles: Los Angeles City Survey* (Los Angeles: Interchurch World Movement of North America, 1920), p. 14; Gladys Patric, *A Study of the Housing and Social Conditions in the Ann Street District of Los Angeles, California* (Los Angeles, 1918), p. 11.
54. Leonard Pitt, *The Decline of the Californios: A Social History of the Spanish-Speaking Californians, 1846–1890* (Berkeley and Los Angeles: Univ. of California Press, 1966), p. 264. See also K. F. Tom, "The Participation of the Chinese in the Community Life of Los Angeles" (Master's thesis, Univ. of Southern California, 1944).
55. Walter V. Woehlke, "Los Angeles—Homeland," *Sunset* 36 (January 1911): 11.
56. George William Baist, *Baist's Real Estate Atlas of Surveys of Los Angeles* (Philadelphia, 1910), plates 4, 5, 12; John Steven McGroarty, *History of Los Angeles County* (Chicago: American Historical Society, 1923), 1: 13, 281.

57. Patric, *A Study of the Housing and Social Conditions*, p. 7.
58. Oxnam, "The Mexican in Los Angeles," p. 23.
59. Ibid.
60. Ashliegh E. Brilliant, "Some Aspects of Mass Motorization in Southern California, 1919–1929," *Historical Society of Southern California Quarterly* 47 (1965): 191–206.
61. James H. Collins, "Los Angeles Grows by a Formula," *Southern California Business* 12 (September 1933): 18–19; Los Angeles Chamber of Commerce, *Los Angeles To-Day: City and County* (Los Angeles, 1927), pp. 3–5.
62. Lofstedt, "The Mexican Population of Pasadena," p. 260.
63. Ibid., p. 262.
64. Elizabeth Hymer, "A Study of the Social Attitudes of Adult Mexican Immigrants in Los Angeles and Vicinity, 1923," (Master's thesis, Univ. of Southern California, 1924), pp. 2, 3, 25.
65. John C. Austin, "Pioneering the World's Second Tire Center," *Southern California Business* 8 (February 1929): 9, 10, 47.
66. U.S. Bureau of the Census, *Fifteenth Census, 1930, Population*, vol. 2, p. 266; Ricardo Romo, "The Urbanization of Southwestern Chicanos in the Early Twentieth Century," *New Scholar* 6 (1977): 185.
67. U.S. Bureau of the Census, *Fifteenth Census, 1930, Population*, vol. 3, p. 287; vol. 6, p. 181.
68. Mary J. Desmond, "New Brownson House," *Playground* 22 (November 1928): 456.
69. U.S. Bureau of the Census, *Fifteenth Census, 1930, Population*, vol. 6, p. 181.
70. Crump, *Ride the Big Red Cars*, p. 236.
71. U.S. Bureau of the Census, *Fifteenth Census, 1930, Population*, vol. 2, pp. 259–263.
72. Mary Lanigan, "Second Generation Mexicans in Belvedere" (Master's thesis, Univ. of Southern California, 1932), p. 45.
73. Walter V. Woehlke, "The Land of Sunny Homes," *Sunset* 34 (1915): 472.
74. Oxnam, "The Mexican in Los Angeles," p. 8. (For the 1912 study, see note 31 above.)
75. Figures computed from data published by Los Angeles Directory Company, *Los Angeles City Directory* (Los Angeles: Southern California Publishing Co., 1920–1930).
76. McEuen, "A Survey of the Mexican in Los Angeles," pp. 74–77.
77. U.S. Department of Labor, Bureau of Labor Statistics, "Labor and Social Conditions of Mexicans in California," *Monthly Labor Review* 32 (January 1931): 86–87.
78. Ibid., p. 89.
79. C. G. Smith, "The Development of the Mexican People," p. 10.
80. Ibid., p. 61.
81. Cited by Walker, "The Conflict of Cultures," p. xiv.
82. Ibid., p. xv. See also Helen Walker, "Mexican Immigrants and Ameri-

can Citizenship," *Sociology and Social Research* 13 (May 1929): 465–471.

83. Los Angeles Chamber of Commerce Files: letters located at the City Hall Library under the title "Industrial Surveys of Los Angeles Chamber of Commerce," Box R330-979. The letters were written by local Chamber of Commerce secretaries and presidents to the main headquarters in Los Angeles.

84. *Los Angeles Times*, November 22, 1922.

85. Ibid., January 2, 1916.

86. Orfa Jean Shontz, "The Land of 'Poco Tiempo,'" *Family* 8 (May 1927): 74–75.

87. Ibid., pp. 78–79.

88. George P. Clements Papers, Los Angeles Department of Special Collections, Univ. of California, Los Angeles.

89. Robert N. McLean, "Mexican Workers in the United States," in *National Conference of Social Work, Proceedings* (Chicago, 1929), pp. 530–531.

90. Patric, *A Study of the Housing and Social Conditions*, pp. 7–9.

91. Hymer, "A Study of the Social Attitudes," p. 52.

92. "Report of the Seventh Annual Conference of the Friends of the Mexicans" (Pomona College, November 11 and 12, 1927), George P. Clements Papers, Box 63, pp. 6–7. See also Alberto Rembao, "What Should Be Done for Juan García?" *Pomona College Magazine* 17 (January 1929): 145–148.

5. The "Brown Scare"

1. U.S. Bureau of the Census, *Fourteenth Census of the United States Taken in the Year 1920*, vol. 3, *Population*, pp. 53, 133; Christopher Rand, *Los Angeles: The Ultimate City* (New York: Oxford Univ. Press, 1967), p. 101.

2. Paul Murphy, "Normalcy, Tolerance, and the American Character," *Virginia Quarterly Review* 40 (1964): 457.

3. *International Encyclopedia of Social Sciences* (New York: Macmillan Publishing Co., 1968), 11: 75–79. See also John Blum, "Nativism, Anti-Radicalism, and the Foreign Scare, 1917–1920," *Midwest Journal* 3 (1950–1951): 47–53.

4. John Higham, *Strangers in the Land* (New Brunswick: Rutgers Univ. Press, 1955), p. 4.

5. Alexander Saxton, *The Indispensable Enemy: Labor and the Anti-Chinese Movement in California* (Berkeley: Univ. of California Press, 1971); William M. Mason, "The Chinese in Los Angeles," *Museum Alliance Quarterly* 6 (Fall 1967): 15–20.

6. Roger Daniels, *The Politics of Prejudice: The Anti-Japanese Movement in California* (Berkeley: Univ. of California Press, 1962); Stuart Creighton Miller, *The Unwelcome Immigrant: The American Image of the Chinese, 1785–1882* (Berkeley: Univ. of California Press, 1969); Alexander Saxton, "Race and the House of Labor," in Gary B. Nash and

Richard Weiss, *The Great Fear: Race in the Mind of America* (New York: Holt, Rinehart and Winston, 1970), pp. 98–120.

7. Hyman Weintraub, "The I.W.W. in California, 1905–1931" (Master's thesis, Univ. of California, Los Angeles, 1947); Elmer Clarence Sandmeyer, *The Anti-Chinese Movement in California* (Urbana: Univ. of Illinois Press, 1939).

8. F. Palmer, "Otistown of the Open Shop," *Hampton* 26 (January 1911): 29–44; Walter V. Woehlke, "Terrorism in America," *Outlook*, February 17, 1912, pp. 359–367; Herbert Shapiro, "The McNamara Case: A Crisis of the Progressive Era," *Historical Society of Southern California Quarterly* 59 (Fall 1977).

9. See, for example, Samuel Bryan, "Mexican Immigrants in the United States," *Survey* 7 (September 1912): 726–730.

10. Higham, *Strangers in the Land*, p. 195.

11. John A. Fitch, "Old and New Labor Problems in California," *Survey* 32 (September 19,1914): 609–610; E. Guy Talbott, "The Armies of the Unemployed in California," *Survey* 32 (August 22, 1914): 523.

12. Bryan, "Mexican Immigrants," p. 729.

13. Ibid. See also "Army and Navy Ordered to be Ready to Invade Mexico," *Los Angeles Times*, April 16, 1912.

14. *Los Angeles Times*, January 20, 1914.

15. For a look at the fate PLM members faced in Mexico, see, for example, William Dirk Raat, "The Diplomacy of Suppression: Los Revoltosos, Mexico and the United States, 1906–1911," *Hispanic American Historical Review* 56 (November 1976): 529–550.

16. For a discussion of Flores Magón's formative years in the United States, see for example Ricardo Flores Magón, *Epistolario revolucionario e íntimo* (Mexico City: Ediciones Antorcha, 1978); John M. Hart, *Anarchism and the Mexican Working Class, 1860–1931* (Austin: Univ. of Texas Press, 1978); Juan Gómez-Quiñones, *Sembradores: Ricardo Flores Magón y el Partido Liberal Mexicano, a Eulogy and Critique* (Los Angeles: Chicano Studies Center, UCLA, 1973). For his activities in Mexico, see James D. Cockroft, *Intellectual Precursors of the Mexican Revolution* (Austin: Univ. of Texas Press, 1968), pp. 111–115. Ricardo Flores Magón, *¿Para qué sirve la autoridad? y otros cuentos* (Mexico City: Ediciones Antorcha, 1978); Ricardo Flores Magón, *Antología*, ed. Gonzalo Aguirre Beltrán (Mexico City: Universidad Nacional Autónoma de México, 1972). For an examination of the PLM's political position, see, for instance, Rafael Carillo Azpeitia, *Ricardo Flores Magón: Esbozo biográfico* (Mexico City: Centro de Estudios Históricos del Movimiento Obrero, 1976), pp. 35–44.

17. Ellen Howell Myers, "The Mexican Liberal Party, 1903–1910" (Ph.D. dissertation, Univ. of Virginia, 1970), pp. 200–201.

18. Armando Barta, *Regeneración, 1900–1918: La corriente más radical de la revolución mexicana de 1910 a través de su periódico de combate* (Mexico City: Ediciones Era, 1977), p. 57.

19. Peter Gerhard, "The Socialist Invasion of Baja California, 1911," *Pacific Historical Review* 15 (September 1946): 295–304.

20. U.S. Department of State, *Papers Relating to the Foreign Relations of the United States, 1911* (Washington, D.C., 1918), p. 409, document dated February 23, 1911, File No. 812.00/848.

21. Document dated March 9, 1911, reprinted in Pablo L. Martínez, *El magonismo en Baja California* (Mexico City: Editorial Baja California, 1958), pp. 16–17.

22. Document dated May 24, 1911, reprinted in Martínez, *El magonismo*, p. 21.

23. 1911 *Manifesto* published by the PLM in Los Angeles (in Univ. of California, Los Angeles, Special Collections).

24. From an essay published in *Regeneración*. Reprinted in Barta, *Regeneración, 1900–1918*, p. 346.

25. Ibid.

26. Ibid.

27. Thomas C. Langham, "An Unequal Struggle: The Case of Ricardo Flores Magón and the Mexican Liberals" (Master's thesis, San Diego State Univ., 1975), pp. 80–90.

28. *Los Angeles Times*, September 15, 1913.

29. Huerta's problems with his enemies in Mexico as well as with Wilson are discussed in a fine study by Michael Meyer, *Huerta: A Political Portrait* (Lincoln: Univ. of Nebraska Press, 1972).

30. *Los Angeles Times*, September 15, 1913. A Mexican perspective on the civil war is presented in the following: Y. Bonillas, "Character and the Progress of the Revolution," *Annals of the American Academy* 69 (January 1917), supp: 18–21; G. Mandujano, "Mexican Revolution," *Pan American Magazine* 31 (May 1920): 13–19.

31. "Revolutions Injure Los Angeles Business," *Los Angeles Times*, November 9, 1913; "Local Carranza Junta Predicts Recognition: Getting Ready to Send Force into Mexico As Soon As Wilson Acts," ibid.

32. *Los Angeles Times*, September 13, 1913; see also "The Situation in Mexico," *Outlook*, August 30, 1913, pp. 1003–1006; "Killing Foreigners in Mexico," *Literary Digest* 50 (March 27, 1915): 674–675.

33. Danger on the Border," *Los Angeles Times*, November 16, 1913.

34. "Los Angeles Is Watching: Mexican 'Reds' Arrested for Carrying Weapons," *Los Angeles Times*, November 18, 1913. The article warned of "Discontented Cholos congregating on the streets and Carranzistas apparently active." The term *cholo*, meaning a lower-class peon, is believed to have been introduced to California during the Gold Rush era and was used by police in this case in a derogatory manner.

35. Ibid.

36. Ibid.

37. *Century Magazine*, however, questioned the wisdom of the United States attempting to resolve the Mexican civil war alone and instead argued for involving other world powers as the only practical solution (W. M. Shuster, "Mexican Menace," *Century Magazine* 87 [February 1914]: 602).

38. Howard F. Cline, *The United States and Mexico* (New York: Atheneum, 1968), pp. 187–188.

39. Arthur Dunn, "War on the West Coast," *Sunset* 33 (July 1914): 150–151.
40. Myers, "The Mexican Liberal Party," p. 229.
41. See mention of Hearst ranch in Friedrich Katz, "Pancho Villa and the Attack on Columbus, New Mexico," *American Historical Review* 78 (February 1978): 115.
42. "For U.S. to Intervene: Benjamin Ide Wheeler Declares Europe Is Waiting on America to Quiet Mexico," *Los Angeles Times*, January 11, 1914.
43. *Los Angeles Times*, June 19, 1914; June 9, 1914. Later that year a *Times* editorial stated that "the only plausible conclusion is that the president plans, if necessary, another 'peaceful' invasion" (December 11, 1914).
44. "Mexican Anarchy and American Duty," *Independent* 81 (March 22, 1915): 407.
45. *Literary Digest* 51 (September 18, 1915): 577.
46. "How Mexico Would Fight Us," *Literary Digest,* 51 (September 11, 1915): 543. The statements are attributed to Harry Dunn, a newspaperman "who has spent seven years in Mexico and knows it fairly intimately."
47. William W. McEuen, "A Survey of the Mexican in Los Angeles 1910–1914" (Master's thesis, Univ. of Southern California, 1914), p. 16.
48. "The Mexican 'Invasion' of Texas," *Literary Digest* 51 (September 18, 1915): 576. See also William Hager, "The Plan of San Diego: Unrest on the Texas Border in 1915," *Arizona and the West* 5 (Winter 1963): 327–336; Michael Meyer, "The Mexican-German Conspiracy of 1915," *Americas* 23 (July 1966): 76–89; James Anthony Sandos, "The Mexican Revolution and the United States, 1915–1917: The Impact of Conflict in the Tamaulipas-Texas Frontier upon the Emergence of Revolutionary Government in Mexico" (Ph.D. dissertation, Univ. of California, Berkeley, 1978), Chapters 4 and 8.
49. "Plan Uprising of Anarchists: Would Seize California and Empty All the Jails," *Los Angeles Times*, September 20, 1915. The following month, the Magonistas moved to the outskirts of the east side, where they established a commune for thirty of their close associates. See Myers, "The Mexican Liberal Party," p. 357.
50. "Plan Uprising of Anarchists."
51. Quoted in Guillermo Pérez Velasco, *Ricardo Flores Magón: Semilla libertaria* (Mexico City, 1975), pp. 329–330.
52. *Los Angeles Times*, December 10, 1915.
53. *Los Angeles Times*, January 23, 1916; February 6, 1916.
54. For some typical reactions to Villa's raid, see: "The Invasion of the United States from Mexico," *Outlook* 112 (March 22, 1916): 642–645; "The Mexican Bandits," *Los Angeles Times*, April 5, 1916; "The President Calls Out the National Guard to Patrol Our Mexican Border," *Current Opinion* 61 (July 1916): 1–2; George Marvin, "Invasion or In-

tervention," *World's Work* 32 (May 1916): 40–62; J. Hopper, "Wilson and the Border," *Collier's* 57 (July 8, 1916): 7–8.

55. "Draw Teeth of War Breeders: Police Take Drastic Action to Curb Villa Adherents," *Los Angeles Times*, March 14, 1916.

56. Ibid. See also James Sandos, "German Involvement in Northern Mexico, 1915–1916: A New Look at the Columbus Raid," *Hispanic American Historical Review* 50 (February 1970): 70–88.

57. "Draw Teeth of War Breeders."

58. Ibid.

59. "Organizes for City's Safety: Police Chief Prepares for an Outbreak of Villistas: Seeks Two Thousand Citizens for Emergency Work," *Los Angeles Times*, March 15, 1916.

60. *Los Angeles Times*, March 16, 1916.

61. Ibid. See also "Villa's Invasion," *Literary Digest* 52 (March 18, 1916): 700.

62. *Los Angeles Times*, March 19, 1916. The punitive expedition is discussed by: Clarence Clendenen, *The United States and Pancho Villa: A Study in Unconventional Diplomacy* (Ithaca: Cornell Univ. Press, 1961); "Mobilizing Against War with Mexico," *Survey* 36 (July 8, 1916): 379; J. G. Cannon, "We Are at War with Mexico," *Independent* 87 (July 10, 1916): 55; "The Pursuit of Villa," *Los Angeles Times*, April 11, 1916.

63. *Los Angeles Times*, April 12, 1916; "Workhouse as Refugee Cure: Would Solve Problem of What to Do with Mexicans," ibid., April 16, 1916.

64. "Would Deport Many 'Cholos': Supervisors Adopt Resolution Asking Federal Action," *Los Angeles Times*, April 12, 1916.

65. Nonetheless, the *New York Times* reported that Army General Funston had requested "mounted forces to help guard the border" (June 12, 1916).

66. *Los Angeles Times*, May 6, 1917.

67. "Police Eyes on Mexican Jollity: Special Squads of Officers Patrol the Plaza," *Los Angeles Times*, May 6, 1917.

68. Ibid. See also "Nip Incipient Riot in Bud," *Los Angeles Times*, May 7, 1917.

69. "Mexicans Face Deportation: Two Held by Government for Advising Revolt," *Los Angeles Times*, May 15, 1917.

70. "Missing Mexicans a Remarkable Mystery: Five Thousand Quit Work and Disappear from Los Angeles County," *Los Angeles Times*, April 11, 1917.

71. Ibid. See also "Villistas Much Nearer Than First Reported," *Los Angeles Times*, April 6, 1917.

72. "Missing Mexicans a Remarkable Mystery" (see note 70). See also "Exodus of Mexicans Is Reported by Sheriff," *Los Angeles Times*, April 7, 1917. The article noted that the sheriff learned that the men who had left "are armed and have been paid to go to Mexico to fight against the Americans."

73. Reference to a sudden exodus of Mexican workers in April 1917 is made by Cornelius C. Smith, Jr., *Emilio Kosterlitzky: Eagle of Sonora and the Southwest Border* (Glendale, Calif.: A. H. Clark Co., 1970), p. 284.

74. "German Influence in Mexico," *New York Times*, June 23, 1916. The article noted that diplomats representing the Allied Powers in Mexico were of the opinion that "German influences have been working on Carranza in an effort to create a situation that might embarrass the enemies of the Central Powers." See also "German Efforts in Mexico," *Worlds Work* 35 (December 1917): 207–210.

75. See, for example, "The Terror on the Border," *Los Angeles Times*, May 10, 1916; "Villista Bandits Not Soldiers," ibid., May 30, 1916; "Talks of Mexico as Germany's Ally," *New York Times*, June 22, 1916; "Teuton Plot Rumor Unworthy of Denial," ibid., June 26, 1916.

76. Karl M. Schmitt, *Mexico and the United States, 1821–1973* (New York: John Wiley and Sons, 1974), p. 151.

77. J. Joseph Huthmacher, *Trial by War and Depression: 1917–1941* (Boston: Allyn and Bacon, 1973), p. 17. For a fuller discussion of the Zimmermann note, see Barbara W. Tuchman, *The Zimmermann Telegram* (New York: Macmillan, 1966).

78. Schmitt, *Mexico and the United States*, p. 151.

79. *Outlook*, February 21, 1917, p. 315. The *Los Angeles Times*, April 6, 1917, reported that "German officers had been training Mexican soldiers for several months."

80. "Unpublished Part of the Zimmermann Note Reveals German Bases," *Los Angeles Times*, April 6, 1917. See also H. W. Van Loon, "The Way of Germany and the Way of Mexico," *New Republic* 7 (July 22, 1916): 304.

81. *Los Angeles Times*, April 1, 1917.

82. Ibid., April 15, 1917.

83. "German Efforts in Mexico," *World's Work* 35 (December 1917): 212; *Los Angeles Times*, April 15, 1917; H. Wray, "America's Unguarded Gateway: New Mexico," *North American Review* 208 (August 1918): 312–315.

84. Smith, *Emilio Kosterlitzky*, p. 265.

85. Paul L. Murphy, *The Constitution in Crisis Time, 1918–1969* (New York: Harper and Row, 1972), pp. 46–52; Thomas F. Carroll, "Freedom of Speech and of the Press in Wartime: The Espionage Act," *Michigan Law Review* 17 (June 1919): 622ff.

86. See H. C. Peterson and Gilbert C. Fite, *Opponents of War: 1917–1918* (Madison: Univ. of Wisconsin Press, 1957); and Harry N. Scheiber, *The Wilson Administration and Civil Liberties, 1917–1921* (Ithaca: Cornell Univ. Press, 1960).

87. William D. Stephens, *California in the War: War Addresses, Proclamations and Patriotic Messages of Governor William D. Stephens* (California Historical Survey Commission, War History Dept., n.d.). Pamphlets include speeches by Governor Stephens during the years 1917–1920.

88. *New York Times*, July 25, 1917.
89. Three articles in the *Los Angeles Times* demonstrated this position: "Must Have All Farm Workers," May 19, 1917; "Bars Down to Mexican Labor," May 24, 1917; "May Import Mexicans to Work on Our Farms," May 30, 1917.
90. *Los Angeles Times*, September 27, 1918.
91. Ibid., June 9, 1918.
92. *Commonwealth* 13 (May 1918): 89, 98. On July 4, 1918, Governor Stephens told a Berkeley audience, "We know the agents of the Kaiser are busy in our midst and every loyal American citizen owes it, as a duty to his country, to maintain vigilance and to help in a relentless campaign to stamp out treachery within our own borders" (*California in the War*, p. 37).
93. *Los Angeles Times*, April 7, 1918; June 8, 1918.
94. Ibid., April 7, 1918.
95. Ibid. See also "To Unite Mexicans," ibid., June 8, 1918. Continued concern with the border region found expression in Wray, "America's Unguarded Gateway."
96. *La Prensa de Los Angeles*, June 15, 1918.
97. Ibid., April 13, 1918.
98. U.S. Congress, Senate, *Investigation of Mexican Affairs: Report and Hearings before a Subcommittee of the Committee on Foreign Relations*, 66th Cong., 1st sess. (1919), p. 1295.
99. *Los Angeles Times*, November 3, 1919.
100. Ibid., November 30, 1919. See also December 13, 1919, article in which the Mexican Minister of the Interior, Manuel Aguirre Berlanga, denied that Mexico had ever contemplated the "adoption of the 'Plan of San Diego' for the purpose of securing portions of the southwestern territory of the U.S."
101. Stanley Coben, "A Study in Nativism: The American Red Scare of 1919–1920," *Political Science Quarterly* 79 (March 1964): 52–53.

6. Work and Restlessness

1. Recently, historians have applied quantitative techniques to the study of the urban working class, but for the most part, these studies—which make use of city directories, birth, marriage, and death records, and census data—have been limited to eastern and midwestern cities and have provided little information about non-European immigrants. This chapter attempts to do for Mexican immigrants in Los Angeles what earlier studies have done for European immigrants in the East and Midwest.
2. Women were not included because so few worked outside the home that the sample was too small to generalize from. It is also extremely difficult to trace women workers over time when using directories because of name changes and because many of them were never listed, while their husbands usually were. Marriage records obviously exclude men who never married, but as Peter M. Blau and Otis D. Duncan have shown in *The American Occupational Structure* (New York: Wiley,

1967), pp. 337–340, the occupational attainment of married men ranks only slightly higher than that of nonmarried men.

3.   A bias often associated with marriage records is that they tend to reflect a rather young population. Sixty-three percent of the Mexicanos sampled for this study were in their thirties. Yet, as T. Wilson Longmore and Homer L. Hitt demonstrate in "A Demographic Analysis of First and Second Generation Mexican Population of the United States: 1930," *Southwestern Social Science Quarterly* 24 (September 1943): 145, the median age of the Mexican population of the United States in 1930 was twenty years, in contrast to twenty-six years for the total U.S. population. Furthermore, the authors found that "the Mexican population contained relatively fewer persons above thirty-four years of age" than the U.S. population as a whole.

4.   For Boston, see Howard P. Chudacoff, *Mobile Americans: Residential and Social Mobility in Omaha, 1880–1920* (New York: Oxford Univ. Press, 1972), pp. 216–231. For Atlanta, see Richard J. Hopkins, "Status, Mobility, and the Dimensions of Change in a Southern City," in Kenneth T. Jackson and Stanley K. Schultz, eds., *Cities in American History* (New York: Knopf, 1972). For San Antonio, see Alwyn Barr, "Occupational and Geographic Mobility in San Antonio, 1870–1900," *Social Science Quarterly* 51, no. 2 (September 1970): 398–403.

5.   Carey McWilliams, in "Getting Rid of the Mexican," *American Mercury* 28 (March 1933): 323, estimated that the city repatriated thirty-five thousand Mexicans from Los Angeles in 1932 alone.

6.   For a literary study of this phenomenon in an earlier period, see Kevin Starr, *Americans and the California Dream, 1850–1915* (New York: Oxford Univ. Press, 1973).

7.   George G. West, "California the Prodigious," *Nation* 125 (October 4, 1922): 325.

8.   Bruce Bliven, "Los Angeles: The City That Is Bacchanalian—in a Nice Way," *New Republic* 51 (July 13, 1927): 198.

9.   The best treatment of this era is Glenn S. Dumke's *The Boom of the Eighties in Southern California*, 4th ed. (San Marino, Calif.: Huntington Library, 1955). See also W. W. Robinson, *Los Angeles: From the Days of the Pueblo* (San Francisco: California Historical Society, 1959), pp. 80–81.

10. Bliven, "Los Angeles," p. 197.

11. Guy E. Marion, "Statistical Facts about Los Angeles," in *Los Angeles City Directory, 1925*, pp. 7–9.

12. James A. B. Scherer, "What Kind of Pittsburgh Is Los Angeles?" *World Week* 41 (February 1921): 382.

13. U.S. Bureau of the Census, *Thirteenth Census of the United States Taken in the Year 1910, Abstract of the Census*, p. 602; *Fifteenth Census of the United States: 1930, Population*, vol. 1, pp. 18, 19, 131; vol. 2, pp. 266–267.

14. U.S. Bureau of the Census, *Thirteenth Census, 1910*, vol. 1, *Population*, pp. 854–855; *Fourteenth Census of the United States Taken in*

the Year 1920, vol. 4, *Population*, pp. 729–731; *Fifteenth Census, 1930, Population*, vol. 1, pp. 248–250.

15. Robert Strout, "A Fence for the Rio Grande," *Independent* 120 (June 2, 1928): 519.

16. Robert N. McLean, "Mexican Workers in the United States," in *National Conference of Social Work, Proceedings* (Chicago, 1929), p. 537.

17. U.S. Congress, Senate Committee on Immigration, *Hearings on Restriction of Western Hemisphere Immigration*, 70th Cong., 1st sess. (1928), p. 47.

18. U.S. Congress, House Committee on Immigration and Naturalization, *Hearings on Western Hemisphere Immigration*, 71st Cong., 2d sess. (1930), p. 81.

19. U.S. Department of Labor, Bureau of Labor Statistics, "Mexican Labor in the Imperial Valley, California," *Monthly Labor Review* 28 (March 1929): 62.

20. Emory S. Bogardus, *The Mexican in the United States* (Los Angeles: Univ. of Southern California Press, 1934); Jay S. Stowell, *The Near Side of the Mexican Question* (New York: Home Missions Council, 1921); and Robert N. McLean, *The Northern Mexican* (New York: Home Missions Council, 1930).

21. G. Bromley Oxnam, *The Mexican in Los Angeles: Los Angeles City Survey* (Los Angeles: Interchurch World Movement of North America, 1920), p. 14.

22. Charles S. Johnson, "Industrial Survey of the Negro Population of Los Angeles, California" (unpublished survey, National Urban League, 1926). Details of this survey were made available to me by the National Urban League office in New York City through Professor Emory Tolbert.

23. Paul S. Taylor, *Mexican Labor in the United States: Chicago and the Calumet Region*, University of California Publications in Economics 7, no. 2 (Berkeley, 1932). See also tables provided in Taylor's "Some Aspects of Mexican Immigration," *Journal of Political Economy* 38 (October 1930): 609–615.

24. As Table 2 demonstrates, some 11,677 Mexicanos in the state were employed in railroad industries in California. Ramón García, a fifty-year resident of Los Angeles and an employee of the Southern Pacific Railroad Company from 1922 to 1965, informed me that all of the laborers in the Southern Pacific yard during the 1920s were of Mexican descent. (Interview with Ramón García, October 15, 1973, Los Angeles).

25. Carl L. May, "Our Anti-Social Mexican Population," *Los Angeles County Employee* 2 (1929): 12.

26. *Mexicans in California: Report of Governor C. C. Young's Fact-Finding Committee* (San Francisco: California Department of Industrial Relations, Agriculture, and Social Welfare, October 1930), p. 82.

27. Paul S. Taylor, "Note on Stream of Mexican Migration," *American Journal of Sociology* 36 (September 1930): 287–288; Emory S. Bogar-

dus, "The Mexican Immigrant and Segregation," *American Journal of Sociology* 36 (July 1930): 74–80.

28. J. B. Gwin, "Social Problems of Our Mexican Population," *National Conference of Social Work, Proceedings* (Chicago, 1926), p. 330.

29. *Mexicans in California*, p. 82.

30. Ibid., pp. 80–81.

31. John McDowell, *A Study of Social and Economic Factors Relating to Spanish-Speaking People in the United States* (Philadelphia: Home Missions Council, 1927), p. 16.

32. Elizabeth Fuller, *The Mexican Housing Problem in Los Angeles*, Studies in Sociology Sociological Monograph, no. 17, vol. 5 (November 1920), p. 6.

33. *Mexicans in California*, p. 105.

34. McLean, "Mexican Workers in the United States," p. 534.

35. Blau and Duncan, *The American Occupational Structure*, pp. 6–7.

36. Oxnam, *The Mexican in Los Angeles*, p. 14. For occupational rankings, I used a model formulated by Stephan Thernstrom, *The Other Bostonians: Poverty and Progress in the American Metropolis, 1880–1970* (Cambridge, Mass.: Harvard Univ. Press, 1973), pp. 290–292. Examples of the occupations found in each of the categories are (1) High White Collar: architects, lawyers, major proprietors, managers, and officials; (2) Low White Collar: clerks, salespeople, and semiprofessionals such as librarians and photographers; (3) High Blue Collar: carpenters, jewelers, mechanics, factory operatives, and tailors; (4) Low Blue Collar: laborers, porters, gardeners, and lumber workers.

37. Emory Bogardus, "Second Generation Mexicans," *Sociology and Social Research* 13 (Jaunary–February 1929): 277–278.

38. Seymour Martin Lipset and Reinhard Bendix, *Social Mobility in Industrial Society* (Berkeley: Univ. of California Press, 1959), pp. 11–12.

39. Thernstrom, *The Other Bostonians*, p. 238; Michael Hanson, "Occupational Mobility and Persistence in Los Angeles, 1910–1930" (unpublished paper, Univ. of California, Los Angeles, June 1, 1970).

40. For a more complete analysis of the economic ranking of occupations used here, see Thernstrom, *The Other Bostonians*, pp. 290–292. Thernstrom's Appendix B lists more than 140 different occupations in the categories used in Table 7 of this book (High and Low White Collar and Blue Collar).

41. Thernstrom, *The Other Bostonians*, pp. 222, 226.

42. For a fuller discussion of the immigrants' journey, see Ricardo Romo, "Responses to Mexican Immigration, 1910–1930," *Aztlán: International Journal of Chicano Studies Research* 6 (1975): 173–194; and Leo Grebler, Joan W. Moore, and Ralph C. Guzman, *The Mexican-American People: The Nation's Second Largest Minority* (New York: Free Press, 1970), p. 62.

43. Computed from U.S. Bureau of the Census, *Fourteenth Census, 1920*, vol. 1, *Population*, p. 125; *Fifteenth Census, 1930, Population*, vol. 2, p. 287.

44. Helen Walker, "Mexican Immigrants as Laborers," *Sociology and Social Research* 13 (September 1923): 58–59.
45. Stowell, *The Near Side,* p. 49.
46. McDowell, *A Study of Social and Economic Factors,* p. 16.
47. G. Bromley Oxnam, "The Mexican in Los Angeles from the Standpoint of the Religious Forces of the City," *Annals of the American Academy of Political and Social Science* 93 (January 1921): 131.
48. Ethel M. Morrison, "A History of Recent Legislative Proposals Concerning Mexican Immigrants" (M.A. thesis, Univ. of Southern California, 1929), pp. 27–28.
49. Carleton Beals, "Mexican Intelligence," *Southwest Review* 11 (October 1925): 24.
50. William W. McEuen, "A Survey of the Mexican in Los Angeles (1910–1914)" (Master's thesis, Univ. of Southern California, 1914), p. 9.
51. Ibid., p. 31. See also Mark S. Reisler, "Always the Laborer, Never the Citizen: Anglo Perceptions of the Mexican Immigrant during the 1920s," *Pacific Historical Review* 45 (1976): 231–254.
52. Ernesto Galarza, "Life in the United States for Mexican People: Out of the Experiences of a Mexican," in *National Conference of Social Work, Proceedings* (Chicago, 1929), p. 402.
53. McEuen, "A Survey of the Mexican in Los Angeles," p. 36; Bogardus, "Second Generation Mexicans," pp. 277–278; Galarza, "Life in the United States," p. 402.
54. See, for example, Alexander DeConde, *Half Bitter, Half Sweet: An Excursion into Italian-American History* (New York: Charles Scribner's Sons, 1971), pp. 14–15. The Italian immigrants, DeConde wrote, "poor and friendless, clung together in slums of eastern cities, fearing to settle in the hostile countryside of rural America."

7. Reform, Revival, and Socialization

1. Carey McWilliams, *North from Mexico: The Spanish-Speaking People of the United States* (Philadelphia: J. B. Lippincott, 1949), p. 302.
2. Manuel P. Servín, "The Post–World War II Mexican American, 1925–65: A Nonachieving Minority," in Manuel P. Servín, ed., *An Awakened Minority: The Mexican Americans,* 2d ed. (Beverly Hills: Glencoe Press, 1974), pp. 160–174.
3. The progressive movement in California is the focus of George E. Mowry's excellent study, *The California Progressives* (Berkeley: Univ. of California Press, 1951). The leader of the California progressives, Governor Hiram Johnson, is the subject of Spencer C. Olin, Jr., *California's Prodigal Sons* (Berkeley: Univ. of California Press, 1968). For a general overview of the progressive movement, see, for instance, Richard M. Abrams, *The Burdens of Progress, 1900–1929* (Glenview, Ill.: Scott, Foresman and Co., 1978); Robert M. Crunden, *From Self to Society, 1919–1941* (Englewood Cliffs, N.J.: Prentice-Hall, 1972); Richard Hofstadter, *The Age of Reform* (New York: Vintage Books, 1955); Henry

May, *The End of American Innocence* (New York: Knopf, 1959; Chicago: Quadrangle, 1964); and Lewis L. Gould, *Reform and Regulation: American Politics, 1900–1916* (New York: John Wiley, 1978).

4. Mowry, *The California Progressives*, p. 153.
5. California, Commission of Immigration and Housing, (CIH), *Annual Report, January 1919* (Sacramento, 1919), pp. 77–78.
6. See California, CIH, *First Annual Report* (Sacramento, January 2, 1915); *Advisory Pamphlet on Camp Sanitation and Housing* (Sacramento, 1915); *Report on Relief of Destitute Unemployed, 1914–1915, to His Excellency* (Sacramento, 1915).
7. California, CIH, *Report on Relief of Destitute Unemployed, 1914–1915* (Sacramento, 1915), pp. 10–11. E. Guy Talbott of the Church Federation of Sacramento estimated that Los Angeles had no less than twenty-five thousand unemployed workers. See Talbott, "The Armies of the Unemployed in California," *Survey* 32 (August 22, 1914): 523.
8. California, CIH, *Second Annual Report* (Sacramento, 1916), p. 238.
9. Ibid., p. 239.
10. Cited in California, CIH, *The Home Teacher: The Act with a Working Plan* (Sacramento, 1916), pp. 4–5. See also Philip Davis, *Immigration and Americanization* (Boston: Ginn and Co., 1920), p. 462.
11. John Steven McGroarty, *History of Los Angeles County* (Chicago: American Historical Society, 1923) 3: 289.
12. California, CIH, *The Home Teacher*, pp. 4–5.
13. McGroarty, *History of Los Angeles County*, 3: 287.
14. California, CIH, *Report on an Experiment Made in Los Angeles in the Summer of 1917 for the Americanization of Foreign-Born Women* (Sacramento, 1917), pp. 21–22.
15. California, CIH, *Second Annual Report* (Sacramento, 1916), pp. 243, 252–253.
16. California, CIH, *Annual Report* (Sacramento, 1925), p. 13.
17. California, CIH, *Annual Report* (Sacramento, 1927), p. 10.
18. California, CIH, *The Home Teacher*, p. 12.
19. Ibid., p. 13.
20. William D. Stephens, *California in the War: War Addresses, Proclamations and Patriotic Messages of Governor William D. Stephens* (California Historical Survey Commission, War History Dept., n.d.), pp. 31, 51.
21. Ibid., pp. 31, 34, 51.
22. Carol Aronovici of the CIH correctly stated in 1921 that "the Americanization movement could not survive during normal times. It was a negative movement . . ." See Aronovici, "Americanization," in *Annals of the American Academy of Political and Social Science* 93 (January 1921): 134.
23. California, CIH, *Annual Report* (Sacramento, 1927), p. 8.
24. McGroarty, *History of Los Angeles County* 1: 283.

25. William W. Robinson, *Los Angeles: From the Days of the Pueblo* (San Francisco: California Historical Society, 1959).

26. McGroarty, *History of Los Angeles County* 1: 283.

27. Ibid., pp. 283–286.

28. Lawrence A. Cremin, *The Transformation of the School: Progressivism in American Education, 1876–1957* (New York: Vintage Books, 1964), p. 156.

29. Ibid., p. 128.

30. Ellwood Cubberly, *Changing Conceptions of Education* (New York: Houghton Mifflin Co., 1909), pp. 15–16.

31. California, *Department of Education Bulletin*, no. 8 (1932): v.

32. Ibid., p. 23.

33. McGroarty, *History of Los Angeles County*, 1: 290.

34. Emory S. Bogardus, "The Mexican Immigrant and Segregation," *American Journal of Sociology* 36 (July 1930): 79.

35. Los Angeles Chamber of Commerce, "Foreign Born Population in Los Angeles," George P. Clements Papers, Box 80, Los Angeles Department of Special Collections, Univ. of California, Los Angeles; U.S. Bureau of the Census, *Fourteenth Census of the United States Taken in the Year 1920*, vol. 3, *Population*, pp. 123–124; vol. 2, *Population*, pp. 53, 561; *Fifteenth Census of the United States: 1930, Population*, vol. 2, pp. 1302, 1377.

36. Quoted in Gilbert González, "The System of Public Education and Its Function within the Chicano Community, 1920–1930" (Ph.D. dissertation, Univ. of California, Los Angeles, 1974), p. 134.

37. Preface by Helen Heffernan, Chief, Division of Elementary Education and Rural Schools in California, "Guide for Teachers of Beginning Non–English Speaking Children," *Department of Education Bulletin*, no. 8 (1932): 1; Joseph M. Santos, "Poverty and Problems of the Mexican Immigrant" (Master's thesis, Univ. of the Pacific, 1931), p. 121; David A. Bridge, "A Study of the Agencies Which Promote Americanization in the Los Angeles City Recreation Center District" (Master's thesis, Univ. of Southern California, 1920), p. 19.

38. Grace C. Stanley, "Special Schools for Mexicans," *Survey* 44 (1920): 714–715.

39. Santos, "Poverty and Problems," p. 120.

40. Meyer Weinberg, *A Chance to Learn: A History of Race and Education in the United States* (London: Cambridge Univ. Press, 1977), p. 158.

41. Ibid.

42. McGroarty, *History of Los Angeles County*, 1: 285.

43. Bogardus, "The Mexican Immigrant and Segregation," p. 80.

44. California, Department of Education, *School Law of California, 1919* (Sacramento, 1919), p. 174.

45. Pearl Ellis, *Americanization through Homemaking* (Los Angeles: Wetzel Publishing Co., 1929), p. 7.

46. Ibid., p. 13.
47. Cited by Gilbert González, *The Relationship between Progressive Educational Theory and Practice and Monopoly Capital*, Occasional Paper No. 1 (Univ. of California, Irvine, 1976), p. 31.
48. McGroarty, *History of Los Angeles County*, 1: 284.
49. Emeline Whitcomb, "Children of Many Nationalities Receive Practical Instruction," *School Life* 11 (March 1926): 138–139.
50. Ibid., p. 139.
51. Blanche A. Sommerville, "Naturalization from the Mexican Viewpoint," *Community Exchange Bulletin* 4 (May 1928): 11.
52. Ibid., pp. 11–12.
53. Joshua A. Fishman, *Language and Loyalty in the United States: The Maintenance and Perpetuation of Non-English Mother Tongues by American Ethnic and Religious Groups* (The Hague: Mouton, 1966), pp. 280–317.
54. Jane MacNab Christian and Chester C. Christian, Jr., "Spanish Language and Culture in the Southwest," in Fishman, *Language and Loyalty*, p. 301.
55. Richard M. Abrams, "Reform and Uncertainty," in William E. Leuchtenburg, gen. ed., *The Unfinished Century* (Boston: Little, Brown and Co., 1973), p. 49. See also Richard Pells, *Radical Visions and American Dreams* (New York: Harper and Row, 1973), pp. 141–142, 144.
56. Robert N. McLean, *That Mexican! As He Really Is, North and South of the Rio Grande* (New York: Fleming H. Revell Co., 1928), p. 145.
57. Linna E. Bresette, *Mexicans in the United States: A Report of a Brief Survey to the Catholic Welfare Conference* (Washington, D.C., 1929), p. 24.
58. Samuel Maldonado Ortegón, "The Religious Status of the Mexican Population of Los Angeles" (Master's thesis, Univ. of Southern California, 1932), p. 61.
59. Ibid., p. 61.
60. See Vernon M. McCombs, "Rescuing Mexican Children in the Southwest," *Missionary Review of the World* 46 (July 1923): 529–532.
61. Bresette, *Mexicans in the United States*, p. 24.
62. Ibid., p. 25.
63. Ibid., pp. 25, 27.
64. Rev. Edwin R. Brown, "The Challenge of Mexican Immigration," *Missionary Review of the World* 49 (March 1926): 195.
65. Robert N. McLean, "Reaching Spanish-Americans with the Gospel," *Missionary Review of the World* 48 (November 1925): 869–874; Jay S. Stowell, *The Near Side of the Mexican Question* (New York: George H. Doran Co., 1921), p. 81.
66. Rev. Charles A. Thomson, "Linking the Two Americas," *Missionary Review of the World* 51 (August 1928): 623.
67. Stowell, *The Near Side*, p. 80.
68. Bresette, *Mexicans in the United States*, p. 36.
69. Ortegón, "The Religious Status," p. 61.

70. John Daniels, *Americanization Studies: America via the Neighborhood* (New York: Harper and Brothers, 1920), p. 245.

71. See for example, Robert N. McLean, *The Northern Mexican* (New York: Home Mission Council, 1930); idem, *That Mexican!* and idem, "Mexican Workers in the United States," in *National Conference of Social Work, Proceedings* (Chicago, 1929), p. 538.

72. Manuel Gamio, *Mexican Immigration to the United States: A Study of Human Migration and Adjustment* (Chicago: University of Chicago Press, 1930); Elizabeth Hymer, "A Study of the Social Attitudes of Adult Mexican Immigrants in Los Angeles and Vicinity: 1923" (Master's thesis, Univ. of Southern California, 1924); Ortegón, "The Religious Status," pp. 14–15.

73. See, for example, Edward R. Kantowicz, "Polish Chicago: Survival through Solidarity," in Melvin G. Holli and Peter d'A. Jones, eds., *The Ethnic Frontier* (Grand Rapids: Eerdmans Publishing Co., 1977), pp. 179–210.

74. *La Prensa de Los Angeles*, January 31, 1920; May 8, 1920.

75. *Los Angeles Times*, January 29, 1921.

76. Ibid., September 17, 1919.

77. Ibid., September 19, 1920.

78. Ibid., September 17, 1919.

79. Ibid., September 17, 1920; *El Heraldo de México* (Los Angeles) August 2, 1921.

80. *Los Angeles Times*, May 2, 1922; May 5, 1922.

81. Ibid., May 11, 1922.

82. Ibid., May 15, 1922.

83. Ibid.

84. *El Heraldo de México* (Los Angeles), January 16–21, 1924.

85. *La Prensa de los Angeles*, November 22, 1917.

86. David Weber, *Foreigners in Their Native Land: Historical Roots of the Mexican Americans* (Albuquerque: Univ. of New Mexico Press, 1973), p. 217.

87. *La Prensa de Los Angeles*, November 22, 1917.

88. *El Heraldo de México*, January 19, 1927.

89. Ibid.

90. Ibid., January 21, 1927.

91. Servin, ed., *An Awakened Minority*, pp. 34–35.

92. *Los Angeles Times*, October 13, 1921.

93. Articles in *La Prensa de Los Angeles*, January 1, 1921, and July 13, 1921, outline some of the activities of Cruz Azul as does *El Heraldo de México*, October 2, 1921.

94. *Los Angeles Times*, October 16, 1921.

95. Ibid., July 13, 1921.

96. *La Prensa de Los Angeles*, July 13, 1921; *Los Angeles Times*, July 7, 1921.

97. *La Prensa de Los Angeles*, September 14, 1918.

98. Ibid.

99. Ibid.
100. *Mexicans in California: Report of Governor C. C. Young's Mexican Fact-Finding Committee* (San Francisco: California Department of Industrial Relations, Agriculture, and Social Welfare, October 1930), p. 123.
101. Ibid.
102. Ibid.
103. Ibid., p. 125.
104. Bogardus, "The Mexican Immigrant and Segregation," p. 78.
105. McLean, *The Northern Mexican*, p. 22; Emory S. Bogardus, *The Mexican in the United States* (Los Angeles: Univ. of California Press, 1934), p. 12.
106. México, Secretaría de Relaciones Exteriores, File on the Los Angeles Consulate, Mexico City: Box IV, 110 Series (73-27), No. 2284; Box IV, 110 Series (73-27), No. 2242; Box IV, 241 Series (73-27), 1930 file No. 03.
107. *Los Angeles Times*, July 2, 1920.
108. *La Prensa de Los Angeles*, April 30, 1921; May 7, 1921; May 21, 1921.
109. Ibid., July 17, 1920.
110. México, Secretaría de Relaciones Exteriores, *Memorias: 1926–27* (Mexico City, 1928), p. 489.
111. *El Heraldo de México*, September 30, 1923.
112. Ibid., October 6, 1923.
113. Ibid., October 19, 1923.
114. Ibid., April 5, 1923.
115. Ibid., April 8, 1923.
116. Ibid., January 3, 1924; January 23, 1924.
117. Ibid., January 29, 1924; February 28, 1924.
118. Ibid., March 8, 1924.
119. Gamio, *Mexican Immigration to the United States*, p. 104.
120. Bogardus, "The Mexican Immigrant and Segregation," pp. 74–80; idem, "Second Generation Mexicans," *Sociology and Social Research* 13 (January–February 1929): 276–283; Manuel Gamio, *The Mexican Immigrant: His Life Story* (Chicago: Univ. of Chicago, 1931); Gamio, *Mexican Immigration to the United States*; Paul S. Taylor, *Mexican Labor in the United States: Imperial Valley*, Univ. of California Publications in Economics 6, no. 1 (Berkeley, 1928); idem, "More Bars against Mexicans," *Survey* 44 (April 1930): 26–27.
121. Milton M. Gordon, *Assimilation in American Life* (New York: Oxford Univ. Press, 1964), p. 108.
122. U.S. Bureau of the Census, *Fourteenth Census, 1920*, vol. 2, *Population*, pp. 801–888.
123. *Mexicans in California*, pp. 72–73.
124. G. Bromley Oxnam, *The Mexican in Los Angeles: Los Angeles City Survey* (Los Angeles: Interchurch World Movement of North America, 1920), p. 22.
125. *Mexicans in California*, p. 62.

126. Constantine Panunzio, "Intermarriage in Los Angeles, 1924–33," *American Journal of Sociology* 47 (March 1942): 692–693; a more contemporary analysis is provided by Edward Murguía and W. Parker Frisbie, "Trends in Mexican American Intermarriage: Recent Findings in Perspective," *Social Science Quarterly* 58 (December 1977): 374–389.

127. Data collected from 1917 and 1918 marriage records in Los Angeles.

128. Hymer, "A Study of the Social Attitudes of Adult Mexican Immigrants."

129. Herman Feldman, *Racial Factors in American Industry* (New York: Harper and Brothers, 1931), p. 121.

130. Hoover's position was put on the public forum by his Secretary of Labor, William N. Doak. See Gardner Jackson, "Doak the Deportation Chief," *Nation* 18 (March 1931): 295–296; and Roy L. Garis, "The Mexicanization of American Business," *Saturday Evening Post*, 8 (February 1930): 46.

131. See Robert N. McLean, "Goodbye, Vicente," *Survey* 66 (May 1, 1931): 182–183, 195; Carey McWilliams, "Getting Rid of the Mexican," *American Mercury* 28 (March 1933): 322–324; Abraham Hoffman, "Mexican Repatriation Statistics: Some Suggested Alternatives to Carey McWilliams," *Western Historical Quarterly* 3 (October 1972): 391–404.

132. Abraham Hoffman, *Unwanted Mexican Americans in the Great Depression: Repatriation Pressures, 1929–1939* (Tucson: Univ. of Arizona Press, 1974).

8. Afterword—East Los Angeles since 1930

1. James Allen Geissinger, "Los Angeles in Festive Spirit," *Christian Century* 48 (October 7, 1931): 1259.

2. Earl Pomeroy, *The Pacific Slope: A History of California, Oregon, Washington, Idaho, Utah, and Nevada* (Seattle: Univ. of Washington Press, 1965), p. 296.

3. James H. Collins, "Los Angeles Grows by a Formula," *Southern California Business* 12 (September 1933): 19. See also Walter J. Stein, *California and the Dust Bowl Migration* (Westport, Conn.: Greenwood Press, 1973).

4. Samuel J. Holmes, "An Argument Against Mexican Immigration," *Commonwealth Club of California Transactions* 23 (March 1926): 23, 26.

5. Lawrence A. Cardoso, *Mexican Emigration to the United States, 1897–1931: Socio-Economic Patterns* (Tucson: Univ. of Arizona Press, 1980), p. 145.

6. Harold Fields, "Where Shall the Alien Work?" *Social Forces* 12 (December 1933): 213–214.

7. Cardoso, *Mexican Emigration*, p. 147. See also Abraham Hoffman, "Stimulus to Repatriation: The 1931 Federal Deportation Drive and

the Los Angeles Mexican Community," *Pacific Historical Review* 42 (May 1973): 205–219.

8. Carey McWilliams, "Getting Rid of the Mexican," *American Mercury* 28 (March 1933): 323.

9. Carey McWilliams, *Southern California: An Island on the Land* (New York: Duell, Sloan, and Pearce, 1946), p. 317.

10. Quoted by Cardoso, *Mexican Emigration*, pp. 146–147.

11. Quoted by Mark Reisler, *By the Sweat of Their Brow: Mexican Immigrant Labor in the United States, 1900–1940* (Westport, Conn.: Greenwood Press, 1976), p. 231.

12. Abraham Hoffman, "Mexican Repatriation Statistics: Some Suggested Alternatives to Carey McWilliams," *Western Historical Quarterly* 3 (October 1972): 391–404.

13. Robin Fitzgerald Scott, "The Mexican-American in the Los Angeles Area, 1920–1950: From Acquiescence to Activity" (Ph.D. dissertation, Univ. of Southern California, 1971), pp. 156, 195. See also Rodolfo Acuña, *Occupied America: A History of Chicanos* (New York: Harper and Row, 1981), p. 323.

14. See, for example, Daniel L. Schorr, "Reconverting Mexican Americans," *New Republic* 30 (September 1946): 412–413.

15. Daniel Martínez, "The Impact of the Bracero Programs on a Southern California Mexican American Community: A Field Study of Cucamonga, California" (Master's thesis, Claremont Graduate School, 1958), p. 17.

16. McWilliams, *Southern California Country*, p. 318.

17. See, for instance, Carey McWilliams, "Los Angeles' Pachuco Gangs," *New Republic* 18 (January 1943): 76–77; Gene L. Coon, "Pachuco," *Common Ground* 8 (Spring 1948): 49–52.

18. Scott, "The Mexican-American in the Los Angeles Area," pp. 222–226.

19. Mauricio Mazón, "Social Upheaval in World War II: 'Zoot-Suiters' and Servicemen in Los Angeles, 1943" (Ph.D. dissertation, Univ. of California, Los Angeles, 1976), pp. 60–91.

20. Ruth D. Tuck, "Behind the Zoot-Suit Riots," *Survey Graphic* 32 (August 1943): 313; "Zoot-Suits and Service Stripes," *Newsweek* 21 (June 21, 1943): 35–36; Marily Domer, "The Zoot-Suit Riot: A Culmination of Social Tensions in Los Angeles" (Master's thesis, Claremont Graduate School, 1955); Emory S. Bogardus, "Gangs of Mexican American Youth," *Sociology and Social Research* 28 (September-October 1943): 55–66.

21. Raúl Morin, *Among the Valiant: Mexican-Americans in WW II and Korea* (Alhambra, Calif.: Borden Publishing Co., 1966), pp. 54–56, 11.

22. Beatrice W. Griffith, "Viva Roybal—Viva América," *Common Ground* 10 (Autumn 1949): 61–70.

23. Miguel David Tirado, "Mexican American Community Political Organization: The Key to Chicano Political Power," *Aztlán: Chicano Journal of the Social Sciences and the Arts* 1 (Spring 1970): 64–66.

24. Charles Wollenberg, "Méndez v. Westminster: Race, Nationality, and

Segregation in California Schools," *California Historical Quarterly* 53 (Winter 1974): 317–333.

25. Julian Nava and Bob Barger, *California: Five Centuries of Cultural Contrasts* (Beverly Hills: Glencoe Press, 1976), p. 363. See Nava's Foreword to Abraham Hoffman, *Unwanted Mexican Americans in the Great Depression: Repatriation Pressures, 1929–1939* (Tucson: University of Arizona Press, 1974), pp. ix–xi. See also Julian Samora and Patricia Vandel Simon, *A History of the Mexican-American People* (Notre Dame: Univ. of Notre Dame Press, 1977), pp. 155–165.

26. Eshref Shevky and Molly Levine, *Your Neighborhood: A Social Profile of Los Angeles* (Los Angeles: Haynes Foundation, 1949), p. 10. See also Eshref Shevky and Marilyn Williams, *The Social Areas of Los Angeles: Analysis and Typology* (Berkeley: Univ. of California Press, 1949), pp. 55–60.

27. Acuña, *Occupied America*, pp. 339–340.

28. Gilbert G. González, "Factors Relating to Property Ownership of Chicanos in Lincoln Heights, Los Angeles," *Aztlán: Chicano Journal of the Social Sciences and the Arts* 2 (Fall 1971): 107–144.

29. Leo Grebler, Joan W. Moore, and Ralph C. Guzman, *The Mexican-American People: The Nation's Second Largest Minority* (New York: Free Press), p. 298.

30. Walter Fogel, *The Effect of Low Educational Attainment on Incomes: A Comparative Study of Selected Ethnic Groups*, Reprint No. 166 (Los Angeles: Institute of Industrial Relations, 1967), p. 31. See also idem, *Mexican Americans in Southwest Labor Markets*, Advance Report 10 (Los Angeles: Univ. of California, Mexican American Study Project, 1967); Frank G. Mittelbach and Grace Marshall, *The Burden of Poverty*, Advance Report 5 (Los Angeles: Univ. of California, Mexican American Study Project, 1967), p. 13.

31. Joel Garreau, "The Nine Nations of North America" (excerpts from his book), *American Demographics* 4, no. 4 (April 1982): 16–17.

Index